AMERICAN HISTORICAL ANTHROPOLOGY

ESSAYS IN HONOR OF

Leslie Spier

Edited by

Carroll L. Riley *and* Walter W. Taylor

With a Preface by W. W. Hill

Contributors

Harold L. Amoss - E. Pendleton Banks

Robert C. Euler - W. W. Hill

Charles H. Lange - David G. Mandelbaum

Harvey C. Moore - Robert L. Rands

Carroll L. Riley - Irving Rouse

Robert F. G. Spier - Walter W. Taylor

American

Historical Anthropology

ESSAYS IN HONOR OF

Leslie Spier

Carbondale and Edwardsville

SOUTHERN ILLINOIS UNIVERSITY PRESS

FEFFER & SIMONS, INC.

London and Amsterdam

IT WAS my good fortune to be associated with Leslie Spier for over thirty-five years in the varying capacities of student, colleague, and friend. During this period I developed an increasing respect for his intellectual achievements. Throughout his lifetime he was an important force in developing and directing the course of American anthropology. This influence was as great as that of some of his better publicized contemporaries. Leslie Spier was a shy person who avoided publicity, the more flamboyant areas of the field, and involvements in anthropological politics. Because of this his impact on the total range of anthropological thought has tended to be underestimated by the current generation. It is impossible in a limited space to do justice to the entire range of his activities. However, in order to place him in proper perspective some brief comments are in order concerning his contributions to three aspects of the discipline, two of which have tended to go unnoticed.

While it may seem superfluous to mention Leslie Spier's research achievements, an area in which he was accorded international recognition, certain facets of his work will bear review because they have relevance for the contemportry scene. First, like other anthropologists of his period, he encompassed the entire field of anthropology, as is amply documented by his publications. That he was productive is attested by such monographic monuments as "Havasupai Ethnography," "Wishram Ethnography" (with Edward Sapir), "Klamath Ethnography," "Yuman Tribes of the Gila River," and "Sinkaietk or Southern Okanagon of Washington" (Walter Cline *et al.*) for which Spier was largely responsible.

These are still referred to as models of completeness in the presentation of ethnologic materials. His facility and thoroughness as a field worker, while generally recognized, was recently reaffirmed by Service (1947 : 360) whose work among the Havasupai postdated Spier's by some twenty years. Service stated: "Geographic isolation has restricted the disruptive effects of white acculturation, so that Spier's ethnography is still accurately descriptive of the Havasupai, except for the few modern changes to be discussed in this paper. Aside from my interpretations as to the meaning of these more recent data, I have added nothing which was not already discussed by Spier in his monograph."

Like others of his era he was interested in historical reconstruction and culture growth and development. His approach to these problems emphasized the intensive investigation of small units and an analysis of data derived from historical sources and the field. For Spier, conceptual schemes were justified only on the area controlled by the researcher. He opposed hypotheses of worldwide scope which depended for verification on data collected at a later date. While he made extensive use of distributional studies, he was fully aware of their limitations, contending that it was impossible to answer the question why until the what and where were known. His approach to the study of cultural dynamics still has application. This is well exemplified in *The Prophet Dance of the Northwest and Its Derivatives: The Source of the Ghost Dance* and *The Sun Dance of the Plains Indians: Its Development and Diffusion*. In these (as well as in other publications) he dealt with differential borrowing; the selective aspects of diffusion as influenced by the donor and acceptor cultures; the roles played by innovating individuals and their backgrounds; and the adaptation of the borrowed elements through reworking and/or elaboration to provide a basis for incorporation into preexisting patterns.

It is noteworthy that while his primary concern was with the areas of historical reconstruction and ethnology, these were by no means all consuming. His diversity of interests is evidenced by his several publications of primitive art, archaeology, studies of physiological growth, kinship, and on the cultural conditioning of bodily habits. Neither did he eschew theory, as is obvious from such papers as "A Suggested Origin for Gentile Organization," "Problems Arising from the Cultural Position of the Havasupai," and "Some Aspects of the Nature of Culture."

An important by-product of Leslie Spier's research was his contribution to methodology. He was impatient with what he called "essay writing," scorned philosophical approaches and what might be designated as intuitional anthropology. Writing in 1959 of Boas' influence on American anthropology (1959: *146*) he extolled his former teacher for providing anthropology with "the scientific approaches of objective empiricism, carefully controlled analysis, firmness of aims, and scrupulous self-discipline in defining the axioms of one's thoughts." While he attributes this to Boas, he was also expressing an article of his own faith from which he never deviated. Spier's procedures were those of the natural and physical sciences: he gathered his data, organized them, and then generalized only so far as the data would allow, no more. More than any of his contemporaries he exemplified the methodologies of the physical sciences which were Boas' legacy and throughout his life he continued periodically to remind his colleagues of their obligations as scientists.

Probably one of Leslie Spier's least known and appreciated contributions to anthropology was in the field of publications and editorial work. He was a firm believer that research should be placed on record for the benefit and use of scholars and he devoted a large portion of his considerable energies to this end. He was instrumental, more than any one person of this period, in creating vehicles for the dissemination of anthropological knowledge. He was solely responsible for initiating the University of Washington Publications in Anthropology; the General Series in Anthropology; the University of New Mexico Publications in Anthropology; and with Edward Sapir, the Yale University Publications in Anthropology and served as editor of all of these for varying periods of time. He was the prime mover in establishing the Publications of the Frederick Webb Hodge Anniversary Publication Fund and served as editor. The *Southwestern Journal of Anthropology* was founded by Spier in 1944, and he continued to edit the *Journal* for sixteen years. He also served for five years as editor of the *American Anthropologist.* His editorial work was characterized by the same meticulousness and objectivity apparent in his research. The amount of energy he expended on manuscripts was prodigious. Most authors will remember a rewritten section, a redrawn map, or a reworked chart. He was acclaimed by linotypists and printers for the editorial perfection of the manuscripts he presented for publication.

While the previous remarks are indicative of Leslie Spier's impact on the growth and development of American anthropology, his greatest and most lasting influence was through the many students he trained, who now continue his tradition of painstaking scholarship and rigorous method. His teaching career extended from 1920 to 1955. Unlike most academicians who spend their lives at one or at best a few institutions, he served at nine universities. While the bulk of his tenure was at the universities of Washington, Yale, and New Mexico, he also taught for varying periods at Oklahoma, Chicago, Harvard, Columbia, and the University of California at Berkeley and at Los Angeles. In many instances he served as visiting professor at the same institution on more than one occasion and this enabled him to leave his imprint on a much wider number of students and colleagues than most teachers. While no adequate data exist, a reasonable guess would be that through personal contact he influenced at least 50 per cent of the professional anthropologists today.

Few men have brought to the classroom his breadth of background, his variety of interests, his wealth of knowledge. He possessed a control of world ethnology which was phenomenal. In part, this was the result of growing up with the discipline. But his mastery of ethnological detail was also augmented by diversified field experience, dedication to editorial labors—no man read more manuscripts during a lifetime—and an insatiable enjoyment of reading in all fields.

The titles of his courses gave the impression that they were descriptive. However, this was misleading. While many empirical data were included, this was merely for the purpose of illustrating principles and methods for the analysis of cultural data. Although Leslie Spier was an excellent undergraduate teacher, his real forte was instruction at the graduate level. Advanced students were stimulated by his wealth of ideas and concern with a diversity of problems. Beyond this his effectiveness lay in extreme patience and a willing expenditure of unlimited time with the individual. It can be truthfully said that no man has written as many dissertations.

W. W. HILL

ACKNOWLEDGMENTS

In a *Festschrift* volume such as this, the editors have a primary debt to the various contributors. In this case, because of long—though unavoidable—delays in publication, we are especially grateful to the contributors for their prompt responses and good-natured patience.

Several members and ex-members of the Department of Anthropology at Southern Illinois University, especially Jerome Handler and James Anderson, helped with the book by reading and commenting on the manuscripts. Riley's introduction also greatly benefited by comments from Laura Thompson, W. W. Hill, and J. Charles Kelley, although they are in no way responsible for shortcomings.

We are also grateful to Loretta Hill and Monte Keniston who spent long hours correcting and collating copy, to Linda Locke who handled final typing of the manuscript, and to Daniel Irwin who drafted charts and maps. A special note of thanks should be given to our wives for their ever-helpful comments and criticisms.

CARROLL L. RILEY
WALTER. W. TAYLOR

March 15, 1967

CONTENTS

AMERICAN
HISTORICAL ANTHROPOLOGY

American
Historical Anthropology
An Appraisal

CARROLL L. RILEY

IN SPITE of man's perennial fascination with human custom and with human beings in general, anthropology as a scientific discipline appeared rather late in time. In part this may be due, rather paradoxically, to the strong interest in the subject matter; intense interest is often tinged with emotionalism and even today the human animal has difficulty in viewing his own kind with detachment and objectivity.

Modern anthropology like many other disciplines had its origin in the classic world though it owes to classic speculation even less than most sciences. For example, historical anthropology may be said to have begun with the writings of Herodotus, Lucre-

CARROLL L. RILEY, is Professor of Anthropology at Southern Illinois University, Carbondale, has studied in the fields of ethnology, archaeology, and physical anthropology and has done fieldwork in Venezuela, Mexico, the American southwest, the Northwest Coast, and the Mediterranean area.

tius, and Tacitus but these men do not seem to have exerted any large amount of influence on Renaissance and post-Renaissance European anthropological thought.

The roots of modern cultural anthropology are varied and rose in part as a result of widespread European contact with peoples of other cultures especially after Columbus. The sixteenth-century Spaniards in fact produced, in Sahagun, one ethnographer and ethnohistorian whose field method was hardly matched until the last three or four decades. Sahagun managed to devise means of reconstructing Aztec culture, using informant techniques and documents with considerable critical ability. Other such reconstructions were less objective though often quite valuable. One interesting trend especially in the early seventeenth century was to have native culture interpreted by acculturated Indians or Mestizos, the best examples being Garcilasso de la Vega and Poma de Ayala. After the first flush of conquest, the Spanish enthusiasm for such studies waned somewhat, though missionaries continued to write ethnographies, sometimes valuable ones. Interestingly, the French, English, Dutch, and Portuguese failed to match the Spaniards in either the volume or the content of ethnographic writings.

Another trend that became exceedingly important, especially to archaeology, was the rise of antiquarianism in western Europe. The antiquarians were originally interested in the Middle Ages, but prehistoric monuments, forts, religious structures, etc. soon began to be systematically investigated. In the eighteenth century Stukeley used knowledge of classical history, architecture, and a crude kind of archaeology to investigate the great English ruins of Avebury and Stonehenge. Such men as Stukeley were, however, greatly handicapped by lack of a coherent method and by certain fundamental assumptions drawn from Christian cosmology that made difficult a serious interpretation of the prehistoric past. For a long time the antiquarian remained a scientific dilettante and today the very term antiquarian is in some disrepute, at least in this country.

Nevertheless, it was antiquarians plus early geologists, anatomists, and natural historians who founded archaeology, modern physical anthropology, and, to some degree, modern ethnology. In the latter half of the eighteenth century Hutton pointed toward a systematic historical geology pushing the origins of the earth far beyond the few thousand years allowed it by contemporary religion. The subsequent discoveries of Smith and Lyell led to an understanding of the slow processes of stratification and erosion and the use of fossils to develop a comparative dating system. Some of these fossils were human remains; as early as 1771 Johann F. Esper had discovered human bones associated with the cave bear in Germany. This discovery was brushed aside but in the next half century discoveries of human skeletons and stone tools, associated stratigraphically with extinct animals, were reported by Schmerling (Belgium), Tournal (France), MacEnery (England), and many others. By the middle of the nineteenth century men like Thomsen and Worsaae of Denmark were establishing a firm method for handling European archaeological material and had introduced such concepts as stone age, bronze age, and iron age for western Europe. Equally important was the work of the antiquarian Boucher de Perthes who as early as the 1830's insisted on a Pleistocene age for man in Europe.

Another trend was the work in the evolution of life forms, especially the contributions of Wallace and Darwin. This, of course, had direct implications for physical anthropology and was needed before such subfields as human paleontology could be properly explored. More important for our discussion, it influenced the study of culture. The underlying assumptions of much of the anthropology of the last half of the nineteenth century and the first part of the twentieth century were evolutionary in nature. When Boas and the later exponents of historical anthropology appeared, they were to react strongly, not in fact to evolutionism as such but to the abuse of evolutionary theory.

The early members of this unilinear Evolutionary School were drawn to it because they felt a need to investigate origins of culture and to establish a theoretical framework to explain cultural difference. Certain ideas, necessary to evolutionary thought, appeared quite early. Adolf Bastian postulated a psychic unity of mankind which under similar conditions produced similar ideas by the process of parallelism, though, like all the evolutionists, he recognized the fact of diffusion. Other early workers attacked various aspects of culture, for example, J. J. Bachofen of Switzerland worked out an evolutionary system for marriage and the family (an initial period of promiscuity followed by female dominance and matrilineality and then a higher patrilineal stage). J. F. McLennan of Scotland also worked on the problem of marriage, incidentally coining the words endogamy and exogamy. Herbert Spenser attempted to synthesize and organize the various evolutionary data into a coherent whole. These and others, however, were only forerunners to the two giants of the evolutionary school; Edward B. Tylor and Lewis H. Morgan. Tylor and Morgan forged evolutionary theory and even such brilliant contemporaries as Durkheim and Freud were, on the whole, content to use cultural evolutionism as a model on which they constructed their own highly original and provocative points of view.

Unilinear cultural evolutionism as used by Tylor and specifically outlined by Morgan had certain basic assumptions that were shared in full or in part by all evolutionists. The concept of evolutionism is based fundamentally on an analogy with biological evolution but actually goes beyond it in assuming a parallel development of cultural homologies. This concept is possible because of the assumption of psychic unity mentioned above. Briefly, the evolutionist felt that man, starting as a cultureless animal, was projected in certain broad directions by forces beyond his control. He gradually learned the rudiments of culture, passing to a stage of *savagery* characterized by exceeding crudeness of technology, an economy based solely on food gathering, a poverty of language, crude religious ideas, and particular kinds of kinship and other social institutions including—in the early phases—group marriage. As man progressed he invented new tools, found new food sources (agriculture, animal husbandry), enriched his language, enlarged his general world view, and changed social institutions to fit the new patterns. Such men lived in tribes based on polygynous families. This stage, called *barbarism,* was succeeded by the stage of *civilization*. Here man learned writing, invented elaborate tools, and began to override the essentially familial structure of society with secular or nonfamily associative units—thus the state developed from the tribe or clan and nonkin specialist groups appeared to cope with the new technology.

The evolutionists then saw the diverse cultures of the nineteenth-century world as groups on various way stations to civilization. Some of them were still savages (Australian aborigines) and were living the life that the ancestors of Europeans had lived and left many thousands of years before. Others were barbarians (most Africans and many American Indian tribes) and some (South and East Asiatics) were on the lower rungs of civilization, the upper rungs being reserved for west Europeans. As the present writer (Riley 1955: 293) summed up this theory,

> Central to this scheme of the evolutionists was the idea that all of mankind would eventually reach civilization by following out this evolutionary path from savagery. The inherent abilities of all people of the earth to attain civilized status was not questioned. The important assumption was that all cultures of the world were sharply ranked according to content and were ranked in all departments of culture. That is to say, savages had less elaborate languages *and* less efficient technologies *and* less developed religion than civilized folk.

None of the evolutionists denied diffusion as a device that would allow particular cultures to skip parts of the journey to civilization but they were primarily interested in the great panorama of generalized evolutionary dynamics and generally paid little attention to its parts. There was probably not, as is sometimes stated, a confusion between holistic and partitive culture. However, this holistic approach led to the great failure of evolutionism. Developmental schemes were either so rigid (as in Morgan's case) that data had to be warped and twisted to fit the theoretical framework or (as was true of Tylor) the investigator studied many cultural phenomenon without more than lip service to the underlying theory and with no serious attempt to fit the facts into the framework. To this was added a somewhat haphazard method, utilizing uncritical missionary and travelers' accounts, accepting what could be tailored to fit preconceptions and rejecting what could not. It was a reaction to such scientific shortcomings that caused the American historical anthropologists to earn their quite undeserved tag of anti-evolutionists.

Another problem for the American school of anthropology was that of racism. The racists, unlike the evolutionists, saw cultural advance as due to inherent biological differences in humans. Formally launched by Arthur de Gobineau, the racist school too had a scale of civilization; the Europeans (especially blond, blue-eyed north Europeans) were at the top, east Asiatics in the middle range and Negroes and Australian aborigines at the bottom. These categories were emphatically not evolutionary; no possibility for the advance of the "inferior" races was left and they were doomed to remain intermediate forms between "Homo nordicus" and his distant cousin the ape. Racial theories of culture actually never attracted the really fine thinkers of either the nineteenth or twentieth centuries, but racism did produce clever propagandists and in the twentieth century became of great political importance. For example, the pseudo-erudition of such men as Madison Grant and H. S. Chamberlain was used to justify changes in American immigration laws. Later these racial doctrines became the justification of the peculiar Nazi concept of historical process and even today they have a certain appeal (see Comas 1961). Boas and his students were especially effective in their attack on this grotesque scientific aberration.

One group of predecessors (and in part colleagues) that had considerable influence on American historical anthropology were the nineteenth-century Americanists themselves. The period following the Civil War was characterized by energetic growth of scientific institutions and in fact is called the Museum Period by

Wissler (1942 : *190*). The appearance of such organizations as the Bureau of American Ethnology (1879) and the anthropology section of the American Association for the Advancement of Science (Morgan was the first anthropologist to be president of this association—in 1879 - 80) undoubtedly stimulated the growth of anthropology in the United States. Even before the Civil War a certain amount of work on American Indians had been accomplished by such men as Albert Gallatin (founder, in 1842, of the American Ethnological Society), H. R. Schoolcraft, and Horatio Hale among others. This work was expanded in the post-Civil War period. Though the early anthropologists were normally drawn from nonanthropological fields, they contributed considerably to the early growth of Americanist studies. An important early figure was the geologist, Major J. W. Powell, who became the first director of the *Bureau of American Ethnology.* Powell was the guiding force behind the first definitive classification of North American native languages. A tribute to his careful and painstaking work has been given by the linguist Harry Hoijer (1946 : *10*).

> The first comprehensive classification of the languages north of Mexico was made by J. W. Powell and his associates, A. S. Gatschet and J. Owen Dorsey, in 1891. Though a number of far-reaching modifications of this classification have been suggested since, the groups set up by Powell still retain their validity. In no case has a stock established by Powell been discredited by later work; the modifications that have been suggested are all concerned with the establishment of larger stocks to include two or more of the Powell groupings.

One of the most promising areas for work in the post-Civil War period was the southwestern United States. Here were found relatively advanced agricultural peoples (Pueblo, Pima, to some degree Navajo) whose culture has certain general resemblances to that of pre-Spanish Meso-America. The situation was confused somewhat by the fact that this region had early been a part of Spanish Mexico and some of the Mexicanization may have been post-conquest in nature. Early Spanish penetration, however, gave considerable historical depth to the cultural data. In addition, the Southwest is an area favorable to archaeology; the dryness of the area and the extensive use of stone and adobe in building have left a vast array of ruins extending over many centuries. With this material at hand, such men as Bandelier, Cushing, Fewkes, Holmes, and Mindeleff combined archaeology, ethnology, and ethnohistory in a broad interpretative way. Characterized by Taylor (1954 : 561 ff.) as the Cushing-Fewkes Period, this era produced such sophisticated works as Fewkes' analysis of Mesa Verde archaeology in light of contemporary Hopi practices and Bandelier's brilliant fictional exposition of the pre-Spanish Frijoles culture, drawing from historic and nineteenth-century Cochiti sources.

Nor were all the fieldworkers Southwestern. Bandelier himself did extensive work on Mexican and Peruvian-Bolivian archaeology. E. G. Squier and D. G. Brinton also attacked Latin-American problems while J. C. Harris (best known for his Uncle Remus stories) was a comparative folklorist and one of those to see the implications of African animal tales carried to the United States and to Latin America by Negro slaves.

Probably the weakest field in nineteenth-century American anthropology was physical anthropology. Very little was known of the peopling of the New World and fanciful theories were advanced to account for the American Indians. In general, American scholars seemed less well-trained than European colleagues both in their knowledge of human paleontology and in their concepts of modern race differentiation.

We have discussed several of the currents of scientific ideas that influenced the early American historical anthropologists. The crucial task of actually identifying this group can no longer be delayed. In brief, it was those anthropologists who centered around Franz Boas and who were interested in collecting, by means of a classic natural history approach, fast disappearing field data; who used careful field methods; who had a great interest in historical interpretation; who tended to be inductive rather than deductive in method—to take into the field relatively few preconceptions; and who generally refrained from advancing grandiose generalizations of human behavior. One may probably refer to them as Boasians; certainly Boas was the one dominant figure.

Sometimes the term American Historical School has been used, but this perhaps implies more unity than was the case. The members of this group quarreled vigorously with each other and some of them even attacked their paterfamilias, Boas. One strong cohesive force was actually negative: it was the disbelief in classic evolutionism, and in the various other extreme schools of anthropology (see below). The most vigorous period of American historical anthropology was that between 1900 and the 1930's when Boas' influence was felt at first hand by most anthropologists in the country and when the intellectual dangers of evolutionism, racism, and extreme diffusionism were still real. Since the Second World War, the profession has swung away from the central core of historical anthropology as floods of newcomers entered anthropology and their interests became more diverse. This broadening of the subject base and the increased cooperation with other disciplines is certainly a good thing but it does increase the centrifugal tendency of this field.

One of our major groups of historical anthropologists today is that of archaeology. By definition somewhat involved with problems of time and space, the archaeologists have also introduced speculative reconstruction of cultures, and have discovered functionalism (a concept used by Boas and others decades before Malinowski). In addition, recent decades have seen considerable work in ethnohistory (for example, the work of E. Wheeler-Voegelin).

American historical anthropology itself is closely tied to the life and career of Franz Boas. Others helped in its founding but the stamp of Boas is clear. As Lowie (1937 : *129-30*) succinctly states:

> Boas' historical position is unique. He is the first anthropologist who combined ample field experience with an unrivaled

opportunity to train investigators. A. L. Kroeber, A. B. Lewis, F. B. Speck, R. H. Lowie, A. A. Goldenweiser, P. Radin, E. Sapir, F. C. Cole, L. Spier, M. Herskovits, G. Herzog, A. Lesser are among those who took their degrees under him, but his immediate influence extended much further. It includes men like A. M. Tozzer, R. B. Dixon, C. Wissler, S. A. Barrett, J. A. Mason, J. R. Swanton, R. Linton, who either studied under him for a limited time or pursued field research under his guidance. Still another category is made up of those who, like B. Laufer, P. E. Goddard, E. C. Parsons, G. Hatt, T. Michelson came to Boas as mature scholars.

This is indeed an impressive list of American anthropologists for the first third of the twentieth century.

The influence of Boas was not only felt by many individuals but extended over the whole anthropological spectrum. Leslie Spier (1943 : *111*) in an article summarizing Boas' contributions made the following comment.

> It has been remarked of Boas' students that they show his influence in the wide range of their own contributions and enterprises, and that this stands in contrast to the products of students of other teachers of anthropology. Where some of the latter students seem to be more systematic because they stayed with one topic, one cannot but feel that this was the result of rather narrow interests or of too limited a conception of anthropology. Where Boas' students have specialized it seems rather that, like Boas himself, they funneled down experiences from the whole of anthropology to concentrate on possibilities within a single branch. Thus what might be mistaken for the dissipation of interest or energy is actually recognition that anthropology must be seen as a coordinated whole.

Although Spier was not necessarily speaking of himself, it might be remarked here that this statement is an admirable description of his own breadth of interest and his holistic concept of anthropology.

Franz Boas entered anthropology after taking a doctorate in physics (Kiel University, 1881). He came into anthropology in part because of an interest in the views of such men as Bastian and particularly of Ratzel, who felt that culture was strongly shaped by geography. Boas in 1883 - 84 had an opportunity to test this latter concept for, as a member of a Norwegian meteorological expedition to Baffin Land, he made an extensive study of Eskimo culture in that area. His experience made him realize the complexities of culture and the uselessness of simple deterministic explanations for culture. This conviction continued all his life and through him became a guiding principle of American historical anthropology.

In the middle 1880's Boas launched his famous study of Northwest Coast peoples. In 1886 he accepted a position on the journal *Science* and in 1888 was appointed to the faculty of Clark University in Massachusetts. The die was now cast and Boas was to concern himself with anthropology for the rest of his life. He spent a few years in Chicago working mainly at the World Columbian Exposition. In 1895 - 96, however, Boas returned East to posts with the American Museum of Natural History and with Columbia University. This latter position was to last for forty years; from this vantage point Boas produced the students and the ideas that made him one of the seminal minds of his time.

American historical anthropology in its beginning years competed with two ingenious and original explanations of the origin and development of much of culture, those of Sigmund Freud and Emile Durkheim. The first of these we can deal with in a few words. Freud, who in the late nineteenth century was opening new vistas in the study of the human mind, made a venture into anthropological theory, combining information collected from work in analysis with current evolutionism. He evolved a bold (in fact breathtaking) vision of early man in a state of chronic trauma, acting out a version of the Oedipus complex and, by means of it, inventing much of religion and many other aspects of culture. In Freud's view, guilt hangs like some miasma over mankind because of the original sin of sons in killing and eating the primal father in order to obtain his wives. Subsequently, mankind has been chained in some terrible psychic prison in which the gloom of expiation is alternated with ecstatic reinactments of the primal sin, the totem substitute for the father being killed and eaten.

Freudian thinking about culture actually has influenced relatively few American anthropologists at least in the development of theoretical frameworks of anthropological systems. The same can be said for the speculations of Freud's colleague and rival, C. G. Jung. The collective unconscious of Jung presumably is a physiological phenomenon operating somewhat as does the complex neural and enzymatic activity that creates instinctive behavior in insects—that is, patterned behavior not dependent on culture. Jungians interpret certain patterns, *i.e.,* the mother (mother goddess), as deriving from this subconscious level of the brain. If true, such a situation would make radical changes in the interpretation of much of culture. There seems to be no particular evidence for such a theory, however, and even some against it (*e.g.,* the nonuniversality of the universal traits).

The influence of Emile Durkheim was more apparent, and actually two different aspects of Durkheimian thought entered certain schools of anthropology. The first concerned Durkheim's study of groups or collectivities, his analysis of which might perhaps be called functionalism of institutions—a realization of the importance of the kinds and numbers of intra-and inter-group contacts for an analysis of a larger social system. Anthropological application of this aspect of Durkheim's work has been fruitful, influencing such people as Radcliffe-Brown, Malinowski, Robert Redfield, Clyde Kluckhohn, W. Lloyd Warner, and Fred Eggan.

Another component of Durkheimian thought—not normally expressed in evolutionary theory but perhaps inherent in it—concerned the absolute difference between the mental processes of primitive and civilized man. This is treated in Durkheim's great anthropological treatise, *Les Formes elementaires de la vie religieuse,* but it was left for his students, particularly Lucian Levy-Bruhl, to develop this theme. To Levy-Bruhl, primitive man functioned on a nonlogical (or prelogical) basis that ignored causality. Essentially, he operated on a mystic level that merged reality and myth or, perhaps to consider this the other way around, combined symbolic systems and external reality in one mystic whole. This ethnocentric assumption, that there is a qualitative mental difference between primitive and civilized man, is actually quite common in the modern world. Shorn of Levy-Bruhl's sophistication and insight this concept appears *ad nauseam* in the Sunday supplements and the popular magazines and seems essentially an article of faith with the uneducated of our own culture. It may represent nothing more than the old tribal concept of "we human beings" versus all outsiders.

A number of later students have attempted to use these specific ideas of Levy-Bruhl or at least have been influenced by them. One of the most able of these scholars was the late Henri Frankfort whose studies of the early Near East are so justly famous. Frankfort suggested that the early civilizations of Mesopotamia and Egypt were mythmaking and failed to make a distinction between symbol and reality. In Frankfort's own words (1961 : 4):

> The ancients did not attempt to solve the ultimate problems confronting man by a single and coherent theory; that has been the method of approach since the time of the Greeks. Ancient thought—mythopoeic, "myth-making" thought—admitted side by side certain *limited* insights, which were held to be *simultaneously* valid, each in its own proper context, each corresponding to a definite avenue of approach.

Actually American historical anthropologists have kept refreshingly free from these ambitious and sweeping generalizations about man, whether primitive or civilized, ancient or modern. In large part, this cautious approach rests on a firm base of ethnographic field work. No one can spend any great amount of time in the intimate presence of primitive peoples without realizing that they function with the same everyday prosaic logic as does civilized man.

It would seem that in general most cultures do not encourage innovation or logical inquiry on any large scale, acting instead to maintain the *status quo* (cultures, here, operate as self-regulating devices). This, however, does not mean that certain cultures impose mythmaking mentalities. Most or all human beings dip into myth but seldom (unless they are confirmed mystics) confuse it with reality. They are indeed apt to lean to a *post hoc, ergo propter hoc* reasoning, but contrary to what is sometimes assumed this—while it is magical—is *not* mystical.

Many of the American historical anthropologists have reservations about still another approach to mental differences (culturally derived) as exemplified by the linguistic work of E. Sapir and of B. L. Whorf. Sapir and Whorf suggested that the basic characteristics of a language themselves strongly channel man's perception and categorization of reality and can further be related to its nonlinguistic culture. Probably the prevalent Boasian feeling here is not so much disapproval but, rather a feeling that drastic differences of grammatical form and of linguistic world view should not be overrated in an evaluation of cultural differences.

If much of the early activity of American historical anthropology was aimed at correcting the grosser errors of the evolutionists and of theories that assumed evolutionism, there was also considerable reaction to doctrines of extreme diffusion. The diffusionists began with two basic assumptions which were, like the assumptions of the evolutionists, unproven and probably unprovable: *1]* Man is uninventive to a very high degree, and *2]* Distance and lack of continuity are essentially unimportant in analyzing similarities between traits or complexes in separated areas. In addition great importance was attached to external form and relatively little to function. The question to the diffusionists is not *whether* diffusion took place but *how* it took place.

The Heliolithic school of G. Elliot Smith, a respected British anatomist turned anthropologist, actually had little effect on American anthropological circles. The idea that all high culture came from Egypt was incredible enough in 1920; with more careful analysis of early Old and New World civilizations it has become untenable. This kind of thinking (which we might characterize as the Prometheus approach to anthropology) did influence members of other disciplines, who read all too uncritically in anthropology. Also certain popular historians—especially H. G. Wells—gave the Heliolithic school a brief endorsement by incorporating it into easy-to-read histories of the world. In more recent years, a number of Promethean theories have appeared, related in spirit if not in actual content, to the Heliolithic school. These all accept the two point *dictum sanctorum* of extreme diffusionism but otherwise vary in plausibility from the carefully qualified historical reconstruction of Gordon Ekholm to the sweeping generalizations of Thor Heyerdahl. The latter writer, parenthetically, reverts to a racial mystique, once more burdening the poor (blue-eyed blond) white man by making him responsible for the origins of New World high culture.

The speculations of Graebner and Schmidt (the Kulturkreislehre) on the other hand deserve careful attention. They represent a painstaking method accepting the generalized diffusionist's assumptions, discussed above, but adding the concept of trait adhesion—*i.e.,* the transmission of trait bundles that maintain their integrity over thousands of miles and thousands of years. According to the Kulturkreise school, culture spread from some original center (or centers?) in a series of waves which, with the passage of time, overlapped one another as they spread to the ends of the earth. These separate waves can be identified by their component elements, which, in turn, can be isolated in any given culture. Although many of the American anthropologists paid lip service to the ingenious theory of this German-Austrian group and most of them admired the level of fieldwork, the Kulturkreise anthropologists did not have noticeable influence. In the final analysis their premises and reconstructions must be taken on faith, and to a group dominated by Boas' ideas, any theoretical system based on faith alone was anathema.

The question of interhemispherical diffusion (or lack of it) was and is of vast importance. It offers anthropology its one chance to compare complex cultures that show striking similarities, *cultures that may never have had significant contact after the terminal Pleistocene.* Here American historical anthropology went immediately to the heart of the problem. Whereas the unilinear evolutionists assumed (as an article of faith) that such similarities would develop anywhere and the extreme diffusionists assumed (as an article of faith) that all such similarity was due to contact, the Boasian group looked on the particular problem as a chance to work with a natural laboratory situation. In order to do this, however, it was essential to determine if the Americas had actually been sealed off from the events of the Old World. Until this determination has finally been made, the further work—so pregnant with theoretical implications—cannot validly be attempted.

By the period 1910 - 20, the concepts of historical anthropology were becoming clear and had, in fact, been spelled out by E. Sapir in his, now classic, *Time Perspectives.* It should be stressed here that historical reconstruction was not attempted by the Boasians for its own sake but because it became a valuable tool for attacking other, more basic, problems in the dynamics of culture. This point of view does not seem to have been really understood by A. R. Radcliffe-Brown who criticized "conjectural history" and talked of sociologically derived laws of culture. Actually, of course, Radcliffe-Brown did excellent "conjectural history" on occasion.

In the 1920's and 1930's, some of the students and colleagues of Boas became interested in the interplay of culture and personality. This took various forms, but one key problem was the discovery of modal or basic personality types. Such would ideally be the result of culture and would also profoundly influence culture. (For examples, see especially Kardiner and Linton, *The Individual and His Society,* 1939.)

Benedict, utilizing a culture and personality approach in a somewhat different way, attempted to describe (at least some) human groups in terms of a single psychic theme. In part borrowing her terms and her ideas from Nietzsche and Spengler, she spoke of the Apollonian Pueblos, the Dionysian Kwakiutl, etc. Though her pictures were overdrawn (Benedict recognized this), she did presage the more definitive *theme* or configuration approach of Opler and Kluckhohn. Here an attempt is made to abstract certain broad underlying themes, synthesizing from observable behavior. If such themes can be discovered and described and their subtle and shifting relationships to one another examined, then we have a new technique—a genotypic technique as it were—for understanding and examining culture.

Other psychological approaches can be passed over more quickly. The Gestalt or configuration school of psychology has been applied to anthropology; it may be fruitful but a discussion would take us too far afield from American historical anthropology. Learning theory, a system with a built-in feedback, has attracted some anthropologists (for example, Whiting and Gillin) who were trained in the historical tradition but does not seem to have made much impress on the American historical anthropology in general. Again we see the reluctance of most American anthropologists to accept simplistic explanations for complex problems. British structural social anthropology has, in the last twenty or thirty years, invaded America in many forms and guises. It is at a polar extreme to American historical anthropology in that it attempts to narrow the scope of anthropology—this at a time when many anthropologists, both physical and cultural, are calling for a utilization of the diverse subdisciplines in attacking anthropological problems (for a discussion of this, see Laura Thompson 1961). Nevertheless, social anthropology at times seems to cross-fertilize with American historical anthropology leading to viable hybrids. At its worst it finally succumbs, giving a death rattle of unintelligible jargon.

Two trends, both having their major growth in the 1930's, have considerably affected the latter day generations of American historical anthropologists. One of these is the quantitative method which P. Radin in a waspish book (*Method and Theory of Ethnology*, 1933) blames in large part on Boas' preoccupation with the methods of the physical sciences. It should be said that from Tylor's time, the attempts to quantify broad cultural data by the use of statistics have failed in spite of the seeming objectivity of such an approach. One example is the University of California trait list publications (culture element distribution lists—see *Anthropological Records*). A trait list can measure presence and absence, but functional integration, intensity, and even to a large extent formal variation are beyond it. Culture cannot be analyzed by IBM methods. It should be stressed that the leading American historical anthropologists generally opposed or early discarded this approach when large cultural entities were to be analyzed. Boas had no doubts about the complex interplay of culture. Spier spoke harshly of trait listing, and even Kroeber, though he was partly responsible for the California experiment, seemed to have entered it in a desultory fashion, with little obvious conviction. This is not to deny that quantification is of vast importance in certain restricted situations, for example, to the archaeologist.

The neo-evolutionism of men like V. G. Childe and L. White has had considerable influence on American historical thinking. Childe, indeed, belongs in the circle of seminal minds; since he was not an American, he perhaps cannot be claimed as an American historical anthropologist—and in any case his background and training were quite different (British and continental archaeological tradition plus a dollop of Marxism). He was exceedingly historically minded, but his main interest was in generalization, and history—or prehistory—simply formed the means and material for these larger problems. His unquenching demand for good work, his essential lack of dogmatism (in spite of a presumed Marxian bias), his willingness to discard a position when it became untenable or improbable, and his reluctance to accept easy unproven generalizations about human nature all go to make him a spiritual brother of Boas and Spier and the others of American historical anthropology.

Leslie White is a study in contrast. His obvious ability and insight is somewhat blunted by a doctrinaire adulation of Lewis H. Morgan and a tendency to polemics when his hero is attacked, criticized, or overlooked. The main difficulty of White, however, is his unwillingness to accept the fact that there is no serious theoretical difference between his own reasonable evolutionism and the Boasian approach. Julian Steward, among others, has utilized evolutionary theory without particular repercussions from his colleagues.

To sum up, American historical anthropology appeared at a time when rich and fruitful theories about men were advanced on every hand but the supporting facts were missing or inadequate. The Boasians shared in the banquet of ideas; they saw clearly the value of studying alternative human answers to universal human problems. Therefore, they devised new methods to accurately collect, record, and analyze field data. With this approach they became especially fitted to investigate certain kinds of basic problems. One such crucial task (still for the future) was outlined by A. L. Kroeber (1955) —delineation of the perimeters of culture with the eventual goal of defining human nature itself.

The American historical anthropologists realized from the beginning that to do field work with exotic peoples they must rid themselves of preconceptions, especially the value systems drawn from their own culture. This commonsense kind of relativism has produced dividends. Not only does it lead to a clearer understanding of other cultures but, as Margaret Mead (1947 : 17) wisely pointed out, it gives new and valuable insights into our own value system and our own pattern of life. On the level of structural-functional analysis the Boasians saw clearly the diversities and intricacies of human learned behavior. They were, therefore, ever reluctant to accept any sort of *simple* or *single* mechanism to explain culture. Perhaps to future anthropologists this will stand as their great and lasting contribution to the science.

Dane Zul

Village in Transition

HAROLD L. AMOSS

THE MOST striking single feature of Afghanistan's landscape is the Hindu-Kush, a high range of mountains extending roughly east and west forming the southern lip of the bowl known for centuries as Transoxania. The Hindu-Kush is a stark rampart which becomes higher and more impassable as it joins the Pamirs to the east. Although elevations of over 20,000 feet are found in the extreme northeast, the central Hindu-Kush has only one group of peaks, the Koh-i-Baba, that rise to just under 17,000 feet.

It is in this central section of the Hindu-Kush that the home of the Hazara, the Hazarajat, is found. It is a high land rising from the valley floors that average around 8,000 feet, completely devoid of trees and brush except along the banks of some of the streams.

HAROLD L. AMOSS is the Director of the Bureau of Community Development at the University of Washington in Seattle. He has done fieldwork in Afghanistan and is especially interested in ethnology, applied anthropology, and culture change.

Everywhere there is vivid and contrasting color, with mineral stained rocks, white patches of perennial snow on the highest peaks, and a deep blue in the sky and streams. The bare mountain sides are a pale green for a short time in the early spring when the new grass appears, and during the summer the poplars along the streams and the cultivated fields are a vivid green.

In spite of the short growing season, poor soil, aridity, and scarcity of level land, the Hazara have been able to adjust to the environment and develop an economy based primarily on agriculture. While they are not particularly good farmers and may not have had a long experience with agriculture, they have utilized a number of techniques designed to derive a living from an inhospitable country. They have constructed irrigation works (but no real terracing), build their houses only on ground unfit for agriculture, and even occasionally cultivate fields high on the slopes of the mountains at elevaitons of 10,000 to 11,000 feet. In addition to growing crops, the Hazara rely heavily on their sheep and goats grazed on neighboring slopes, and make full use of wild plants and animals, both game and fish. Perhaps as important as anything to Hazara success in living in the harsh environment of the Hazarajat has been their cheerfulness in the face of adversity, their willingness to exist close to the subsistence level and their reliance on a personal God.

As in any agricultural community, the annual work cycle is related to the growing season. Men prepare the fields and plant during the spring, weed by hand and irrigate the crops during the summer, harvest in very early fall and do little but take care of livestock during the winter. Women assist in the fields during the growing season and take care of their households throughout the year. Older children of both sexes work alongside their parents in the fields, while the younger boys and girls tend the flocks of sheep and goats on the mountainsides.

The presence itself of the Hazara in the Hazarajat presents an interesting problem of culture history and the movement of peoples, for it is obvious that the Hazara form an enclave surrounded by alien peoples. The Hazara are Mongoloids, speaking a group of dialects (*Hazaragi*) whose major component is Persian, and are Shia Muslim in religion. A majority of their neighbors to the north, Uzbecs and Turcoman, are also Mongoloids but are somewhat larger physically, speak a variety of Turkish, and are predominantly Sunni in persuasion. To the east and south of the Hazara are Caucasoids who speak either Persian or Pashtu and are predominantly Sunni. To the west are the Char Aimak, who are Mongoloids and speak Persian. Although there are some interesting similarities between the Hazara and the Char Aimak, there are numerous cultural traits separating the two. From the Hazara viewpoint the most important of these differences is religion, as the Aimak are Sunni. Thus in terms of race, religion, and language the Hazara are sharply separated from their neighbors.

There are two logical explanations for the situation; either the Hazara represent an older society engulfed by newer arrivals and perhaps pushed into this refuge area, or they themselves are intruders who dispossessed the former inhabitants. Elizabeth Bacon, who studied this problem intensively in connection with her interest in Mongolian social structure, concludes that the Hazara are descended from Mongols who entered the Hazarajat at various times between 1229 and 1447 (Bacon 1951 : *241*). The Hazara appear to have displaced a sparse Tadjik population from parts of this mountainous area. The upper end of the valley near Sar-i-Chishma west of Maidan graphically illustrates this presumed order of appearance in this area of three groups, Hazara, Tadjiks and Pashtuns. The apparently older Tadjiks have been squeezed into the middle reaches of the valley with Pashtuns at the lower end and Hazara occupying the upper end. Further data on the history of the Hazara tribes must await additional investigation of the various dialects of Hazara Persian and the form of Islam found among them.

The Hazara are divided into tribes occupying recognized tracts. Tribal names refer either to the claim of descent from a remote ancestor or to a descriptive term. It is difficult to be sure of a total number of tribes because not all Hazara agree on tribal designations except for the largest tribes. For example, the Besudi Hazara informants employed in this research did not recognize the tribal name Timuri (not the Timuri of Herat Province), identified as a small tribe living on the eastern border of Besudi territory by Hudson and Bacon (Hudson 1941 : *243*). These Timuri may be considered by some to be a lineage rather than a tribe. Tribal identification is employed by the Hazara themselves but reference to less remote ancestors, as is done by the lineage group, is more useful for purposes of organization. It is said there are slight differences of dress and speech between tribes, but comparative study of these differences has not been made.

The Hazara who are the subject of this study live at the eastern end of the Hazarajat in the Besud District of the Province of Kabul. The subgovernor of Besud, appointed by the central government, is a non-Hazara because of a long history of antagonism between Hazara and the politically dominant group in the national government—the Afghans. Incidentally, the provincial government does not station a Hazara soldier within his own tribal territory. Not only have there been pitched battles between the two groups in the past but the Hazara have traditionally allied themselves with the enemies of the Afghans. In this connection it is of interest to note that there are still supposed to be around five hundred Hazara who speak some Urdu as a result of service in the British-Indian Army (Ferdinand 1959 : *36*).[1]

The provincial government's link with the individual village is the headman (*arbab*). Formerly, this man functioned as the representative of the village; he was its spokesman, official host, and leading citizen. His office was hereditary but continuing tenure or even being chosen depended on personal qualities of leadership. The villagers could reject a son of the previous headman and elect his brother instead, or if the occasion arose that none of the sons were qualified in local eyes for headmanship, the village might place itself under the jurisdiction of the headman of a neighboring village. It was necessary for a headman to have enough wealth to act as the official host of the village. However, the institution was self-supporting because the villagers made contributions to the headman for use in an official capacity and the headman could expect presents from distinguished visitors in return for his hospitality.

The office of the headman appears to be in the process of changing (Ferdinand 1959 : 36). He no longer represents solely his people, but must attempt to be the local representative of the provincial government. The self-sustaining financial mechanism at this time is the percentage of taxes that does not go forward to the governor but remains in the headman's hands. However, his villagers expect him to use a part of this income to purchase the goodwill of officials when necessary. Great skill is needed for the headman to balance these two antagonistic roles and serve the needs of bureaucratic government on one hand and elemental, localized needs of the villagers on the other. The general feeling today is that the headman is moving more and more over to the side of the government, and there is a corresponding decrease in the affection and respect he receives from the villagers.

Among the Besudi, and this is probably true for most eastern Hazara, the headman has not a great deal to do with policy decisions at the village level. He is given regulations from the provincial government to administer in the village, and the mechanism for articulating the desires of local families is an informal board of elder males (*riš safīd*-greybeard). In a small village or a particular neighborhood of a larger village there may be only one elder; in other cases there may be several so that the composition of this board changes from time to time. This small group of greybeards acting in this manner is a widespread institution of nomadic peoples. Formerly the headman, the *mullahs* (religious specialists), and the *sayyids* (those who claim descent from the Prophet) were accorded high status and were called upon to arbitrate disputes. Now however, while there is little change in the high status of *mullahs* and *sayyids* among Besudi, there is a tendency to relieve all three of the responsibility of adjudication and to depend more on the judgment of the greybeards. There is an additional means for resolving dispute open to the Besudi by applying to the governor for judgment, but they seldom avail themselves of this method.

Hudson and Bacon have described the village as the basic unit of social organization among all Hazara tribes (Hudson 1941 : 244). Among the Besudi this is true only among small villages where the village is coextensive with the lineage. In larger villages where several lineages are found confined to their own neighborhoods, the village becomes more of a means of identification than a unit of social organization. The same term, *deh,* is used both for the small village and the neighborhood consisting of a single patrilineal lineage. It is true that a Besudi individual will first identify himself by his village, but it is the corresponding social unit, the lineage, which is basic to Besudi social organization.

Again according to Hudson and Bacon there are consolidations of administrative units under the leadership of a *malik* among other non-Besudi eastern Hazara. They report that there is no special name for this subdivision of a tribe (Hudson 1941 : 247). Among the Besudi certain headmen, because of personal attributes, are able to influence and in part control lesser headmen. There is a concept of a social unit intermediate in size between the lineage and the tribe which seems to approximate a canton. The term, *khol,* encompasses all people who live in the upper reaches of a stream drainage. The upper boundary of the *khol* are the divides between drainage areas, and the lower borders are placed at a point where members of the *khol* feel that there is no longer a continuity of group. The feeling of a relationship that exists between the members of a *khol* is considerably weaker than that of the family, lineage, or even the tribe. The term appears occasionally in place names and reflects cooperation in certain ways, *i.e.,* intermarriage, use of the same flour mills, and cooperative digging and maintaining of irrigation works.

One of the characteristic problems of emerging nations today is the movement of people from marginal agricultural regions to the cities. Economic advantages, greater opportunities for education and social interaction, relief from traditional regulation, and curiosity draw them to the city. Added to these advantages pulling people to the city are forces pushing them out of their traditional homes. It becomes difficult to satisfy traditional needs due to increased taxation or stronger competition from more successful agricultural areas, and when these needs change in response to better transportation and increased communication, the pressure to migrate becomes stronger. The tendency for cities to grow at the expense of the rural areas is true of Afghanistan. Because much of the Hazarajat is truly marginal agricultural land, the movement of Hazara into the cities, especially the capital city of Kabul, is pronounced.

An eastern Hazara village in the District of Besud was chosen for a three-part study consisting of a cultural inventory, and a study of both those who remained in the village and those who left for Kabul. Although excellent for other aspects of the study, the village proved to be too small to provide data on which a satisfactory analysis of individual personality in terms of migration and social change could be made. In June, 1957, there were fifty-nine persons said to be living in Dane Zul, down from a previous high of eighty-four. Not all of the fifty-nine could be found at any one time as many were making brief trips to Kabul in hopes of finding permanent work there.

There is no available information on how long Hazara from the region around Dane Zul have been moving to Kabul, but large-scale immigration appears to be a relatively recent phenomenon associated with the growth of the capital city and its increase in goods and services (Burnes 1842 : 231).[2] A sudden decision to move is not made; rather it is based on a number of visits and care is taken to follow a relative, live with him or near him, and to obtain employment through him. This means that the Hazara are found in certain sections of Kabul and in fairly restricted lines of work. While a few Hazara become entrepreneurs by setting themselves up in small businesses like bakeries (the King's baker is an Hazara from Dane Zul), generally these city Hazara are economically vulnerable because of general underemployment and the sporadic call for common labor. They generally work as coolies, snow shovelers, water carriers, and lower level house servants.

Dane Zul's principal contact with non-Hazara people is with Pashtu-speaking nomads, called *kuchis*. These nomads spend the summer in the mountains of the Hazarajat and then retreat before the snows to the warmer regions of Pakistan. Each *kuchi* group uses the same route year after year and summers in the same area. The Hazar-Buz (thousand goats) Clan returns each summer to the Dane Zul region.

Ferdinand, using *kuchi* informants, concluded that *kuchis* started appearing in the Hazarajat sometime during 1863-79 and after 1892 began to enter the Hazarajat in large numbers (Burnes 1842 : *19*). At first contact between Hazara and *kuchis* appears to have been peaceful, but tensions soon arose on two counts. The *kuchi* flocks began to compete with the animals of the sedentary Hazara for the meager grass on the mountainsides and trade relations led to bad debts and tensions. Today, the Hazara barters grain and *roghan* (animal oil) for such items as cloth, shoes, sugar, tea, rice, kerosene, salt, soap, and matches.

When tension between Hazara and *kuchi* has erupted into fighting and brought to the attention of the government, it has usually been adjudicated in favor of the *kuchis*. However, the government is now trying to control one of the principle sources of conflict between *kuchis* and Hazara—the *kuchi* practice of moneylending at usurious rates. Relations between the two groups illustrate the old tension between sedentary farmer and nomad, and between members of two distinct ethnic and religious groups. The relationship is economic in nature with little intermarrying or social intercourse. Hazara informants insist they do not speak Pashtu forcing the *kuchis* to learn Persian.

The people of Dane Zul live in a rigorous climate with poor

soil and have an inheritance system that fractionates land holdings. While the tax rate is no greater for them than it is for farmers in other parts of the country, the Hazara live so close to the level of bare subsistence that even a tax rate that is equitable on a national basis is onerous for them. These special factors and the general ones relating to the relationship between an urban center and its hinterland are the genesis of Hazara influx into Afghan cities.

As earlier mentioned, a Hazara family moving to Kabul does not do so in a sudden, final act. There is exploration, discussion, and return for visits after the move has been made. The new city dweller attempts to justify his decision and to influence others to join him. Not only do those who have left the village keep in close touch with the home village, but gypsies, nomads, peddlers, and travelers make their way along the mountain trails bringing news and information. Indeed, it is doubtful if twenty-four hours elapse before the village gets word of most important events. Word is brought directly from Kabul by word of mouth, and it is also relayed from the nearest village having a radio receiver. Although Afghanistan's literacy rate is rising, it is still too low to make the written word an effective news medium. But Radio Kabul is a powerful source of news and information. Dane Zul does not have a receiver and learns most of its news from Lolinge about twenty-five miles away. The point is that Dane Zul is not isolated but receives a veritable bombardment of news and opinions. The question becomes what is happening to it as the result.

Dane Zul is a poor village living very close to the breakeven level. Given the physical environment and the present level of technology, there are few minor innovations that would improve the way of life. But the villagers are being introduced to new ideas about the kind of life that is now possible and the means of attaining that life. There were not many alternatives in the past. They had made about all of the improvements they could make under the circumstances, and their idea of the proper values could be summarized by the catch-phrases, respect of age, male dominance, conformity, self-control, piety, and respect for tradition.

Now men want more for their families. They want roads as a first step toward economic progress and schooling. And they want the things that can be obtained by aggressiveness, business acumen, and opportunism.

These things are obtainable by moving to the city and almost a third of Dane Zul has taken this way to reach these goals. Among those who remain in the village are the traditionalist, the relatively successful farmer, the local exploiter, the one who is tied to the rhythm of the soil, and those who would leave but have no relatives to provide entrée for them. But even these have been affected by Kabul. Traditionally, the community's reference group was likely to have been the headman and the greybeards. Now it is largely drawn from responsible male relatives who have migrated to the city.

As yet there has been no appreciable change in the material culture of Dane Zul. The same crops are grown by the same techniques. Except for an occasional windowpane of Belgian glass the houses are identical to those that the Hazara took over centuries ago when they presumably entered the area. *Barak,* a dense, feltlike cloth, is still woven from lambs' wool on a horizontal loom by women. Money sent back by absentee landowners and presents brought on visits are all used for practical purposes. The face of the land will not change until the innovations presently sought in the village—roads and schools—are developed.

But there is clear change in the level of expectations even among those of Dane Zul who have stayed behind. It is true that many of the new dreams are based on living in Kabul, but many feel that somehow they will be able to achieve their goals right there in Dane Zul. It is now a period of transition when the newer values are becoming institutionalized. Doubts are raised over the role of the headman, and the traditionalist council of greybeards is losing influence. But the most powerful social control among these people, shame, still has meaning (Hudson 1951: 250-51). This consciousness of improper behavior is felt most readily in situations where affection and respect are concerned. Close relatives and those in authority, if they enjoy the affection of those under them, can bring forth shame and thereby tend to confine behavior to a somewhat narrow range of alternatives.

If deviant behavior is seen as that which violates institutionalized expectations, deviant behavior is difficult to identify in Dane Zul at this time, because not all of the methods of social control formerly important have been replaced. There is little evidence of antisocial behavior because of the safety valve of Kabul, and the fact that internalization of others' approval or disapproval is still important. Finally, deviant behavior implies conformity, and in a period of changing values, the question becomes conformity to what. A group may reject traditional normative reference groups and accept alien value systems with or without the socially approved means to realize these values. The process of transition itself poses problems of identifying the basis of conformity. Dane Zul is a quiet village obeying the provincial administration and retaining some of the older virtues that resulted in conformity. There is a revival of piety if the new mosque in the village is any indication. (It may possibly function as a reaction against the real or imagined secularism of Kabul). The conscientious observance of reciprocal duties towards members of the lineage is being eroded by migration. There is really at the moment little on which to evaluate conformity and deviance in Dane Zul. While it is clear that the community as a whole is reaching out for some of the newer goals of a growing Afgan city, there are several individuals who do not share this change in orientation. One is a man of about thirty-five who spends a good deal of time in Kabul. He is attracted by city life; yet he has never moved. He loves to hunt and has a reputation as such. While most of his wants are supplied by Dane Zul, there are still other needs that create an ambivalence for him. Another man, somewhat younger, has moved his family to Kabul and has an adequate job there. Yet his fondest dream would be to return to the village with his city-earned wealth and remain there as a *mullah.*

Dane Zul was always too small to develop a class system but

certain families were more important than others based upon descent from a former *khan* (tribal chieftain). Now achieved status is becoming valued primarily as a vicarious experience enjoyed through relationship with the city Dane Zuli. This kind of status system is important only within the Hazara group as all other ethnic groups of Kabul place the Hazara at the bottom of the social scale.

It is assumed that ambivalence towards a system of expectations, whether it is institutionalized or merely becoming so, results in strain. In this case, retention of the older order or acceptance of the new is made at a price. It is hard to define deviant behavior among the people of Dane Zul because of the difficulty of establishing norms, but anxiety and frustration are very evident. Every family house unit has a lock on its door now. In this connection it is said that the locks frustrate nonvillage thievery, but they would seem more likely to be a protection against fellow villagers, especially now that so many property owners are away in Kabul. One former resident of Dane Zul, now living in Kabul, was compelled to return to the village during the harvest of 1957 because he suspected that a relative, who was responsible for his farm property, was stealing some of the harvest. Stealing from a relative would have been very unusual in the past, and it appears now to be related to very complicated attitudes toward those who have left the village and acquired relative wealth. One informant learned that his father-in-law had died in Dane Zul, but because of the requirements of his job he could not leave Kabul. On his next visit to the village, he encountered reserve and hostility because he had not fulfilled his duty toward his deceased relative. Older people in the village could not understand that anything was more important than returning home at the death of a relative. This event illustrates the kind of tension that develops between traditional and new value systems.

The large-scale migration that is emptying Dane Zul has introduced both new values and goals and raised expectations. Yet in doing so, it has brought new frustrations and strains. Once these changes were introduced, the process became irreversible. Depopulation of the Hazarajat will present a complex and growing problem to the Afghan government. In spite of Afghanistan's progress in developing industries, agriculture should continue to be in the foreseeable future the mainstay of the country's economy. Admittedly, all available land around Dane Zul is being cultivated, so that the Hazara moving to the city have caused little drop in total agricultural production. Yet if this trend persists, there will be a loss of agricultural acreage very similar to what happened in Vermont when farmers moved to the more attractive farmlands of the Midwest. New land is being reclaimed from the desert in other parts of Afghanistan and advances in agricultural techniques will for a time offset the loss of the Hazara farmland, but Afghan planners must think of long-range possibilities and make some provisions for them in their calculations.

On the opposite side of the coin, there is the economic advantage to the country of having for industrial development access to this source of labor which is strong, used to hard work and living under difficult conditions. However, the introduction of large numbers of Hazara into industry might have profound effects on Afghan society.

With the exception of Kabul, there is little evidence of a middle class in Afghanistan. In the capital city, however, there is an incipient middle class, drawing its members largely from government employees. Industrialization will augment this incipient class and threaten the traditional relationship between the highest and lowest classes. At the same time, the establishment of industry has helped all over the world to create a new group of workers able to exercise growing political power. Economic and political factors will affect social values and help to tear down the tribal flavor of much of Afghanistan's society.

NOTES

[1]   "In the beginning of this century a Hazara regiment or battalion (?) was formed in Quetta under the Indian Army. Even today many Hazara from the southern regions (Jaghori, etc.) go to Quetta for occasional work, sometimes only for the winter, but also for a year or two" (Ferdinand 1959: *36 - 37*).

[2]   "All the drudgery and work in Cabool is done by Hazaras, some of whom are slaves and some free: in winter there are not less than ten thousand who reside in the city, and gain a livelihood by clearing the roofs of snow and acting as porters," Burnes (*1842 : 231*), as cited by Ferdinand (*1959 : 20*).

Pau Cin Hau

A Case of Religious Innovations Among the Northern Chin [1]

E. PENDLETON BANKS

BETWEEN 1910 and 1940 a religious movement spread through the Northern Chin Hills of Burma. Under the name of Pau Cin Hau (it is also known as Pau-Chin-Hau, Pau Tin Hau and Laipianism) and based on the dream-visions of a man of that name, it introduced monotheism to the animistic Chin. Originally the movement emphasized the curing of illness, substituting prayers to one god for the earlier pattern of expensive sacrifices to several spirits, but it developed into an organized and well-rounded religion, complete with rituals, buildings, sacred objects, and a priesthood or elite group. In many villages a majority of the people joined Pau Cin Hau, and it gave indications of becoming the dominant religion of the Northern Chin; however, Christian

E. PENDLETON BANKS, Professor of Sociology and Anthropology at Wake Forest College, Winston-Salem, North Carolina, has worked in Burma. Social anthropology, ethnology, race relations, and culture change are his principal fields of study.

missionary activity, which flourished during the same period, became even more successful than Pau Cin Hau. Following the death of the prophet in 1948 the organization of the movement all but disappeared and many of the members left the movement or became inactive.

Religious movements, especially those arising in a nonliterate society during a period of acculturation, have long interested anthropologists. Attempts have been made to classify such movements and to provide a body of theory to account for them (*e.g.,* Linton 1943; Wallace 1956). It may prove to be of value to examine this example more closely with the dual purpose of clarifying Chin culture history and of testing some of the theoretical formulations. No assumptions need be made initially that Pau Cin Hau is a nativistic movement or a revitalization movement; to find a place for it in the conventional nomenclature will be one of the tasks of the investigation.

The published materials for this inquiry are meager, being limited (to my knowledge) to a brief description in the *Census of India* for 1931 and an occasional mention in publications on Burma (*e.g.,* Stevenson 1944). General ethnographic and historical information on the Chin is far from plentiful; some work has been done on the Lushai, Kuki and other relatives of the Chin on the Indo-Pakistan side of the border, but for the Burmese Chin we are dependent on one old ethnography (Carey and Tuck 1896), one recent ethnography (Lehman 1963), and a few contributions on specialized topics—economics (Stevenson 1943) or linguistics (Luce 1959). Heavy reliance must be placed, therefore, on information collected in the field.

Chronology

The first task of the inquiry is to establish a chronology for the significant events connected with the origin and spread of Pau Cin Hau. Here I gratefully acknowledge a debt to Leslie Spier, who demonstrated in his classic study of another religious movement,

The Prophet Dance (Spier 1935; see also Spier 1927) — as in the bulk of his writings — that both culture historical and theoretical conclusions must be based on painstaking reconstruction and on locating precisely in time and space the crucial occurrences of a pattern.

According to the *Census of India* account (*Census of India 1931 II : 217 - 18*) the movement was founded by Pau Cin Hau as a result of a series of dream-visions that occurred between 1900 and 1903. Field data, however, reveal a tradition that Pau Cin Hau had earlier acted as disciple to a prophetess named Pi (an honorific) Nuam Dim, daughter of Hau Zui. According to this tradition, Tiddim, the chief village of the Northern Chin Hills, was ruled in the late 1880's by Khua Cin, a powerful and cruel chief, who held sway over two hundred villages and oppressed the poor. Nuam Dim had a vision in which Pa Sian (God — "Pa" is the usual male honorific) told her that he was angry with Khua Cin and that his vengeance would take the form of killing Khua Cin's son, wiping out his family line and destroying his *inn ka*. The *inn ka* is a sort of verandah that all Chin houses have. Made of planks and jutting out over a hillside, it is the center of family activity and the location of the status feasts which play an important part in Chin life. A man's status is symbolized by the size of his *inn ka* and by the location of his seat when visiting another *inn ka*. Khua Cin's *inn ka* was very large, made with extra wide planks — "the width of a *za bo*," or extended hand breadth — and located where the modern football field is.

Nuam Dim told others of her vision and met with hate and scorn from the people of Tiddim and threats of death from Khua Cin. At this point Pau Cin Hau enters the scene. Then aged sixteen or seventeen, he was chosen by Pa Sian to prophesy the date when the *inn ka* would be destroyed. On the predicted date the *inn ka* "broke like thunder" and the other details of the prophecy were fulfilled. Nuam Dim, vindicated, fades from sight — the date and manner of her death are unknown — and Pau Cin Hau after a considerable interval becomes the prophet.

Pau Cin Hau was born around 1872, a member of an upper-class family which had moved to Tiddim from Mualbem, a large village eleven air miles south of Tiddim. According to his own account (*Census of India* 1931 *11 : 217 - 18*) he was ill from 1888 to 1902, and from 1900 onward had a series of dream-visions that inspired his religious teaching. Interestingly, he does not mention Nuam Dim or the events connected with Khua Cin, which must have occurred about 1888. As a result of the dream-visions he was cured of his illness in 1903. His first attempts to share his experience with others were unsuccessful: "I stood alone in my faith for three years during which time the members of my own family, even, reviled instead of encouraging me but gradually as my neighbours and even people from distant villages saw me still enjoying sound health my religion began to spread until after six years people from all parts of the hills became my fellow worshippers" (*Census of India* 1931 *11 : 217*). It would appear that 1906 - 9 was the initial period of diffusion.

Around 1930, Pau Cin Hau moved from Tiddim to his ancestral village of Mualbem. By that time the movement was well established, and since it is not mentioned in the 1911 or 1921 census reports, the 1920's probably represent the period of greatest growth. In 1931 the number of followers of Pau Cin Hau in the Chin Hills District was estimated by a government official at 35,700, distributed as follows: Tiddim Subdivision, 26,000, Falam Subdivision, 9700, and an undetermined but probably small number on the Indian side of the border (*Census of India* 1931 *11 : 218*). It is significant that the great majority of the followers lived within the same Subdivision as the prophet, *i.e.,* within forty or fifty miles. This is not unexpected, considering that the only communications in the Chin Hills in those days were mule trails and footpaths and that the movement spread by means of personal visits of disciples. The movement reached Lumbang, which is now fifty-five miles by road from Tiddim, only in 1933. It came via Vaw Klak, which is fourteen airline miles southeast of Tiddim and thirteen airline miles north of Lumbang. Twenty-seven miles in twenty-five years represents what is certainly a modest rate of diffusion (1.08 miles per year, which is very close to the rate of diffusion of Neolithic material culture traits; see Edmonson 1961).

Available estimates do not indicate any marked change in the number of followers during the next three decades. Stevenson (1944) gives the number as 30 per cent of the population of the Manipur River valley between Tiddim and Falam, which would be between 30,000 and 40,000, and government officials estimate there were about 40,000 in 1960. The expansion of the movement seems to have halted well before Pau Cin Hau's death, which occurred in 1948.

The figures for the later years are probably misleading and should not be taken at face value as indicating a flourishing state of affairs. By that time Christianity and Pau Cin Hau had divided the population of many villages in the Tiddim Subdivision. The usual reply of a non-Christian to the inquiry of a government officer or census taker about his religious affiliation was "Pau Cin Hau"; yet it might have been years since he took an active part in the movement. The situation at Lumbang, a village nineteen miles north of Falam on the Falam-Fort White road, illustrates the present state of the movement. Nearly half the population identify themselves as Pau Cin Hau; yet the meeting place is in ruins, there are no *palik* and few Pau Cin Hau ceremonies are held. Everyone who is not Pau Cin Hau is Christian, and Pau Cin Hau is thought of as an anti-Christian movement by both Pau Cin Hau and Christians; but in many families the parents are Pau Cin Hau and the children are Christian. The movement is more active in villages close to Tiddim and Mualbem, but even there the active followers think of themselves as a faithful minority struggling against apathy to keep the movement alive.

Dogma and Ritual

It is difficult to get a clear statement of Pau Cin Hau beliefs from informants; indeed, it appears that the movement does not possess an elaborate theology. Myths are lacking, except insofar as the traditional accounts of the deeds of Nuam Dim and Pau Cin Hau have a mythical aspect. A good place to begin is with the dream-visions of Pau Cin Hau as told in his own words:

> The first of these dreams and visions was in 1900 when in my dream I saw a twisted rope suspended between the heaven and the earth. Many people were trying to climb it but no one was successful. I knelt in prayer and ascended the rope as far as the thirtieth heaven, then descended to the earth and still by means of the rope, which had penetrated the ground, descended deep into the heart of the earth.
>
> A year later I heard the voice of God calling me by name and commanding me to look forward to the future when many mysterious things would occur. I saw visions of railway trains, steamships and other Western inventions although I had never been away from the hills and had no knowledge that such things existed. There were visions of great battles, of stone-clad horses and horsemen. There were English, Indian and many unknown nations engaged in the struggle. I saw amongst other things the unknown nations falling dead and disappearing from view while my own people who were with me, though still alive were left cowering in the valleys between the hills, covered with dust and rubbish. I tried to cover my face with my hands but in spite of myself I had to continue gazing into a mirror held by an Englishman so that the vision remained in my mind's eye for three days and three nights.
>
> In 1902 I had another dream. In this dream I saw an Englishman who appeared to me to be divine. He wanted me to learn lessons, taught by means of stones in the shape of letters, which put together formed a book. I tried to learn the same and eventually succeeded and my eyes then opened. . . .[2]
>
> . . . In the following year, in another vision I saw many races of people flocking together in a huge plain. Then there appeared a being who came riding the sun as a horse, the bridle and other trappings of which glittered like gold. Then I shouted "Behold and obey the order of God" and while all bowed themselves to the earth he called my by name twice in succession "Pau Chin Hau, Pau Chin Hau, will you worship me?" I said "who are you?" and he replied, "The Lord who made heaven and earth, men and

animals, the sun, the moon and the stars and who has power to cure all sickness."

I had faith in him and in a moment was cured from my illness of fifteen years. During those years for the cure of that illness I had paid the sum of Rs. 400 in making sacrifices of various kinds of animals to the nats or demons. The cure of God was complete and cost nothing (*Census of India* 1931 *11:217*).

From this account and the testimony of informants it would appear that followers of the movement believe in one all-powerful, creator god (Pa Sian) and that the most important aspect of the relationship between Pa Sian and his worshippers is the curing of sickness. Pau Cin Hau himself states that his main contribution was to replace the numerous spirits formerly worshipped by the Chin with a single god, thus abolishing the expensive sacrifices and offerings that used to be required and showing the way to the cure of disease (*Census of India* 1931 *11:217-18*).

There are seven different types of ritual practiced by Pau Cin Hau followers, classified according to occasion and function:　*1]* "sweeping or cleaning the house," introducing Pau Cin Hau to a household;　*2]* the curing ritual;　*3]* the Sunday ritual;　*4]* prayers for the welfare of the village;　*5]* the planting ritual;　*6]* the New Year; and　*7]* Pau Cin Hau's birth- and death-day. These will be described briefly on the basis of informants' reports.

1] *"Sweeping or cleaning the house":*　When the head of a household expressed a desire to join the movement, a party of followers, led by *palik,* would perform this ritual in his house. The *palik* were the elite of the Pau Cin Hau movement (the term is obviously derived from Burmese *palei'* which is derived from English "police," a derivation explicitly recognized by informants). They paid a fee for the privilege; there were differences in rank among them, some being referred to as "commissioned officers." *Palik* wore a distinctive red headdress and were entitled to fees and other perquisites (See *Census of India* 1931 *11 : 218*). The members of the party began by dancing in a circle in a counterclockwise direction on the host's *inn ka.* They danced with their hands held in front of their foreheads and with a peculiar (by Chin standards) stomping gait, singing songs. Then they divided into three groups to drive out the three spirits that, in traditional Chin belief, inhabit every house—one on the *inn ka* near the water trough (a massive object made from a single log that usually stands along one edge of the *inn ka*), one in the house, and one beneath the house near the back. Frequently the "cleaning" was climaxed by taking down and throwing away some of the animal skulls that are ordinarily displayed on the front of a Chin house. Hunting trophies and *mithan* (a bovine animal kept solely for feasting and sacrifices) skulls were left, but skulls of animals killed for spirit-worshipping ceremonies were removed. The *palik* were paid a fee of three kyats (about sixty cents).

2] *The curing ritual:*   When a person was sick, a single *palik* was sent for. He prayed to Pa Sian for the recovery of the patient. It is interesting that the curing process, which Pau Cin Hau felt was the most significant contribution of his movement, was carried out with a minimum of personnel and formal ritual. A small fee, usually in the form of *zu* (millet beer), would be paid the *palik*.

3] *The Sunday ritual:*   Pau Cin Hau members used to meet every Sunday; at Lumbang, a private home was used for a while, then a meeting hut was built at one of the *tlangs* or dancing grounds of traditional Chin religion under a large banyan tree (*Ficus religiosa*). These Sunday meetings included a circle dance like the one described for the cleaning ritual, presumably danced outside the hut, and a series of public prayers by the members. These prayers followed no particular formula but were extemporaneous—"they shouted whatever came into their heads, like Baptists." A group of empty *zu* pots were kept in the hut and occasionally the prayers were shouted into the pots. Sometimes *zu* was drunk during the meeting.

4] *Prayers for the welfare of the village:*   Certain locations on village lands, usually marked by large rocks or trees, were thought to be inhabited by spirits in traditional Chin belief. *Palik* sometimes conducted prayers at these places for the welfare of the village, possibly analogous to the cleaning ritual. A large pig would be killed and eaten and *zu* was drunk. I do not know on what occasions this ritual was held or who furnished the pig and *zu.*

5] *The planting ritual:*   The Chin are swidden agriculturalists, and the time of planting at the beginning of the southwest monsoon in May is an important occasion. *Palik* were called upon to conduct prayers for the success of the new crop at planting time. This ritual was conducted at one of two locations known as *pawn hmun;* the location chosen depended on whether the fields to be planted were above or below the village. The *palik* were paid with *zu* for this ritual, which was considered a service performed for a specific family.

6] *The New Year:*   Traditionally the New Year (mid-October) was celebrated by the Chin with a festival that lasted three days or more. It marked not only the beginning of a new calendar year but also the time of harvest and the beginning of the dry season. Many animals were killed and much *zu* prepared, and the feasting, drinking and dancing went on day and night. Pau Cin Hau himself considered that this was the only traditional community-wide ritual retained by his movement; his followers referred to it as the "Festival of God" and went to their meeting place for prayers at the conclusion of the celebration (See *Census of India* 1931 *11 : 217 - 18*).

7] *Pau Cin Hau's birth- and death-day:*   A ceremony is performed on the anniversary of Pau Cin Hau's death, December 28. It is intended also to commemorate his birth, which also occurred in December, exact day unknown. No further details are available, except that this ceremony is considered by followers to be one of the two important rituals (the other being the New Year ritual).

There seem to be two patterns for these rituals, neither particularly elaborate. One, which we may call the public pattern, seen in 3], 4], and 6] and probably 7], includes dancing, songs and/or prayers, and *zu* drinking, the participation of many or all of the *palik* and other followers, and sometimes feasting, present in 4], 6] and probably 7]. The other, the private pattern, is seen in 2] and 5]—curing and planting—which are interpreted as being services to individuals or families. Here one *palik* could officiate (although others might be called in, especially in connection with curing), a fee was paid, prayers were said and *zu* was drunk, at least by the *palik*. The cleaning ritual   1] contains elements of both patterns: it was a service to one family and a fee was paid, but otherwise it followed the public pattern.

Of the ritual elements, the prayers or songs offer the most interesting possibilities for further study. (I suspect that these terms are interchangeable, except for the extemporaneous prayers uttered during the Sunday ritual). I recorded several of the songs in Tiddim dialect but did not succeed in getting satisfactory translations of most of them; informants commented that the style and choice of words made them hard to translate. I saw a copybook, much used and worn, in which some of the songs were written in Pau Cin Hau's alphabet and in the Roman transcription. I did not hear any of them sung.

According to tradition, nine of the songs were composed by Pau Cin Hau and an indefinite number have been composed by his followers. The songs are called *nuam dim la*—Nuam Dim's songs—or *pa sian la*. Here are translations of two songs.

> If you do not follow me, the person who does not want to listen will see what happens to the nobles' *inn kas*.
>
> The world is wrinkled with age and I am not going to give my message again; this is the last time I introduce myself to you and to the people of the world.
>
> As noble as the sun, I am supreme as the sun, no one can compete with me; they do not want to follow my advice.

> Do not do as you please, like a wild bird; anything that opposes
> me will be destroyed by me.

As to content, these and the other songs for which I obtained
translations appear to be exhortations to follow Pa Sian, coupled
with threats to those who refuse. These songs are supposed to have
come to Pau Cin Hau (and presumably to some of his followers)
in dream-visions. Some of them contain admonitions to proper
conduct, but the oracular tone and vagueness of language make it
hard to say just what proper conduct is. The form of the songs is
quite consistent. Each song contains two lines, when written by
Chin informants, and each line contains two or more clauses or
sentences; if more than two, the extra clauses usually paraphrase
each other. The lines are uniform in length, most having eighteen
or nineteen syllables, with an extreme range of fifteen to twenty-
three, so that they could be sung to the same melody or to an
interchangeable set of melodies. Unfortunately I was unable to
find anyone who could sing the songs, although I was told they are
still sung occasionally. In form and style the words resemble those
of other Chin songs; composing new songs, especially love songs,
is a favorite pastime. A musicological study of Pau Cin Hau and
other Chin songs would be rewarding.

Analysis

This inquiry would be incomplete if no attempt were made to
analyze the phenomenon of Pau Cin Hau; on the other hand, to
analyze in the absence of certain pieces of information (for example, details of Nuam Dim's life) —to say nothing of the lack of an
adequate ethnographic study of the Northern Chin—is to run the
risk of error.

One of the noticeable features of Pau Cin Hau is that, arising
during a period of culture contact, it includes traits that can be
traced to Christianity and other departments of Western culture.
The table lists the more obvious Western traits, as well as those
that have clear antecedents in pre-Pau Cin Hau Chin culture.

Western and native traits in Pau Cin Hau

WESTERN	NATIVE
Monotheism	The name *pa sian*
Extemporaneous prayers	Use of headdress in palik's costume
The word *palik*	Location of meeting place in *tlang*
A building as meeting place	Dancing (but not the exact step)
Services on Sunday	Songs
Propagation by disciples	Use of *zu* pots in ritual
Steamships, etc., in Pau Cin Hau's visions	*Zu* drinking
Basis of Pau Cin Hau's alphabet	House spirits involved in "cleaning house" ritual
	Dream-visions in curing
	Time and place of planting ritual
	New Year festival

A glance at the history of Chin contact with the British and American agents of Western culture makes diffusion a plausible hypothesis, especially if we assume that these ideas came to Pau Cin Hau after 1900. According to Carey and Tuck (1896 *1 : 118 - 26*) the chief of the Kanhow "tribe" (probably a lineage; there is a circumstantial account of the splitting of the Sokte lineage based at Mualbem into a senior and junior branch, the latter taking the name of Kanhow from its first chief and becoming fully independent under Kochin's successor, Howchinkup) from 1868 to 1890 with his capital at Tiddim was Kochin (undoubtedly the Khua Cin of Pau Cin Hau tradition). The British having occupied areas in India not far away from Chin territory, Kochin found himself in 1871 assisting the Maharajah of Manipur and the British in putting down a rebellion of the Lushai, who are linguistic relatives of the Chin. Substantial contact with the British, however, came only after the Third Anglo-BurmeseWar of 1885. The British won the war in a few days and with it the right to occupy Upper Burma; realizing the right took several years, however. Negotiations were opened with the Chin in 1887 - 88 and raids and telegraph wire cutting on the part of the Chin called forth punitive columns on the part of the British. Based on Kalemyo the British finally penetrated deep into Chin territory, motivated by the fact that a Burmese rebel leader named Shwe Gyo Byu Mintha had fled into the Chin Hills,[3] and captured Tiddim in March, 1889 (Carey and Tuck *1 : 29 - 30*).

In 1890 a permanent post, complete with political officer, was established at Haka, a fort built at Fort White, about twenty-five miles from Tiddim, and mule trails were constructed. In 1891 - 92 two parties of Chin chiefs were taken to Rangoon, entertained, and pointedly shown the sights that demonstrated British power; un-fortunately the people back home refused to believe the chiefs' description of what they had seen and greeted their stories with scorn. (It is surely plausible to see these stories as the source of Pau Cin Hau's vision of steamships and railroads ten years later.) A rebellion broke out in 1892 and was put down the following year, and by 1896 the Chin had been officially disarmed (the presence of many antique firearms today indicates that the disarming was far from complete) and the country of the Northern Chin brought under "administration" (Scott 1900 *1 : 441 - 51*).

It must be kept in mind that direct personal contact between Chin and Europeans during the early days of British rule was minimal. The British administration was spread very thin in Burma, and the Northern Chin Hills was a remote and insignifi-cant area, entitled to a political officer and a garrison of Indian troops. Opportunities for acculturation were relatively limited. Headhunting and intervillage warfare were abolished and taxes collected; modifications were made in the system under which war captives (especially Burmese) had been enslaved. Indirect rule, however, tended to preserve the social structure, with the heredi-tary chiefs serving as magistrates and tax collectors for the British.

As far as I can tell, there were no immediate economic dislocations. The main effect of the presence of the British was to notify the Chin that thenceforth they would be subordinate to the local representatives of a remote and powerful society with a culture that was for the time being a great mystery, a closed book.

Parallel with British conquest were efforts by missionaries, mainly Americans representing the American Baptist denomination, to reach the Chin with the conscious intention of bringing about acculturation. The missionaries had learned in the days of Adoniram Judson in the early part of the century that the non-Burmese peoples responded more readily to Christianity than the Buddhist Burmese. Before the Third Anglo-Burmese War they had been confined almost entirely to coastal areas. They lost no time in taking advantage of the expansion of British domination. In 1887 a mission station was established at Thayetmyo, 290 miles southeast of Tiddim, to serve as a base for work among the Northern Chin, and in 1888 a station for the Southern Chin was opened at Sandoway, 335 miles south of Tiddim. Finally in 1899 the first station actually in Chin territory was established at Haka, fifty airline miles south of Tiddim (Merriam 1900: *114-16*).

A couple named Carson operated the station at Haka, assisted by a physician named East, who traveled throughout the Chin Hills. There were also some native (Karen) preachers who spoke Chin. Carson died in 1908 and was succeeded by Mr. and Mrs. J. H. Cope. In 1910 the station was moved to Tiddim because more converts were there. Cope learned the Chin language early, reduced it to writing using a Roman alphabet and opened schools; he was later appointed honorary Superintendent of Education by the British and pupils in the government schools still learn to read from primers written by him.

There is no firm evidence that Pau Cin Hau was directly involved in this religious activity; according to Mrs. Cope, he was not a convert and indeed always opposed the missionaries. But it is likely that he was exposed at least to a secondhand influence by the time he began to have visions; and the most probable source is the traveling physician. Here was a ready-made conjunction between monotheism and curing. If Pau Cin Hau's exposure was second-hand and he did not participate in any services or hear any sermons, we have an explanation of the curious discrepancies in his teachings: the absence of Jesus, the cross, the Bible, baptism, etc. It would appear that we are dealing with an authentic case of stimulus diffusion. This is certainly the case with Pau Cin Hau's alphabet (see note 2).

If Nuam Dim is to be credited with originating any of the Pau Cin Hau doctrines, however, difficulties arise. Although one informant insists that her prophecy and the breaking of the *inn kas* occurred before the arrival of the British, it is tempting to equate this episode with the British capture and destruction of Tiddim in 1889; and this can be done without straining the chronology of known events. It is highly improbable that Nuam Dim could have been influenced by Christianity in the 1880's. Whatever contributions she made to the movement, then, must have been either traditional Chin traits or innovations of her own. I am inclined to believe that her true significance was in providing Pau Cin Hau during his adolescence with an initiation into the techniques and language of mysticism.

If this analysis is to be more than a search for the origins of the traits associated with the Pau Cin Hau movement, a theoretical framework is needed. Wallace (1956*b*) has provided a useful framework in his theory of "revitalization movements." Revitalization movements are defined as "deliberate, conscious, organized efforts by members of a society to create a more satisfying culture" (Wallace 1956*b*: 279). On the assumption that he is dealing with a generic type of cultural event, Wallace outlines a theory that attempts to explain such movements in terms of stress, culture change, and psychodynamics. Among other things he provides a scheme of stages through which a typical movement will pass. In the treatment that follows I shall use Wallace's terminology.

including his labels for the stages (most of the terms are self-evident; see Wallace 1956*b* for definitions and further discussion).

I STEADY STATE

We are handicapped at the outset in lacking a clear picture of the steady state of Chin society and culture prior to Nuam Dim and Pau Cin Hau. Socially and politically the Chin were accustomed to what some societies would consider catastrophic changes. Warfare with the Burmese, and in earlier times with the Shans, was the normal condition, with each side raiding the other for slaves; Chin women were in such demand among the Burmese that the conventional (but probably false) explanation for their practice of tattooing their faces was that it was done to make them unattractive to the slave raiders. Raids were often followed by reprisals; the Burmese burned Tiddim in 1850 (Carey and Tuck *1 : 118 - 21*). Intervillage headhunting raids and battles were frequent, and the nearest thing to stability was reached when a lineage established control over several villages as in the case of Kochin's Sokte-Kanhow. Certainly the concept of a steady state with shifts and fluctuations around a moving equilibrium is more appropriate to the Chin situation than older, more static concepts of equilibrium. Chin religion, however, seems to have been more of a constant, consisting of a belief in a number of spirits to whom animal sacrifices were made at planting time and in case of illness; shamanistic practitioners who diagnosed illnesses and interpreted omens through trances or dreams mediated the religion (Carey and Tuck *1 : 195 - 99*).

II THE PERIOD OF INCREASED INDIVIDUAL STRESS

This is difficult to document for the Chin during the period before the Pau Cin Hau movement originated. Presumably there was considerable stress connected with Nuam Dim's prophecy and its fulfillment, and Pau Cin Hau's own experience was stressful, if only because of his long illness. It would be reasonable to assume that the British conquest and domination were experienced by the Chin as stressful events, but we have no direct evidence of regressive behavior or other typical reactions to stress on the part of Chin individuals. The period of real stress came later when the missionaries were active and many villages became battlefields for the struggle between Christianity and Pau Cin Hau. Thus it may in the end be easier to explain the *spread* of the movement than its *origin,* and we may be forced into the apparent paradox of seeing the Pau Cin Hau movement as a stress-inducing factor in the situation that led to its own growth.

III THE PERIOD OF CULTURAL DISTORTION

Here again it is easier to see why cultural distortion should have taken place toward the end of the nineteenth century than to show that in fact it occurred. Lehman (1963) provides what may be the essential clue, suggesting that in earlier contacts with Shan and Burmese culture the Chin's usual reaction was an overwhelming sense of the inferiority of their own culture, followed presumably by a reappraisal of at least some of their patterns (though there was little direct adoption of foreign patterns; for example, Buddhism failed completely to penetrate the Chin Hills). Simple exposure through contact with a handful of British officials and the early missionaries may well have been enough to sensitize the Chin to the shortcomings of their own culture (for example, the failure of their tactics to defeat the British) and to develop in them feelings of dissatisfaction with traditional patterns. Further, their social structure had been built on the pattern of gaining status through hunting, headhunting, and the holding of extravagant feasts; and even though the British did not attack the status system directly, the *Pax Britannica* must have led to a search for substitute patterns for the attainment of status and for self-expression. Cultural distortion certainly occurred later when a sizeable number of Chin became adherents to Christianity.

IV THE PERIOD OF REVITALIZATION

1. *Mazeway Reformulation.* Wallace finds it useful in analyzing the cases of religious inspiration that usually accompany revitalization movements to introduce the concept of the "mazeway," which is defined as a kind of cognitive map that an individual has within his brain, including concepts of himself and other people and objects, values both positive and negative, and ways of obtaining desired ends. When for various reasons an individual's mazeway becomes unsatisfactory—when, for example, it no longer conforms to external reality because that reality has changed—he may give evidence of mental or personality disorder, as well as somatic illness. Occasionally such an individual undergoes a sudden personality change, which may include the disappearance of somatic symptoms, and in Wallace's terms we may say that "mazeway resynthesis" has taken place; he has worked out a new mazeway and restored his biopsychic equilibrium. What makes this relevant here is that in the revitalization movements studied by Wallace there was usually a prophet or leader who underwent mazeway resynthesis and went on to reformulate the culturally patterned mazeway of his society. The process of individual mazeway resynthesis was usually interpreted as religious inspiration and described by the prophet and his followers as a revelatory communication from the supernatural (Wallace 1956a). The personal history of Pau Cin Hau fits very well the pattern described by Wallace. There is the period of illness and withdrawal from effective functioning, which in Pau Cin Hau's case lasted fifteen years; unfortunately we do not know his symptoms in detail. There is the dramatic episode, the dream-visions, spread over three years and culminating in the vision of a god riding a horse with golden trappings. There is the immediate and miraculous cure of the prophet, combined with the instructions to tell others of his discovery of the true nature of the supernatural. And the doctrines to be promulgated represent a new direction for Chin culture. In understanding all of this it becomes almost irrelevant that we can

point to a foreign cultural source for Pau Cin Hau's innovations; what is significant is the psychocultural process that is taking place.

2. *Communication.* Wallace found that the prophet was usually given explicit instructions to communicate his experience to others; this is the case with Pau Cin Hau. And Pau Cin Hau's encounter with skepticism and resistance is typical. Apparently Pau Cin Hau owed his success to perseverance and to charisma, for eventually people sought him out to hear his message. One of the remarkable features about the movement was that it spread beyond the usual Chin horizon, the local community. Even if its spread was not impressive in terms of miles, it had to overcome boundaries of language, intervillage enmity, and so forth.

3. *Organization.* True to form, the Pau Cin Hau movement developed an organization, the *paliks* and the local congregations. This was in the end its weak point. Perhaps the organization was so disrupted by the Japanese invasion of 1942, when Tiddim, Fort White and Falam were occupied, whole villages were evacuated, and many Chin cooperated with the British in carrying on guerrilla operations, that it could not recover. Perhaps the failure of the prophet to renew his message with further visions was a factor. There is evidence that some of his disciples attempted to have dream-visions of their own but that these were rejected as unauthentic.

4. *Adaptation.* This refers to changes in the movement to adapt to new conditions, resistance, etc. Pau Cin Hau began as a new religion, attacking the traditional Chin animism. As it grew it encountered the growing influence of the Christian missionaries and in response shifted its target. In the end it became a truly nativistic movement, a rallying point for the conservative and antiforeign elements in Chin society. At Lumbang the nominal adherents of Pau Cin Hau in 1960 were the less acculturated, who lived in houses with thatched roofs. The Christians were the progressives, who placed a high value on education and on trying new farming methods and crops, and whose houses had slate or

corrugated iron roofs. And an informant from Tiddim, born in the 1930's, was surprised to learn that Pau Cin Hau was a twentieth-century development; he had always thought of it as *the* Chin religion.

5. *Cultural Transformation.*   Here is another of Pau Cin Hau's failures. He set out to preach a new religion but tended to limit its significance to the field of curing. His message did not contain the detailed reformulation of an entire culture found in the message of Handsome Lake, for example (see Wallace 1956*a*). While his followers ended by applying the new religion in contexts other than curing—planting and the New York festival—in most contexts they continued to follow traditional Chin patterns. In contrast, the Christian converts displayed a thorough reorientation; for example, they gave up the drinking of *zu* and the traditional dances and feasts that accompanied hunting. It may have been this more thoroughgoing transformation that attracted these Chin who were more sympathetic with innovation and contributed to the weakening of the Pau Cin Hau movement. If Pau Cin Hau had preached a more complete reformulation of the culture he might have been more successful; but it is likely that he would have encountered official British resistance sooner or later and that would have been fatal. As it was, Pau Cin Hau avoided the political and suffered no restriction from the British.

6. *Routinization.*   The reduction of Pau Cin Hau's intense and vivid insights to a prosaic set of observances took only two or three decades, and occurred well before the prophet's death. The absence of new inspiration on his part and the failure of a new prophet to arise, as Pau Cin Hau had arisen after Nuam Dim, made the observances more and more mechanical.

V   THE NEW STEADY STATE

It is perhaps premature to speak of the final outcome of the movement. Pau Cin Hau appears as a relatively insignificant ingredient in the orientation of Chin society and culture today. Christianity is still a dynamic element. The Protestant missions are being carried on mainly by Chin preachers, who are less successful on the whole than the American missionaries but who are able to hold together a number of viable congregations. The Roman Catholic church has increased its work since World War II, building missions and schools and staffing them with Europeans. Both Pau Cin Hau and Protestant congregations are losing members to the Roman Catholics; it is perhaps not entirely irrelevant that the Catholics do not forbid the drinking of *zu,* and that they offer an attractive sequence of educational opportunities which include the excellent Catholic secondary schools in Mandalay and Rangoon.

Since Burma became independent in 1948 the Burmese have taken over the administrative machinery set up by the British; to the Chin this means they are still under foreign rule. There have been economic changes; a few roads, jeeps and trucks, increased trade with the valley, a growing but still minute demand for manufactured goods. There is a chronic shortage of food and an increasing dependence on rice, which has to be imported from the valley. More and more Chin, including a few who are obtaining a university education in Rangoon, are looking for secular answers to the problems their society faces. It is unlikely that a Pau Cin Hau, with tales of visions and supernatural revelations, would get much of a hearing with these people today; perhaps it would be more realistic to say that if a new revitalization movement should arise it would be phrased in political terms, with or without supernatural content. The Chin are not immune to the stirrings of nationalism that have been felt by the Karen, Kachin, Shan, and other minorities in Burma. The fact that an independent Chin nation impresses the outsider as an unrealistic goal is probably irrelevant. At present, however, the state of Chin culture reflects continuing acculturation, mediated by the Burmese, and a tendency to look to secular progress, as evidenced by new roads, schools and hospitals, as the key value.

Conclusion

We have reviewed the chronology of a Northern Chin religious movement, including its immediate antecedents in the nineteenth century, and analyzed it in terms of conventional culture history and of Wallace's theory of revitalization movements. There are still some details of Pau Cin Hau history that are obscure and much that remains unknown about Chin ethnography; nevertheless it has been possible to show that the movement is an example of revitalization movements. Wallace's scheme stands up well in this case; but it may be suggested that the Period of Increased Individual Stress and the Period of Cultural Distortion may follow, as well as precede, the appearance of a prophet, and may account not so much for the origin of a movement as for its development and spread. In using such a theory as Wallace's to elucidate cultural events it is necessary, as our inquiry has shown, to study the details of what actually occurred as minutely as the data allow, and to expect modifications due to particular historical circumstances. It is hoped that the analysis given here demonstrates this point, as for example in showing the circumstances that converted a movement that began as a kind of cultural revolution into a conservative, nativistic movement.

NOTES

[1] The field work upon which this study is based was done in Burma in 1960–61 while holding a Fulbright Lectureship at the University of Rangoon. Gratitude is hereby expressed to the Fulbright Program of the U. S. State Department and to the U. S. Educational Foundation in Burma for this opportunity. I must also acknowledge gratefully the assistance of the following: Dr. Hla Bu and U Htun Myaing of the U. S. Educational Foundation in Burma; Prof. B. A. V. Peacock, Head of the Department of Anthropology of the University of Rangoon; Mr. Francis Sang Cin of Lumbang, assistant, guide, and interpreter; Mr. Za Hre Lian, Minister for Chin Affairs, Union of Burma; Mrs. Elizabeth S. Cope, who shared generously her memories of thirty years as a missionary in the Chin Hills; and those who served so helpfully as informants. Thanks are due to the administration and Graduate Council of Wake Forest College for financial aid in carrying out this research.

[2] Pau Cin Hau developed a semi-alphabetic script for the Chin language following this vision. He spent many years revising it and taught it

to some of his followers; some documents (notably the texts of Pau Cin Hau ritual songs) were written in the script and possibly some materials were printed, though I was unable to find any specimens of printing. Pau Cin Hau's script lost out to the Romanized alphabet developed by J. H. Cope, an American Baptist missionary, which was adopted by the government and taught in the schools. A copy of Pau Cin Hau's script appears in *Census of India* 1931 11 : 195. A detailed analysis of the script will be published elsewhere; it may be noted here that the script contains both Roman and Burmese symbols and bears a strong (if coincidental) resemblance to Sequoyah's Cherokee syllabary.

[3]   So reads the official account; but it is unlikely in the first place that a Burmese would have attempted to take refuge with the Chin and, in the second place, that he would have retained his head very long if he had. Perhaps the British needed a pretext to justify their expensive and bloody campaign.

Ethnographic Methodology

A Tri-Chronic Study in Culture Change, Informant Reliability, and Validity from the Southern Paiute.

ROBERT C. EULER

This is a slightly altered version of a paper read at the annual meeting of the American Anthropological Association in Mexico City in December, 1959. I should like to express my deep appreciation to Dr. Henry F. Dobyns and to my wife, Elizabeth, for their critical comments on it.

ETHNOHISTORY, AS a technique of research in the United States, has received great impetus in the past two decades through the federal Indian Claims Commission Act framed by the late Felix Cohen and passed by the Congress in 1946. Anthropologists and historians, and anthropologists at long last turned historians, have been able to achieve significant results in reconstructing the aboriginal culture-history of many American Indian and other societies.

In the course of these accomplishments ethnologists have had to examine realistically the reliability and validity of historical documentary sources as well as of the ethnographic studies carried

ROBERT C. EULER is Chairman of the Department of Anthropology at the University of Utah in Salt Lake City and is concerned with archaeology, ethnography, and ethno-history especially in the southwestern part of the United States.

out in past years primarily by students of the Boasian tradition. How though are these documents to be analyzed for objectivity and accuracy? How can we be sure that earlier ethnographers, although admittedly historically oriented, actually recorded data about aboriginal contact rather than acculturative conditions? Murdock (1959 : 43), for example, in discussing ethnographic surveys in Africa, placed no dependence upon "*the oral historical traditions* of the African peoples themselves." He remarked that "indigenous oral traditions are completely undependable much beyond the personal recollections of living informants, unless they happen to be of the very unusual type, characteristic of Polynesia, ..." This is a sweeping condemnation, intimating as it does that most native informants, wherever found, are less than accurate. Whether or not it is a valid criticism, ethnologists have been prone to accept with little qualification, not only historical sources but have been especially dependent upon informants' statements about the past.

It has thus become necessary for us to question not only the reliability but the retention in oral tradition of knowledge of both aboriginal and changing cultures by present native informants. How far backward in time or in contact periods can contemporary respondents actually recall? In some cases this can be determined, but with increasing frequency, as factor control diminishes, field ethnologists have fewer adequate means of judging. Moreover, we have recently become concerned with certain theoretical aspects of the relations of ethnohistory to history and ethnology. When we peruse archival documents relating to Indians and written by early European travellers and explorers, are we undertaking historical or ethnohistorical research? While an answer to this question is not the primary concern of this paper, it is pertinent and will be discussed together with the problem of informant reliability and retention.

In 1956 and 1959 I investigated the ethnohistory of the Southern Paiute Indians of the Great Basin area in the western United States. The earlier studies were sponsored by the United

States Department of Justice and those in the latter year by a grant-in-aid from the Penrose Fund of the American Philosophical Society which I here gratefully acknowledge. This research involved a combination of archaeological, historical, and ethnological techniques; significant data were collected concerning the aboriginal culture of the Southern Paiute, some changes which occurred through time, and the results of these changes upon the oral history of these Indians. Three time levels were involved.

I: TIME LEVEL

Many historical documents pertaining to the Southern Paiute and their habitat in Utah, Arizona, and Nevada were studied and these revealed new data concerning their aboriginal culture. These several sources covered a hundred year time span from 1776 to 1875.

II: TIME LEVEL

In 1910 the late Edward Sapir, then at the University of Pennsylvania, collected more than one hundred pages of field notes detailing the ethnography of the Southern Paiute. These were never published and upon Dr. Sapir's death were deposited with the late Dr. Leslie Spier. Dr. Spier, during the course of my research, handed a copy of these notes to me with the suggestion that they be edited for publication.

Sapir's informant, Tony Tillahash, was a young student at Carlisle Indian School when Sapir worked with him from January to June of 1910, in Philadelphia. It might be argued that a young man far from home and, it may reasonably be assumed, functioning in a stress situation would not be the best of respondents about the aboriginal life of his people. It must be noted, however, that Tony came from an even then comparatively isolated group of Southern Paiute living on the Kaibab Plateau along the north rim of Grand Canyon in Arizona. His parents had had little contact with Anglo-American settlers. In addition, he gave evidence of having a consuming interest in the past of his people. Sapir quite reasonably assumed that he was recording data relating to contact or even to precontact life. Additional correlative ethnographic data from this same general time level came from the published writings of Kroeber (1925), Lowie (1924), Park (1938), Julian Steward (1938), Isabel Kelly (1934), and Omer Stewart (1942).

III: TIME LEVEL

When I was in the field both in 1956 and 1959, I had the rare opportunity of working with the same informant Sapir had used almost half a century earlier. Tony Tillahash then was an alert man in his seventies. Together we went over Sapir's field data detail by detail, *without the informant knowing that I had these notes in my possession.* In addition, I was able to obtain oral statements from fifteen aged Southern Paiute now living in other sections of their former territory.

The factual data obtained from these three different time levels add much to scientific knowledge of the Paiute. They are now being prepared for publication. Moreover, they allow some conclusions to be drawn about informant validity, reliability, and retention, a matter of very great concern to anthropologists whose scientific generalizations necessarily rest largely upon protocols obtained from native informants.

A comparison of the documentary records with the informant protocols from the two later time levels permits conclusions as to the validity of informant statements about aboriginal culture elicited forty to sixty years after aboriginal conditions as a whole had disappeared, and about culture change in general. A comparison of the 1910 with the 1956-59 informant protocols from the same man permits conclusions to be drawn as to the reliability of informants over a period of nearly half a century, and about cultural stability in general. All pertinent data from the three times levels have been reduced to marginal punch cards and coded in general accord with the Human Relations Area Files *Outline of Cultural Materials* (Murdock *et al.* 1945) for purposes of analysis.

Historic European contact with the Southern Paiute began, insofar as we know now, in 1776 when the Franciscan father Silvestre Velez de Escalante traveled from Santa Fe, New Mexico through Southern Paiute territory (Bolton 1950). In 1826-27 the American fur trapper Jedediah Smith recorded two trips through Paiute country (Sullivan 1934), and beginning about 1830 there was considerable commercial traffic through the region over the Old Spanish Trail as portions of Escalante's route had come to be known (Hafen and Hafen 1954). The first American military party in the area was that of Fremont (1845) on his return from Oregon and California in 1844. Early in the summer of 1848 emigrant and gold rush travel began through the territory. We are fortunate to have the diary of Orville C. Pratt, a lawyer of Rochester, New York, who traveled the route in the fall of 1848, and the records of several persons traveling with wagon trains in 1849 (Hafen and Hafen 1954). The 1850's saw the coming of settlers and Mormon missionaries to the Southern Paiute (Simpson 1876), and aboriginal culture was appreciably altered, although after that date we cannot overlook the data from Edward Palmer in 1866 and 1877 (Heizer 1954) or that from John Wesley Powell and G. W. Ingalls (1874) of the same period.

These early accounts, it is true, are not full, and in many instances are blatantly ethnocentric. If, however, we examine them primarily in terms of concepts of culture and culture change rather than solely from the point of historical descriptive narration, we can learn much of the nature of cultural contact. As we compare these historical data with the ethnographies of the first three decades of the twentieth century there are found to be general areas of agreement, especially in material culture. Socio-political data, recorded by some ethnologists, however, seem to present a picture of postcontact rather than native conditions. The 1910 Sapir notes, the only body of material I have correlated precisely with the historical documents, reveal 96 per cent agreement. That is, wherein the eighteenth- and nineteenth-century histories of trappers, soldiers, settlers, missionaries, and eoanthropologists like J. W. Powell, and Sapir's data both referred to similar categories of Southern Paiute cultural traits and patterns, the agreement was virtually complete. Given such a high degree of correlation in areas of culture by both Sapir's informant and the documents cited above, the validity of the information given in 1910 but not sought or recorded in the histories, also was probably objectively reflective of native life. It may also indicate, subject to more precise comparison, that acculturation was accomplished primarily in socio-political spheres. The data from many earlier ethnographers can be understood temporally only when related to all available historical data no matter how insignificant or egocentric these may appear. To give but one concrete example from a neighboring group, the Yuman-speaking Havasupai, it may be noted that the careful, scholarly work of Spier (1928) portrayed a postcontact political structure as aboriginal because he was unaware of the impact of one Anglo-American school teacher upon native leadership patterns eighteen years before he himself (*i.e.,* Spier) worked there in 1918 (Iliff 1954).

As to the second question posed at the outset of this paper, that relating to the amount of native oral tradition recallable to informants of today, it has been indicated that the data given by Tony Tillahash in 1910 are to be considered applicable to contact or precontact conditions. When detailed statements concerning the same subjects were elicited from Tony in 1956 and in 1959, data analysis revealed a 92 per cent correlation. In another 4 per cent of the data Tony was hesitant, but, following some conversational interaction with his wife in the presence of the questioner, he gave essentially the same answers he had earlier given to Sapir. More explicitly, 96 per cent of the data had been retained virtually intact over half a century. In only 4 per cent of his responses did he give negative replies and these, rather than contradicting his former statements, merely indicated that he had forgotten. This minor deficit may perhaps be accounted for by a shift in the informant's interests over the time span rather than his fallibility. Such changes in interest are important, and are frequently overlooked by ethnographers. The older informant of 1956 might conceivably know more about his own people but undoubtedly, as an older man, his interests, and hence what he would stress, would be different from those of the young informant of 1910.

To be sure, this man may be an unusual respondent; he continues to maintain a great interest in the past and *was* able to elaborate upon some of the narrower statements he had given to Sapir. One must also consider the possible effect Sapir may have had upon him. It could be argued, certainly, that once an informant had been used and trained or at least conditioned by an ethnologist, especially under the conditions of the Sapir-Tillahash relationship, that that informant might continue to maintain an interest in the culture-history of his people and respond positively in later interviewing situations. Yet, in this instance, the body of evidence suggests an excellent reliability and retention.

Has this research essentially been ethnohistorical in nature? My colleague, Henry F. Dobyns of Cornell University has discussed this theoretical point in manuscript (1959). "Ethnohistory," he stated, "is (or should be): *An advancement of the understanding of culture or culture process by analysis of human group behavior through time utilizing protocols of an historic nature,* preferably analyzed for purposes other than those originally intended by the authors, and categories based upon modern ethnographic field investigation."

The analysis or mere recording of historical narrative data, even though it be the history of an ethnic group, does not become ethnohistory until it is related to theory of cultural process, precisely what is being attempted with the bulk of the Southern Paiute historical data referred to above.

Historical Reconstruction
Problems in Cochiti Culture History

CHARLES H. LANGE

THERE IS but one way of achieving any appreciable degree of reliability, or scientific accomplishment worthy of the name, in the reconstruction of culture history. There is no alternative to a strict adherence to the fundamental principle of proceeding from an initial, most often limited, base of known, factual data to the ordinarily far more extensive realms of the unknown. To depart from this fundamental policy in the reconstruction of culture history is to reiterate fantasies and falsehoods that commonly characterize folklore and legendary accounts of a tribal or cultural past.

Hypothesis, conjecture, and even considered guesses should never be discouraged nor discounted; on the other hand, they must

CHARLES H. LANGE is Professor of Anthropology at Southern Illinois University, Carbondale. He has done fieldwork in Central Europe as well as in the southwestern part of the United States and is Director of the Cochiti Dam salvage archaeological project in New Mexico.

be recognized for precisely what they are—nothing more than working frameworks within which additional data may be sought and subsequently ordered. These frameworks must be constantly checked against and weighed in reference to each individual bit of newly acquired evidence. When hypothesis, conjecture, or any similarly tentative or unsupported idea becomes carelessly inter-woven or confused with known, objective data, the resulting con-clusions cannot withstand scientific scrutiny.

The contents of this paper are divided into two distinct sec-tions; both are relevant in their respective ways to the reconstruc-tion of culture history of the Indians of Cochiti Pueblo, New Mexico.[1] In the first section, a brief summary is presented of what is known of Cochiti culture history. In the second, the discussion shifts to a review of the considerably larger body of data that now seems either likely or even highly probable but, in any case, remains to be ascertained before the Cochiti phases of Puebloan culture history may be considered complete and settled. Included in this review is a discussion of selected problems involved in the search for these additional data.

The Known

Today, Cochiti Pueblo is a village composed primarily of one-storied adobe houses, located just west of the Rio Grande in north central New Mexico. The village occupies the same position, on the first terrace above the flood plain, as that reported for it by the first Europeans in the area, the Spanish explorers of the middle and late sixteenth century. Surface collections of potsherds from within the present village limits (L.A. 126 [Laboratory of Anthro-pology, Museum of New Mexico, Site No. 126]) demonstrate that this occupancy covers not only the entire span of history in this region but extends back into prehistory at least to the early thir-teenth century.

There is no evidence that any Spaniard of the Coronado expedition (1540-42), or the Rodriquez-Chamuscado expedition

(1581-82), or the Espejo expedition (1582-83), actually visited or even saw Cochiti Pueblo. Knowledge of this village apparently consisted of only hearsay until the time of Gaspar Castaño de Sosa's visit in 1591. This interpretation is based upon the studied opinion of Schroeder and Matson (1965 : *170*) who have concluded that Luxán's (and Espejo's) Cachiti, a pueblo visited by the Espejo expedition in 1582, was erroneously identified as Cochiti by Hammond and Rey (1929 : 82). Schroeder and Matson have indicated that the name, Cachiti, was actually a corruption of the Keresan word, Katishtya, used for San Felipe Pueblo; strict interpretation of the meager journal entries in terms of the regional topography also gave preference here to the substitution of San Felipe for Cochiti. In past summarization of this phase of Cochiti culture history (1959*b* : *9*), I accepted the identification and interpretation by Hammond and Rey; however, in view of these new data, I favor the opinion of Schroeder and Matson that the first visit of Europeans to Cochiti Pueblo was not by Espejo in 1582 but rather by Castaño de Sosa in January, 1591.

The approximately square plaza has been and remains the physical center, as well as the cultural center, of the village, though in recent decades, there has been a growing tendency to disperse new homes at greater distances from it. Other, lesser plazas have been mentioned in the earlier literature (*e.g.*, Bourke and his companion, Strout, in 1881, in Bloom 1938 : 234-37; see also Lange 1959*b* : *46-48*), but these have been of little, if any, real significance within the memory of present-day Cochiti. Recent decades have also witnessed the steady decline of multi-storied dwellings in Cochiti; after World War II there was but a single second-story wall standing, the sole remaining vestige of this formerly common feature. A few gabled roofs of corrugated iron sheeting, noted in the early 1920's by Goldfrank (1927 : 7), continue to intrude among the traditional Puebloan flat roofs.

This intrusion was, until recently, emphasized by the fact that the Roman Catholic Mission of San Buenaventura, the largest structure in the pueblo, had such a gabled roof since 1912. (It is of interest to note here that, for several years after World War II there had been a movement among the Cochiti to collect funds with which to remove this gabled, metal roof and restore the mission church to its appearance during the nineteenth and earlier centuries. A most active leader in this prolonged drive was Alfred Herrera, the Cochiti Governor in 1963; the movement specifically, and the tribe generally, suffered a great loss when this outstanding individual collapsed with a heart attack at the conclusion of all-day ceremonies and died in the autumn of 1963. The community will greatly miss his wise and effective leadership; it is gratifying to record, however, that after many years of planning and talking, the reconstruction of the church, partly as a memorial to the late governor, was undertaken and completed in the fall and winter of 1963 - 64.)

Former dry-farming and flood-water acreage bordering the foothills west of the village and in similar locations elsewhere on the reservation was abandoned after construction of new and larger irrigation canals by the Middle Rio Grande Conservancy District in the early 1930's. Irrigated fields and pastures presently extend above and below the village on both sides of the Rio Grande. Beyond these fields, extending to the boundaries of the reservation, are the communally owned rangelands.

At present, Cochiti is the essentially permanent residence of three or four hundred individuals, with an additional two hundred tribal members living elsewhere at any given time. The village is virtually unique among Puebloan tribes because of the residence there, since early colonial times, of a number of Spanish-American families. Originally invited to reside in Cochiti in return for their assistance against Navaho and other raiders, the descendants of these families have lingered on. Relationships with the Indians have varied with individuals and circumstances; while bitterness has arisen from time to time in such matters as land holdings, water rights, community labor, and interference in tribal affairs, the relationships have been, on the whole, quite congenial, with a number of firm friendships, as well as occasional intermarriages, resulting.

Among the Cochiti people, themselves, two principal phenotypes may be recognized, with a range of blends between the two forms apparent in many individuals. First, there are those people who conform to a generalized "Pueblo" type. The body tends toward a heavy, short build; the face is round and full, with a flattened nose; in contrast, there are those with a slender, wiry body and sharper, more aquiline facial features. While the first physical type, with variations, dominates in the Cochiti population, the second type, with its deviations, is by no means unusual. These types and mixtures, significantly, are also present in varying proportions, among other Puebloan tribes, especially in the Rio Grande Valley, and also among neighboring Spanish-American populations, all of these having contributed through the years to the gene pool of the regional population as manifested in various communities.

Linguistically, the Cochiti constitute one of five Eastern Keresan-speaking tribes, the others being San Felipe, Santa Ana, Santo Domingo, and Zia. While members of any one of these tribes may chide other Keresans for their linguistic peculiarities, relatively easy communication prevails among them. This is less true, however, when communication is attempted with people of the Western Keresan villages of Acoma and Laguna; considerable difficulty, at least initially, is commonly experienced in trying to converse with these individuals. No form of wider linguistic affiliation is recognized by any of these Keresan speakers; when communicating with non-Keresan speakers, obviously alien tongues—Tanoan, Zuñian, Shoshonean, Athabaskan, Spanish, or English—are necessarily used unless, of course, the other person speaks Keresan.

In recent literature, Miller and Davis (1963 : *310*) introduced their remarks on "Proto-Keresan Phonology" as follows.

> Keresan is spoken in seven varieties at seven Indian Pueblos in New Mexico. . . . The languages, or dialects, are closely related, and have a time depth of about five hundred years. The greatest differences are found between the two most distant Pueblos, Acoma and Cochiti; the two dialects are mutually unintelligible

except to speakers who have had an opportunity to become accustomed to the speech of the other Pueblo.

The "time depth of about five hundred years" in the foregoing quotation was based upon an earlier paper, in which, following Swadesh (1954), Davis (1959:73) stated, "Results obtained from applying glottochronology to unwritten languages, however, have been generally consistent with archaeological evidence." He then proceeded to add refinements to earlier studies of Keresan, including that by Spencer (1940) in which Eastern and Western Keresan distinctions were recognized, together with the possibility that Zia, linguistically, was Western rather than Eastern (*p. 77*).

Applying lexical and phonetic data in his comparisons, Davis first selected ninety-seven items from the Swadesh 100-word list plus three random items from the 200-word list. In the table, his results are summarized in terms of the number of cognates among these 100 items as determined for each pair of Keresan dialects (*pp. 77-78*).

Relationship of Keresan dialects

	Acoma	*Cochiti*	*S. Domingo*	*S. Felipe*	*S. Ana*	*Zia*
Laguna	98	86	88	88	91	91% cognates
Zia	89	93	96	97	99	
S. Ana	89	92	96	96		
S. Felipe	86	95	98			
S. Domingo	86	94				
Cochiti	84					

Next, within the context of the above comparisons of cognates, Davis found frequent phonetic differences, or what he termed phonetic correspondences. Each correspondence tended to set off one group of Keresan dialects against another. For example, the *t : r* correspondence distinguished Acoma and Laguna from other Keresans, implying at least a partially independent linguistic development for the Western Keresan. Also, he found,

There is sufficient linguistic evidence to show that the phonetic change which resulted in the *t : r* correspondence was a change from *r* to *t* in the Acoma and Laguna dialects, rather than from *t* to *r* in the others. This means that at the time the change occurred, Acoma and Laguna acted as a unit and either were one people or else were in intimate contact one with another and isolated from other Keresan speakers (*p. 78*).

Of eight phonetic correspondences well supported by the data, Davis found three that grouped Acoma and Laguna; two that grouped Cochiti, Santo Domingo, and San Felipe; one that united Santo Domingo and San Felipe; one that isolated Cochiti; and one that isolated Acoma.

In summary, Davis felt there was a primary division between Acoma and Laguna and the others. For the others, interrelationships among them seemed to parallel their present geographical distribution. There was also some tendency to divide Acoma, Laguna, Zia, and Santa Ana as a unit from San Felipe, Santo Domingo, and Cochiti as another entity. Further, Cochiti appeared to have more linguistic divergence than might have been anticipated from its topographic location (*p. 78*).

Glottochronological time depths within the Keresan stock must be viewed in the context of a considerable degree of cultural contact among the various pueblos. Most of the cognate counts yield time depths well within the historic period, and obviously do not represent the actual time of separation of the two dialects. Even the lowest cognate count, that between Acoma and Cochiti, yields a time depth of only about five hundred years. This must be considered as a minimum length of time that has elapsed since Keresan was an undifferentiated language. The actual break-up may have begun considerably earlier (*pp. 78 - 79*).

In conclusion, Davis noted, "The picture is rather complex, and may have been made even more so by the intermingling in the past of more than one dialect within a single village." The following figure has been based, though redrawn, on that of Davis (*p. 78*), to show a probable Keresan family tree.

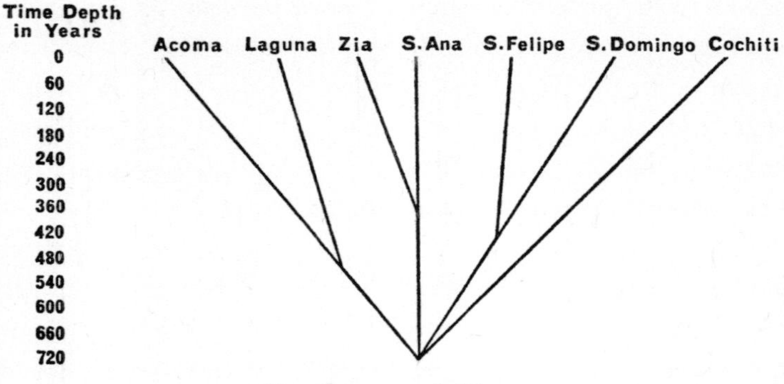

1. Family tree of Keresan

Economically, the Cochiti have conformed throughout historic times to the general Puebloan pattern of being essentially agricultural; this pattern, however, has been significantly supplemented by hunting, gathering, and fishing activities which have fluctuated in importance with changing times and circumstances. As in the case of most Pueblos, the Cochiti emphasis upon agriculture increased steadily from the time of initial Spanish colonization (1598) up to about the time of World War II.

This trend reflected the initially slow, but cumulatively significant, increment of various European crops (especially wheat), fruits (peaches and apples), and garden vegetables to the aboriginal complex (maize, beans, squash, and pumpkins). Other important European additions to the agricultural economy were domesticated animals (cattle, oxen, horses, mules, sheep, and goats) for which the newly acquired alfalfa also assumed real importance as expanded acreages of irrigated fields gradually replaced dry farms and flood-water plots. European metal tools—axes, hoes, and shovels—facilitated the replacement of earlier, simpler irrigation systems with larger and more efficient canals and ditches. Other noteworthy additions included the plow and wheeled cart; crude as these were when judged by mid-twentieth-century standards, they constituted significant improvements over the matériel and methods of pre-European times.

Continued increased importance of agriculture in the early

decades of the present century may be at least partially explained as a compensating trend for the decline in hunting activities. As the non-Indian population steadily encroached upon the hunting ranges and as the numbers of game animals dwindled within the remaining hunting ranges, Puebloan interest in hunting, as well as actual dependence upon it, generally lessened.

Beginning in the 1930's but not gaining actual momentum until the years of World War II and its aftermath, a mounting interest in wage earning and an ever-greater involvement with such employment have typified the Cochiti economy. In a steadily increasing number of cases, this has meant residence away from Cochiti. Cases range from single individuals, more commonly absent for sporadic and limited periods of outside employment, to those where all members of the wage earner's family also leave for what often amounts to an essentially permanent residence away from the pueblo for these individuals. This trend, in turn, means a growing disassociation from, and consequent lack of concern with, the social, religious, political, and other facets of tribal culture.

Socially, the Cochiti possess a patrilineal moiety organization, based upon kiva membership, and, at the same time, a matrilineal clan system. Down through the years, there has been general adherence to the rule of exogamy in both moiety and clan, though this has been especially true in regard to clan. In the late nineteenth century, Adolph F. Bandelier (1890: *301*) and, later, Edward S. Curtis (1926: *86*) thought they had found evidence of former moiety endogamy, but, by the time of their investigations, respectively, there was little or no evidence to support such a claim. In matters of clan endogamy, these deviations have occurred in small numbers for as far back as written records provide data, some seventy-five years. In virtually every instance, such marriages took place in clans during periods when there was an unusually large membership. There is little doubt that these deviant marriages, actually constituting incestuous unions in terms of clan exogamy rules, primarily involved individuals who, though members of the same clan, could justify their unorthodox behavior on the basis of sufficiently distant relationship, or none at all, when the matter was reckoned according to the view of the Catholic Church. (For a more complete discussion, see Lange 1959*b* : 377-82, 389-94.) Quite obviously, these cases have tended to occur more frequently among the more acculturated Cochiti; for such individuals, traditional values regarding clan exogamy have been more easily subordinated to the more recently recognized (and perhaps more convenient) views of Catholicism and European culture in general.

Marriages have been primarily intratribal among the Cochiti, though, again, there has been a steady, but small, incidence of marriages with other Keresans, other Puebloans, other Indians, and both Spanish- and Anglo-Americans (listed here in descending order of general preference among the Cochiti). In recent years, there has been at least one instance of intermarriage with a Negro. Marriages with non-Cochiti and especially with non-Keresans and non-Puebloans, tend to be short-lived or, often, to result in residence away from the village. Marriages by Cochiti with other Puebloans show no clear-cut preponderance as far as the two sexes are concerned; similarly, there seems to be no dominant pattern of residence within or away from Cochiti in reference to the sex of the individual Cochiti specifically involved. Both Cochiti men and women have brought in alien spouses who have been well accepted in the tribal life; some, for example, have satisfactorily held responsible secular and ceremonial offices. Conversely, Cochiti men and women have themselves been well integrated elsewhere in the life of their respective spouse's village.

While such integration has most commonly involved isolated, individual cases rather than families, clans, or similar groups, there can be no doubt of the considerable cumulative impact of such persons as effective agents of diffusion. Consequent innovations may take the form of vocabulary or other linguistic modifications, ceremonial additions or embellishments, pottery forms and designs, or countless other manifestations. About 1910, three families moved to Cochiti from San Ildefonso Pueblo; they were all adopted by the Cochiti Oak Clan, their original clan, or clans, not being represented at Cochiti and the Cochiti presumably preferring that the newcomers not establish an entirely new clan en masse in their new community. For the most part, the newcomers became affiliated with the Pumpkin Kiva, or moiety. Their collective impact upon Cochiti life, considered either genetically or culturally, has been of unquestionable significance during the intervening five or more decades.

The Cochiti tribe may still be properly designated a theocracy though the effective control of tribal life by the religious hierarchy is undeniably weaker than at any known time in history. Prospects point to a continued decline of this power as, one by one, the various secret societies, medicinal or otherwise, become extinct. The numerical strength of these groups at present is uniformly low, though, in itself, this does not constitute any great shift from past situations. Reconstructions of society rosters for almost the entire past hundred years indicate that society memberships have consistently been of a relatively restricted, rather than a general, nature. Recent years, however, have seen only an occasional recruit in any society; as older members die, the likelihood of extinction seems inevitable for a number of societies. Compared with the situation of only a few decades ago, the current roster of societies already reveals several gaps; known society extinctions include: Snake, Fire, Po'shai-añi, Tubá ji, Warriors (Ompī), Hunters, and, most recently, Giant.

Functions of the first four societies, essentially medicinal in nature, have in part been absorbed by remaining societies and have in part been lost. With the disappearance of the Hunting Society and the hunt chief, these duties and functions have been partially assumed by the Shī'kame Society (represented for some time now by a single member) and, once again, partially lost. Only within the last decade, the Giant Society, as noted, has disappeared from the culture, the aged and highly venerated headman having died and the sole remaining member moving away from the village, together with his family, presumably with no intention of returning. Thus, the annual election of secular officers, in reality a designating of these men by the heads of the three medicine societies, has had to be done differently. The fiscale and his lieutenant continue to be named by the Shī'kame headman; the governor and his lieutenant, however, are now named by the cacique (Flint Headman) who, with the demise of the Giant Society, has added this function to his previous one of naming the war captain and his lieutenant.

These organizational losses and related changes at Cochiti during recent decades have also resulted in the weakening of an overall duality in ceremonial and other facets of Cochiti culture. This duality has come to be rather intimately associated with Puebloan culture in general. Highly significant among these changes at Cochiti has been the disappearance of the Warriors Society and the war chief, or Nahī'ya. His functions have been partially taken over by the war captain and his lieutenant, partially by the cacique, and in part simply lost from the culture. Accordingly, the cacique, or town chief (*i.e.*, domestic, or peace, chief), remains as the dominant figure in the native theocratic structure.

The powers of the cacique, however, depend today more directly upon his personality than ever before. In contrast to former times, when traditional patterns were relatively intact and tribal members accorded more authority to the office of cacique, per se, these personal qualities were not as vital in terms of tribal leadership. With the accelerated and exaggerated changes of recent years, as well as the foreseeable future, it is clear that the cacique must exercise effective leadership in religious activities or lose prestige and influence proportionately.

To what extent continued consolidation and sloughing off will occur in the future can only be surmised; long-term continuance of present Cochiti patterns obviously presupposes a degree of society recruitment currently nonexistent. How soon the traditional system will collapse due to its increasing overburdening of the ever-fewer surviving participants, and how soon it will be replaced, perhaps, by some form of constitutional government, are difficult questions to answer. Such a development as the latter alternative might well be considered as virtually inevitable; the timing of its occurrence, however, is much less certain. Various Puebloan patterns have, in the past, proved persistent well beyond the considered calculations of many prognosticators.

In compiling an annual calendar of events at Cochiti, one notes that native religious observances, partially tied to natural phenomena such as the solstices, have been frequently merged with celebrations of the Catholic Church and general Euro-American culture to influence strongly the cycle and character of a given year's activities. It is indeed rather ironic that Catholicism, with its ultimate goal of completely supplanting the native religious life, has, by diverse policies, actually served to perpetuate a number of facets and details of the native religion—by basic definition its inherent adversary (Lange 1954 : 294 - 95).

While agriculture formerly exerted a much stronger influence upon the lives of the people, today's wage-earning activities, as noted earlier, have tended to free individuals from not only the patterns of the often restrictive agricultural routines—both economic and ceremonial—but also from the obligations of general village activities, many of which have had communal, or group, implications.

In general, there has been (and continues to be) a definite trend away from theocratic strictures which have traditionally surrounded the communally, or group, oriented society based essentially upon a combined economy of agriculture, hunting, and gathering. In the displacement of these features of the traditional cultural patterns, there has come unprecedented opportunity for an individual Cochiti to exercise ever-greater freedom of choice in a variety of cultural facets. By more highly acculturated individuals, this growing freedom is envisioned and assumed with increasing satisfaction and eagerness. For the less acculturated, there is a very real sense of uneasiness as traditional communal provisions for personal security either disappear entirely or become less and less effective in meeting life's problems.

Hypotheses, Needed Data, and Associated Problems

In introducing the data in this portion of the paper, several experiences reported by the 1955 Seminar in Archaeology, which dealt with "The American Southwest: A Problem in Cultural Isolation," are noteworthy.

> Another problem was the separation of what was "known" from what was "believed"; this was a constant danger during the period of factfinding. Though bothersome, this was of only passing annoyance because it was generally possible to demonstrate degrees of reliability for our data. . . .
>
> Perhaps the greatest of our hazards, and the least successfully avoided, was the constant temptation to "tie up" every loose end of American archaeology we noted; the breadth and range of Southwestern culture contacts invite broad and freewheeling interpretation. (Jennings, *et al.* 1956 : 67 - 68).

While this seminar dealt with a somewhat different range of data, with emphasis almost exclusively upon archaeological evidence, the general pertinence of these reactions is readily apparent in the present task of reconstructing Cochiti culture history.

Earlier in this paper, Cochiti Pueblo (L.A.126) was noted as existing in its present position throughout the historic period and for as much as three centuries further back into the prehistoric period (to the early thirteenth century). What we do not yet know, however, is the exact nature, either sequentially or in specific individual content, of the component layers—or, indeed, even if there are significant layers—of stratigraphy in the Cochiti refuse and other occupational deposits. As of the moment, our knowledge is limited to rather minimal evidence revealed almost exclusively by surface finds. This lack of stratigraphic data will unquestionably be remedied in time, and it is hoped that real progress in this regard will be achieved in the very near future.

Intriguing new data and perspectives relating to problems of stratigraphy and prehistoric and/or historic background at Cochiti have resulted from recent archival research and fieldwork by

Schroeder and Matson (1965) in the course of newly editing the journal of Gaspar Castaño de Sosa. Turning now to that journal (1965 : 140), the following entry for January 17 - 20, 1591, is of particular importance for Cochiti culture history.

> On the 17th we set out from this pueblo [San Ildefonso, according to Schroeder and Matson, CHL] and went to another place (*valle*) with inhabitants of a different nation, who are called Queres [*Queresas*]. We slept on the road with very much snow. The next day [18th, CHL] we went to the aforesaid place, where there were four pueblos in sight of each other. We were in them two days. They gave their obedience to His Majesty; governors and *alcaldes* were appointed in them; crosses were set up in all the pueblos with the ceremonies previously described.

Schroeder and Matson are firmly convinced that this "place" in which four pueblos were in sight of one another was an indirect reference to Cochiti, in the vicinity of the confluence of the Rio Grande and the Rio de Santa Fé. Accepting present-day Cochiti Pueblo as one of the four (of this, there can be no reasonable doubt), the problem now lies in identifying the other three.

De Sosa's journals provide no additional data regarding the size of any of these four villages; there is no explicit statement as to whether or not *each* pueblo was visible to the other three or only to one or two others which would still qualify them as "in sight of each other." Visibility, itself, was never clearly defined so that we do not know if this meant literally within view, or merely that a village's presence could be detected through smoke columns or some similar manifestation.

From excavations and surveys made during the field seasons of 1963, 1964, and 1965 of the Cochiti Dam Archaeological Salvage Project (see note 1), two sites—L.A.6455 and L.A.70, Bandelier's "Pueblo del Encierro" (1892 : 179), excavated west and east of the Rio Grande, respectively, and both less than a half-mile below the present Cochiti Dam—revealed potsherds which would place them within the time span of De Sosa's late sixteenth-century visit.

Another possibility is the partially excavated L.A.9154, Ojito

Cañoncito (Nelson n.d.), on the north bank of the Rio de Santa Fé, near the present-day Cochiti Springs and straddling the eastern boundary fence of the Cochiti Reservation. This is a site of perhaps seventy-five rooms, which shows sufficiently late sherds to justify its consideration. Bandelier (1892 : *179*) reported three sites across the river (east) from Cochiti. One of these he identified as Tash-ka-tze, "Place of Potsherds," (L.A.249). Surface collections at the Museum of New Mexico, however, show wares from this site to be rather early for strong consideration. The question of whether L.A.9154 is one of the other two, or whether there are two others in addition to L.A.9154, is difficult to ascertain since periodic flooding by the Rio de Santa Fé and the Rio Grande plus the leveling activities associated with the clearing and/or improvement of irrigated tracts have combined to obscure, if not obliterate, sites in this particular vicinity. L.A.34, on the north bank of the Rio de Santa Fé, is almost too late and too small to be considered in this discussion. However, the pottery from the site is definitely historic and pre-1680. Its consideration, especially in view of De Sosa's brief commentary, cannot be entirely discounted.

Still another possibility is the large site in the Cañada de Cochiti, west of the Rio Grande. Called Kuapa by the Cochiti, Nelson designated the somewhat divided site as "Kuapa I" and "Kuapa II," and this division has been perpetuated in the Museum of New Mexico's designations, L.A.3443 and L.A.3444, respectively. This very extensive site, located on the present-day Rancho de la Cañada, has long been considered by the Cochiti as the ancestral home directly antecedent to their present village. Surface sherds again indicate an occupancy sufficiently late to qualify the site as potentially one of De Sosa's four pueblos.

As noted, however, the positive identification of at least three of these four pueblos may prove extremely difficult; clues suggesting likely identification of any of the numerous archaeological sites in the area, other than Cochiti Pueblo, itself, are disappointingly scanty. De Sosa's journals do reveal sufficient familiarity with present-day San Ildefonso and Santo Domingo that these may be safely eliminated from consideration. Up until, and as of, that time, 1591, the physical presence of European items in these villages, where De Sosa's party spent a little over two days, would have been virtually nonexistent. Further, the chances of archaeologically recovering such rare specimens, if, indeed, there ever were any, would be extremely limited. (This lack of significant impact of the Spaniards upon the Rio Grande Pueblo Indians, in general, prior to the arrival of Oñate's expedition in 1598, has already been noted by Reed [1956*a* : *594*], among others.)

It is interesting to note, in conclusion, that there are no other known historic references to multiple Cochiti villages; their own accounts of the tribal past tell of several pueblos, most commonly beginning with Tyuonyi (L.A.82), in Frijoles Canyon, and ending with the present village site, with several pueblos having been occupied in the intervening territory, a total distance of less than fifteen miles. The impression is consistently given in these accounts, however, and occasionally stated explicitly, that these villages were inhabited sequentially in the course of the tribal migrations.

It may be safely assumed, if Castaño de Sosa was indeed correct in his observations and notations, that the other three Cochiti villages, though occupied, were on the verge of being abandoned. The few survivors in each village must very shortly thereafter have withdrawn to the principal pueblo, or at least to the village which has subsequently been consistently referred to as Cochiti in the historic and ethnographic literature. As a final comment, it is, of course, entirely possible that survivors from these villages withdrew not to Cochiti, or at least not only to Cochiti, but to other, even non-Keresan, pueblos.

Such a contraction of population in the Cochiti area would have been compatible with similar movements at that time elsewhere in the Rio Grande and Chama valleys. For example, Schroeder and Matson (1965 : *131 - 32*) have noted the abandonment of villages in the Chama area by the Tewa people and subsequent regrouping in the present Tewa Basin during the middle and late sixteenth century. (See also Wendorf 1953 : 94.) Drouth conditions during that period have been considered largely responsible for these movements.

Another, but related, level of investigation involves the need to gather comparative data from various pueblos in the middle Rio Grande valley, Keresan and non-Keresan, known to have been occupied during historic times. Of great value, for example, would be the intensive study of stratigraphy at Jemez Pueblo. Jemez, unlike the usual descriptions of Cochiti for the early historic period, was repeatedly characterized as a cluster, or series, of pueblos. For example, at the time of Coronado, it was described as consisting of seven villages (Winship 1896 : 510, 525). Recovery and interpretation of stratigraphic reflections of this multiplicity constitute tremendously challenging and potentially highly rewarding research for the future—but the sooner the better.

Another research facet of a stratigraphic project at Jemez would be to determine how much and precisely what kind of evidence is obtainable which would be directly illustrative of the 1840 immigration into Jemez of their relatives, the last twenty survivors from Pecos Pueblo. This movement, merging the residents of the two remaining Towan-speaking communities, is a historically known event of the middle nineteenth century (Parsons 1939 : 11 : 906). Less specifically known migrations from one village to another should similarly be reflected in the archaeological deposits of the recipient villages. Total or partial migrations are known to have occurred with considerable frequency. The Laguna move to Isleta, the Tano to First Mesa Hopi, San Ildefonso to Cochiti, Galisteo peoples to Santo Domingo, Cochiti, and other Rio Grande pueblos, and Hopi to the Rio Grande and vice versa are but some of the better known historic group movements.

Perhaps a special case, of particular interest in Cochiti culture history, was the construction and occupation of "Old Cochiti" (L.A.295) on the precipitous Potrero Viejo, by residents of Cochiti, San Marcos, and several other neighboring pueblos in fear of retribution after the Pueblo Revolt of 1680. This village, known also as Pueblo Viejo and, to the Spanish, as Cieneguilla, was occupied until its capture and destruction by the Spaniards in 1693. Excavations were conducted there by Nels C. Nelson of the American Museum of Natural History in 1912 - 14. Because of the precisely known chronology of this occupation and the established identity of the involved tribes, data from this site are of unique value. (Dr. Nelson and the American Museum of Natural History very generously turned over to me the fieldnotes, photographs, and remaining specimens from the excavations at Pueblo Viejo so that these may be utilized and ultimately incorporated in any eventual publication on the prehistory and history of the Cochiti region.)

To these cases mentioned here, innumerable movements of individuals, families, clans, and other social segments may well have left discernible evidence which may yet be recovered if we remain constantly aware of the possibility and consequently alert to its potential presence. Knowing that such movements have occurred at specific times within the historic period, techniques must now be perfected for detecting and recovering such evidence. Thus, leads and controls may be developed for working on similar, yet more difficult, problems in the prehistoric period for which knowledge must usually rely on traditions and the resulting hunches, impressions, or considered guesses.

Problems of distinguishing evidence of trade from that of actual migrations have long been recognized, though satisfactory solutions or interpretations are the exceptions rather than the rule. Thus, it would seem that one of our greatest needs is to establish under precise controls the stratigraphic sequence of each of the historically occupied villages. While not entirely unique, the recent work by Herbert W. Dick at Picurís Pueblo presents a model, in terms of the excavations and also in terms of the rapport established and the consequent cooperation by the officers and people of Picurís. Aside from working out certain problems with frequent opportunity to check data against historical documentation, valuable insights could be obtained for the optimal interpretation of prehistoric stratigraphy and other evidences for which there can be, by definition, no documentation. (Of interest here, particularly in the potentially greater interpretive insights to be derived from computer analysis, are the data presented in the doctoral dissertation of William A. Longacre, University of Chicago, on the subject, "Archaeology as Anthropology, A Case Study.")

Turning once more to the people themselves, Puebloan, Keresan, and Cochiti, there are only meager data available within the compass of physical anthropology. Anthropometric data for Cochiti, specifically, are almost completely lacking, either for the present population or for that of any time period in the past. One minor exception to this statement is a series of forty-six adult males from Cochiti, reported upon by Howells (1936: *16-17*). However, only a very brief summary was published; it is reproduced here in its entirety.

An anthropometric report dealing with a series of thirteen men from San Ildefonso and a series of forty-six men from Cochiti. The two gross series may be called physically identical, in spite of the difference in linguistic stock. Deletion from the Cochiti series of a number of individuals with Mexican ancestry leaves a supposedly more pure-blooded group numbering thirty-three, which differs slightly from the San Ildefonso series and the total Cochiti series, mainly in having a relatively larger face. The principal features of the group are a long nose and upper face.

Comparison with samples from other Pueblos, obtained by Hrdlicka [1908, CHL], reveals no distinct deviation on the part of these two villages from the general Pueblo physical type. Those villages which by gross estimate appear physically most like Cochiti are Laguna, Isleta, Acoma and San Juan. Similarly, the groups most unlike Cochiti are Zuñi, Hopi, Santo Domingo and Taos. There is thus no completely consistent correspondence with linguistics or other cultural lines of division.

Similarly, data from the "new" physical anthropology—polymorphisms and genetic and serological information—are all essentially lacking. The present population is, of course, available for sampling, the series potentially including a number of non-

Cochiti present because of extratribal marriages and the resulting offspring. The excavations of the 1963 Cochiti Dam Archaeological Salvage Project yielded about one hundred skeletons, including seventy-five from L.A.6455, alone, already noted as possibly one of the Cochiti villages visited by Castaño de Sosa in 1591. Further possibilities for extending the time depth in physical anthropological data have been obtained from excavations at L.A.70 and L.A.9154 during the 1964 and 1965 seasons.

Results of such comparative studies involving both archaeological skeletal series and present populations might well be anticipated as conforming to, or reinforcing, the general observations of Seltzer (1944: *32-33*) in regard to his "Southwest Plateau" physical type, "largely distributed over parts of Arizona and Northern and Western New Mexico."

A study of the time relationships of the units forming the "Southwest Plateau" stock strongly suggested the existence of a continuity of "Southwest Plateau" stock from the Basket Maker period clear up to recent times. There was no evidence to show, from any data available at the present, that there was any other physical stock at the same level of importance as the "Southwest Plateau" Indians in the make-up of the Basket Maker-Pueblo peoples. The presence of other physical types and deviations from the typical "Southwest Plateau" pattern among the Pueblos and especially the later Pueblos could be attributed for the most part to modifications of the original strain due to the absorption of new blood through intermittent small contacts, intermarriage, selective genetic factors, or to the result of stimuli persistently present in the environment. There is no suggestion of any sweeping change in physical type or of any enormous influx of new blood into the Basket Maker-Pueblo peoples until perhaps in the latter part of the Pueblo IV [1300-1600, CHL] period, except in the Rio Grande region. In this latter area, the new elements arrived earlier and in greater strength than in the western part of the upland plateau region and served to obliterate the original "Southwest Plateau" type.

As shown in Spuhler's review of "Some Problems in the Physical Anthropology of the American Southwest" (1954:

604-19), data of virtually all types are only sporadically, if at all, present for the Southwestern area as a whole. This dearth of material has been pointed up in a number of instances, most recently, perhaps, by Reed (1963:130-32). Comparative and control data on both phenotypes and genotypes are urgently needed not only for Cochiti as a "local population" (Kraus 1954:621), but for virtually all present-day Pueblo tribes as potentially discrete components of the "Southwest Plateau" stock. Consistently uncooperative with attempts at such investigations in the past, at least a portion of virtually all Puebloan tribes would undoubtedly continue to resist efforts along these lines at present. On the other hand, it is quite probable that even now a beginning, at least, could be made with most Pueblo populations, nonresident if not resident; it is also quite probable that adequate samples, if not complete series, could be obtained from at least a few villages, of which Cochiti could well be one.

Linguistically, the unknowns appear to lie, in terms of culture history, not so significantly within any particular Pueblo's form of Keresan, as in our lack of knowledge of what affiliation, if any, Keresan has with other languages. This larger, overall view is, of course, obtainable only when there is an adequate foundation provided by specific data from the seven individual Keresan Pueblos. Of value here is the synthesis of Keresan internal relationships presented by Davis (1959) and recapitulated in the preceding portion of this paper. Sapir (1929) suggested the grouping of Keresan with the widespread and culturally heterogeneous Hokan-Siouan stock, but no supporting data for this proposal were ever offered.

Hoijer, in his "Introduction" to *Linguistic Structures of Native America* (1946:9-29), recognized this lack of evidence and, accordingly, endorsed the earlier, self-styled "initiatory and tentative" work of Powell (1891:83) which classified Keresan as an independent linguistic family. Within the Keresan family, Hoijer noted a distinction between Western Keresan (Acoma and Laguna) and Eastern Keresan (Zia, Santa Ana, San Felipe, Santo

Domingo, and Cochiti). Subsequently, in correspondence and conversation, Newman and Maring have expressed agreement with Hoijer's appraisal of Keresan. Finally, and most recently in print, there has been the confirming evidence offered by Davis (1959 : 78), already cited here. Until linguists agree that some further affiliation has been indisputably demonstrated, there is no alternative to that of leaving Keresan as an unaffiliated language, even if such a status may appear frustrating, or possibly even contradictory, to prevailing principles or underlying premises of glottochronology or lexicostatistics.

The prospect of such a final solution (leaving Keresan linguistically isolated) may be similarly unsatisfying in terms, specifically, of Keresan culture history. Thus far, however, no non-Puebloan culture has been convincingly demonstrated to be either a Keresan component or affiliate. Consequently, there is no perspective and no potential clue regarding past shifts, developments, or other changes of either Puebloan or non-Puebloan forms. Origins, for the moment at least, appear to be rigidly confined to the Basket Maker-Pueblo, or Anasazi, cultural continuum. (In contrast, the Hopi, as members of the more widely distributed and culturally heterogeneous Shoshonean, or still more inclusive, Uto-Aztecan, linguistic stock, invite interesting conjecture and intriguing hypotheses.)

Reverting from the foregoing discussion to the specific Keresan linguistic genealogy presented in Figure *1*, it will be noted that the time scale suggests a separation of something over seven hundred years for Cochiti, *i.e.,* separation from other Keresans as of the early 1200's—a date roughly compatible with that indicated for the oldest occupation of the present-day Cochiti site by analysis of surface potsherds. If one next compares this concurrence with the series of migratory moves of the Cochiti and their Keresan relatives, the result is not particularly disparate.

Hodge (1907 : 317) described the Cochiti moves as follows: from Tyuonyi, in the Rito de los Frijoles; to Yapashi, Pueblo of the Stone Lions, on the Potrero de las Vacas; to Ha-atze, on the

Potrero de San Miguel, or Potrero del Capulin; to Kuapa, in the Cañada de Cochiti; to the present site of Cochiti. His identifications, somewhat elaborated upon here, were actually very close to those reported by Bandelier (1892 : 21); indeed, it is quite probable that Hodge based his account upon Bandelier's data. However, Bandelier added pueblos on the north and south banks of the Peralta Canyon arroyo as this entered the Rio Grande from the west. The present village lies somewhat north of the Peralta arroyo, and there is no evidence of an occupation immediately south of the arroyo. However, flood control and irrigation construction in recent decades have served to reroute this arroyo somewhat to the south—a fact which may or may not account for this seeming discrepancy.

Additional data, partially confirming and partially conflicting with the foregoing migration material, were gathered by Harrington (1916 : 440 - 41). He listed, in sequence, seven Cochiti villages, beginning with Tyuonyi and ending with the present site of Cochiti. His discrepancies consisted of two unidentified, *i.e.,* unlocated, pueblos—the first occupied between Yapashi and Ha-atze, and the second occupied between Kuapa and present-day Cochiti. To what extent L.A.35 (Nelson's Pueblo Cañada), L.A.70, L.A.6455, or some other large glaze site of the area, may someday be identified as either of these unknowns remains problematical and most likely an unsolvable question. In summary, it may be well to make explicit the obvious: there is, as of the moment, no archaeological verification of the accuracy of five, six, seven, or any other number of ancestral villages of the Cochiti.

Another discrepancy appears to lie in the difference between the linguistic appraisal by Davis (1959 : 78 - 79) and the traditional claims that 1] Cochiti, San Felipe, and Santo Domingo lived together in the Rito de los Frijoles and began their southerly migration from that canyon together; 2] subsequently, however, Santo Domingo broke away and continued to the south, crossing to the eastern bank of the Rio Grande where there were potentially better fields; and 3] at a still later date, San Felipe separated from Cochiti and also moved southward. Douglas (1932:179) went so far as to call Cochiti "half a tribe," the other half being San Felipe. Geographically, this sequence of events may be explained by the fact that Santo Domingo had already taken possession of the land immediately south of the area occupied and used by the Cochiti. This caused the San Felipe migrants to leapfrog still farther south, establishing the village which has existed in the same relative position (either east or west of the Rio Grande) up to the present time.

The greater similarity of the Cochiti dialect to that of Santo Domingo rather than to that of San Felipe, to be sure, a seemingly rather fine distinction, may very well have arisen during the subsequent period. While separating from Cochiti after Santo Domingo, San Felipe's more distant position through the succeeding years may have served to facilitate some drifting apart of these two dialects whereas Santo Domingo's greater proximity to Cochiti during the same time span could have had approximately the opposite result linguistically. Thus, these two dialects, Cochiti and Santo Domingo, either regained some measure of similarity or at least maintained what existed at that time in contrast to the Cochiti and San Felipe dialects, which, more isolated from one another, tended to drift further apart.

The remainder of this discussion is concerned, briefly, with the data and approaches which hold promise for further revealing and ordering the culture history of Cochiti Pueblo. Innumerable significant problems at various levels still await solution, despite our considerable present knowledge. Some questions involve Cochiti as a component of Keresan culture history (Lange 1958*b*), within the context of what may well be considered as Puebloan Co-tradition.[2] Still other questions are of a more restricted nature, pertaining rather exclusively to Cochiti alone.

The solution of problems in Cochiti culture history is obviously facilitated by the availability of voluminous data, in regard to both Cochiti and other Puebloan tribes. Indicative of this general wealth of information is Parsons' monumental *Pueblo Indian*

Religion. Since the publication of this two-volume work in 1939, ethnographic knowledge of many Puebloan cultures, or facets of these cultures, has increased immeasurably. (It should also be pointed out, however, that many of the fundamental questions posed by Parsons in the concluding portion of her study remain unanswered and, in some instances, still unstudied—despite an appreciable surge of fieldwork among Puebloan tribes since 1939.) In the midst of these ample data, we are, at the same time, hampered partly by confused evidence in the sense of conjectural or erroneous interpretations and partly by a total lack of evidence.

The need for data, of both an extensive and an intensive nature, has already been commented upon for physical anthropology and linguistics. In the area of material culture, the range of deficient data (as well as a commendable attitude regarding the rectifying of the situation), was well summarized by Reed (1956*b*: *16* - *17*) as he concluded his paper on "Types of Village-Plan Layouts in the Southwest." Citing a suggestion by Jennings that the shift in pueblo village plan "from front-facing arrangement to inward-looking plaza type might reflect the 'freezing' of Pueblo society into ultra-conservatism," Reed expressed sympathy for this "kind of explanation" and added the hope that the explanation might be made to fit the chronology. Presenting his scheme of village plans in time and space, Reed acknowledged the collaboration of Schroeder, noting his attempt to correlate additional data with Reed's scheme. Reed termed Schroeder's correlation as something "which I am not ready to indorse, although it also is the *kind* of explanation I want." Reed concluded,

> Possibly with further consideration, a general hypothesis can be worked out along this line (and following up the penetrating suggestions which have been offered in the last twenty-five or thirty years by Strong, Steward, Florence Hawley, Eggan, and others), which will fit with the historical facts indicated by material culture. *Town plans will surely prove as important as potsherds for this kind of syntheses* [Italics mine, CHL].

While in overall agreement with Reed's data and interpretation, I have expressed in an earlier paper (1958*b*: *37* - *38*) one particular reservation regarding his classification of Keresan village plans. I still question Reed's classification of Keresan plazas as parallel- or street-aligned (though the same typology was followed by Dozier 1961 : 99); a few comments from my earlier paper follow.

> However, the precise nature of these plazas varies considerably from village to village, and even within single villages, so that the stranger may have difficulty in some instances in identifying a plaza unless unusual events are occurring there at the time of his visit. Among the Keresans, a rather well defined plaza, set apart from the mission church building and *Campo Santo,* is present in Cochiti, San Felipe, Santa Ana, Zia, and Laguna. The plaza in both Santo Domingo and Acoma is hardly distinguishable from other principal streets. However, in none of these villages is there any confusion in the minds of the residents as to the location of "the plaza."

In further consideration of village plans, or layouts, maps, and aerial photographs, such as those presented by Stubbs (1950) in his book, *A Bird's-Eye View of the Pueblos,* are of great value. Caution must nonetheless be exercised in distinguishing older arrangements from those resulting from the rather recent trend in several pueblos toward dispersal of dwellings. In these matters of maximum, or optimal, interpretation, wherever feasible utilizing the combined data from archaeology, ethnology, and other fields, the comments of Taylor (1948; 1954) again come to mind.

Two papers in which material culture data have been well coordinated with those of nonmaterial culture, for Keresan tribes as well as other Puebloans, have been contributed by Florence Hawley Ellis: "Big Kivas, Little Kivas, and Moiety Houses in Historical Reconstruction," Hawley 1950*a : 286 - 302*), and "Pueblo Social Organization and Southwestern Archaeology," (Ellis 1951*a : 148 - 51*). Again, however, the transformation of such hypotheses as these into verified culture history still awaits elucidation of the stratigraphic deposits in all historic pueblos. In the meantime, they do no harm and are actually of value in keeping such problems in prominence as work progresses in the reconstruction of historic and prehistoric movements of Puebloan peoples.

Other papers by the same author deserve mention here: "The Role of Pueblo Social Organization in the Dissemination of Catholicism" (Hawley 1946); "Keresan Patterns of Kinship and Social Organization" (Hawley 1950*b*); "Patterns of Aggression and the War Cult in Southwestern Pueblos" (Ellis 1951*b*); "An Outline of Laguna Pueblo History and Social Organization (Ellis 1959); and "A Reconstruction of the Basic Jemez Pattern of Social Organization, with Comparisons to Other Tanoan Social Structures" (Ellis 1964). As suggested by the titles, these papers have provided syntheses of comparative data for the Puebloans generally and for the Keresans particularly. Valuable insights have been given on cultural dynamics and social structure within the context of these cultures; while details of fact and/or interpretation may, in time, be altered in light of new evidence, it is certain that no future reconstruction of Puebloan or Keresan culture history can fail to concern itself with these papers.

Further selected examples of noteworthy efforts at historical reconstruction in Puebloan culture include those by White on Keresan medicine societies (1930 [though somewhat modified by White, himself, in subsequent publication, as in his 1942 Santa Ana monograph]) and on "Keresan Pueblo Prayer Sticks" (1963); by Anderson on the Kachina Cult (1955); by Kurath on Pueblo Indian Matachines (1957), a specific study of ceremonial origins; by Dutton in her long-awaited meticulous analysis of the kiva murals excavated at Kuaua (1963); by Underhill in her consideration of the broader topic of "Intercultural Relations in the Greater Southwest" (1954); by Eggan in his more restricted and detailed *Social Organization of the Western Pueblos* (1950), the concluding section of which on "The Eastern Peublos and Their Interpretation," it is to be hoped, will be expanded either by Eggan or someone; and by Foster in his overall study of the details of America's Spanish heritage (1960).

Finally, mention should be made of the efforts of Dozier to

correlate ethnological data (1958) with the archaeological reconstructions by Reed (1949; 1956*b*), Wendorf (1954), and by Wendorf and Reed (1955). To these should be added the "Summary of Northern Rio Grande Archaeological History," provided by Stubbs in the report on excavations at Pindi (1953 : *152-55*). These bibliographic citations are meant to be neither exhaustive nor even highly selective. Additional significant and relevant papers by some of the aforementioned authors, as well as by others interested in this broadly inclusive and complex subject, might very well have been included.

At this point, the discussion might best be returned to the principle noted in the introductory paragraph—the need of progressing from the known to the unknown in reconstructing culture history. This procedure is, of course, nothing new; it merely needs to be consciously applied whenever possible. As Spier noted in the Preface and General Summary of his paper, "An Outline for a Chronology of Zuñi Ruins" (1917),

> The purpose of the study was to provide a background for ethnological investigations among the Zuñi (*p. 209*).
>
> .   .   .   .
>
> It seems worth while briefly summarizing the preceding pages in order to emphasize the distinction between the body of data of which we are reasonably sure and the outline chronology which is in part an hypothetical structure. It does not seem fair to leave an impression of greater certainty in the results than the data seem to us to warrant. (*p. 326*).

In a later paper (1919), "Ruins in the White Mountains, Arizona," Spier was able to state the following, advancing, as it were, from the hypothetical structure noted in the earlier summary.

> My excavations into the base of modern Zuñi revealed its growth since the foundation just prior to the Spanish advent. Taking the earliest pottery types there as a point of departure, we concluded that the Zuñi inhabited the pueblos, Hawwikku, Kettcippawa, Kyakkima, and Mattsakya, together with the unidenti-

fied "Aquinsa," immediately before concentrating in their present town. All of our evidence indicates that neither Pinnawa nor Hallonawa were Zuñi ruins of the historic period as had been supposed by earlier investigators. (*pp. 386 - 87*).

As demonstrated earlier in the present paper, Cochiti culture history is actually known to a considerable degree in terms of both time and space. Frontiers of the unknown may be viewed, in part, as existing beyond, or outside, this main body of known data, most especially, perhaps, in regard to chronology. In part, the frontiers of the unknown may also be viewed as internal, especially in regard to ethnographic details.

Data of the first category are essentially archaeological and pushing back this frontier will involve, as mentioned earlier, extending the earliest known date of recognizable Cochiti occupancy beyond the early thirteenth century. The key to success in this effort lies in meticulous analysis of the contents of the stratigraphy under the present-day village. Until this has been accomplished, all efforts to associate the presently occupied village with prehistoric remains, either in the vicinity or in more distant localities, amount to little more than conjectures.

Data of the second category are primarily ethnographic, or, perhaps more precisely, ethnological, since the research must sooner or later be extended to Puebloan cultures other than Cochiti itself. We know of numerous instances of contacts between Cochiti and other tribes, and we strongly suspect many others. These cases, and still others which may be initially revealed in the course of further ethnohistorical field and archival research, are desperately needed before the culture history of Cochiti Pueblo may be considered to be at all complete.

Concurrently, data should be sought on the details of the innovative process (Barnett 1953), particularly as pertains to the late nineteenth and early twentieth centuries—prior to the more intensive impact of acculturation (Dozier 1961) experienced by the Cochiti and other Rio Grande Pueblos in recent decades.

In this regard, it seems appropriate to conclude with comments from Kluckhohn's paper (1954 : 692 - 93) on "Southwestern Studies of Culture and Personality," in which he, in turn, quoted from earlier writings of Boas.

> . . . the Southwest is now ready for studies of the type suggested long ago by Boas. He wrote in 1897:

> The object of anthropological research being to elucidate psychological laws on the one hand and to investigate the history of human culture on the other, we must consider it a primary requirement that only such phenomena are compared as are derived psychologically or historically from common causes. . . .

> In other words, one of the main rewards of intensive study of a culture area such as the Southwest is that such study eventually frees investigators to raise genuinely scientific questions—problems of process. Once the influences of various cultures upon others in the same area and the effects of a common environment (and its variant forms) have been reasonably well ascertained, one can then operate to a first approximation under an "all other things being equal" hypothesis and intensively examine the question: why are these cultures and these modal personality types still different—in spite of similar environmental stimuli and pressures and access over long periods to the influence of generalized area culture or cultures? We are ready now, I believe, for such studies, but no one is yet attempting them seriously.

Times are changing, and Puebloan cultures—basic attitudes and value orientations—are also changing, perhaps more slowly, but nonetheless perceptively. Extended and detailed research in a number of cultural facets is no longer resisted so categorically. It seems safe to anticipate continued progress in anthropological research at Cochiti Pueblo, assisted immeasurably by the growing collaboration from the people, themselves. In the not too distant future, it is to be hoped that, in turn, other Pueblo tribes will become more amenable to such research and that the study of culture history at Cochiti will be augmented by numerous other examples, all contributing to our reconstruction of Puebloan culture history.

NOTES

[1] The present paper represents an assessment, somewhat in midstream, of research that has been in progress for almost twenty years and which is planned as continuing for perhaps as many years more. Several articles on various aspects of ethnography and acculturation at Cochiti Pueblo have appeared in a number of journals; one book, *Cochiti: A New Mexico Pueblo, Past and Present,* was published in 1959 (see accompanying bibliography).

My subsequent research at Cochiti has been essentially archaeological in nature; it has included test excavations, site survey, and surface collecting on the Rancho de la Cañada (1957, with a grant from the Museum of New Mexico and with the cooperation of Mr. James Webb Young), site survey, surface collecting, and a minor excavation at Bandelier National Monument (1958 and 1959, as a collaborator of the National Park Service), and site survey, surface collecting, and an excavation on the Cochiti Indian Reservation (1958, with a grant-in-aid from the American Council of Learned Societies and with permission of the Cochiti Tribal Council).

During the summers of 1963, 1964, 1965, and 1966, excavations and survey activities have again been conducted on the Cochiti Reservation under my direction. This on-going research has been made possible by the Cochiti Dam Archaeological Salvage Project of the Museum of New Mexico under contract with the National Park Service and under permit of the Cochiti Tribal Council.

Since 1955, my research has also been greatly facilitated by the interest and support of the Museum, Graduate Council, and Department of Anthropology, Southern Illinois University.

I am indebted to Rodger Heglar, Joel M. Maring, and Albert H. Schroeder for their critical reading of this paper in its preparatory stages. I greatly appreciate their assistance; the total paper, of course, remains solely my responsibility.

[2] Regardless of one's views in the controversy existing for some years as to the legitimacy of applying elsewhere Bennett's concept of a cultural co-tradition in Peruvian archaeology (1948), this concept, or, a modification of it, might very well be of positive value in providing a meaningful time and space framework within which Puebloan culture history could ultimately be analyzed, ordered, and described. (For a basic orientation on this topic, consult the bibliography provided in Wheat 1954).

Pattern and Culture Area
Maintaining the Family Cycle in India

DAVID G. MANDELBAUM

THE TOPIC which Leslie Spier selected for his presentation of the Annual Research Lecture at the University of New Mexico in 1954 was "Some Aspects of the Nature of Culture." The topic was stated broadly enough so that he could include some of the leading ideas which, as he saw it, had developed out of anthropological research. One of these is the concept of culture area, useful as a preliminary way of classifying cultures but also a potential guide to more penetrating analysis.

He put the nature of the concept in this way. "As a consequence of long ages of diffusion, there is not an infinite variety of cultures in the world. Rather, at any moment in history we find a somewhat limited number of fundamental forms. These do not occur at random, either in time or space. It is thus possible to define both a cultural tradition and the spatial distribution of a

DAVID G. MANDELBAUM has worked in the fields of ethnography and applied anthropology in Canada and India. He is Professor of Anthropology at the University of California in Berkeley.

common culture pattern" (1954, *p. 12*). In using such terms as fundamental form, cultural tradition, common culture pattern, Spier brought in much more than the manifest traits which have commonly been taken as the criteria for culture area classification. He goes on to mention the integrating principles which have been formulated for some areas. Each society, he notes, puts together its assemblage of culture traits in a unique way, yet there are also certain integrating themes, such as the wealth concept of the American Indian tribes of northwest California, which are as characteristic of that area as are the more visible traits of material subsistence.

The present paper takes all of India as a culture area and examines common patterns and principles of marriage. Included in this analysis are the vast majority of villagers and townspeople on the subcontinent; excluded are the tribal peoples of the northwest, northeast, and interior regions. Also excluded are the (relatively few) matrilineal societies, mainly of Kerala. Though marriage rituals among the Muslims of the subcontinent differ from those of Hindus and there are differences in some of the explicit rules of marriage (but hardly greater than differences among Hindu groups), the principles of marriage alliance are broadly similar among followers of the main religions. Common governments and ancient scriptures have made for certain cultural uniformities of great importance, but the hand of government has had little direct influence on marriage and the cultural consistencies in marriage extend to many more Indian peoples than follow the regulations of Sanskritic scripture.

Cultural variation is built into village society in that the people of each jati,[1] that is each endogamous group, in a village are expected to have some customs peculiar to their group. Further, there are often noticeable culture differences between one village and its neighbor; major differences occur across geographical regions and linguistic groupings. But it is nevertheless essential for an understanding of India to recognize the similarities of behavior and expectation which transcend the myriad differences among regions and within villages. "Their basic identity is best seen in the perspective of the continent as a whole" Spier wrote of the culture areas of North America. Students of India have special need to take a continental perspective because the great cultural diversity within India on the one side and the misleading popular generalizations about supposed all-India traits on the other, tend to distract the ethnologist from examining the common themes which do prevail.

Marriage patterns, in all societies, are part of the cycle of family development dictated by the biological facts of life. A family is formed, it grows in size as children are born, eventually its members disperse to found or to join other families. Among most Indian peoples, this cycle takes a characteristic form because of the prevalent ideal of filial and fraternal solidarity. This ideal prescribes that a son stay in the same family household with his father and with his brothers for some time after his marriage. Descent is patrilineal and residence typically patrilocal. A bride leaves her natal family at her marriage to live with her husband's natal family. The married couple spend at least the first years of their married life in the home of his parents.

Some, especially among the higher jatis and wealthier classes, live in the joint family until after the death of the father. Among poorer families, usually those of lower caste rank, economic factors often militate against large joint families of long duration. But even among them, each newly married couple lives with the groom's family for a time and during that time that family is a joint family. I have discussed the typical form and variations of the family in India elsewhere (1948); the process of maintaining the family in its characteristic form is also part of the general Indian pattern, as we now go on to observe.

Maintaining the Family Cycle

Males come in to the family at birth and remain until separated by death or partition. If husband and wife find themselves unable to bring forth a son biologically, they may try to bring one into the family socially. Adoption is the most common way of doing so; it is a procedure firmly rooted in formal law and common practice. An adoptive father takes a boy from his own jati, frequently he prefers to take one who is already related to him.[2] Another alternative, less commonly taken because of considerations of cost and temperament, is that the husband take another wife, or several, in order to beget a son.

Still another alternative is open to a prosperous landowner who has a daughter but not a son, perhaps because none has survived. He can arrange a marriage for his daughter to a man who will join his family. The son-in-law helps work the family lands which eventually pass to the daughter's children. This is an inferior kind of marriage for a man, to go to live on the bounty of his father-in-law. Yet there are some such instances in most places since an impoverished young man will reckon that the attractions of the estate make up for whatever stigma for him may be involved in the marriage. Whatever means are used by the members of a family to assure the inflow of males, they do not usually have to ponder difficult choices or manipulate touchy social considerations. They have only to celebrate a birth with proper ritual, or, being convinced that a birth is not forthcoming, to secure a suitable alternative with main dispatch and little fuss.

Marriage, the transfer of a female from one family to another, is commonly a matter of transcendent concern and much activity in both families. It is an inescapable choice point and usually brings into the balance every aspect of the family's status, resources, and social relations. It cannot be avoided because the person of a pubescent daughter in a household, unwed and unclaimed, is uncomfortable, even dangerous for the other members of the family. It is uncomfortable because her continuing presence betokens either neglect of duty on their part or grave personal defect on hers. It can be dangerous because her untethered sexuality may bring social disgrace, perhaps supernatural retribution, on the whole family unless she is promptly bound in marriage (see Kapadia 1958 : *140*).

The need for marrying off a grown son is not quite so urgently felt, partly because there is not the same spur of fear about his unbespoken sexuality and partly because his status and the family's reputation do not suffer as much if he remains unmarried. Still, his family should do its duty by him and do justice to him by getting him married. Marriage is a sacrament, ordained and imperative, which every normal man and woman should undergo.

A marriage mobilizes the family's social resources. Through marriage the members extend and renew their kin ties and may establish new bonds of kinship. Celebrating a marriage requires that all who can be genuinely counted as kin or allies participate through giving gifts, performing services, or just being present for the occasion. The closest kin must take part in all these ways. Other related families should send at least one representative if only to keep alive the kinship bond. The family's clients, who provide goods and services in the traditional jajmani relations, contribute their services; the barber often acts as go-between and ceremonial assistant, the potter, washerman, and other clients fulfill their roles in the ritual and receive gifts in return. In a village near Lucknow, for example, client families of ten different jatis perform ceremonial roles in the marriage of a landowner's child; in a village of southern Mysore clients of seven jatis assist in marrying off their patron's child (Majumdar 1958 : *43 - 49*; Epstein 1960 : *230*). A patron family, in its turn, need not attend the wedding of a child of their sweeper's family, but that wedding elicits some gifts from every patron of the sweeper family.

Marriage as Test of Status

On all social levels, a marriage is a test of a family's status. Then more than at any other time, a family's alliances stand forth proven and personified by gifts and attendance; its status hinges on its strength in allies and clients. Hence a marriage provides the prime opportunity for demonstrating and for validating family status. A family, like other social units in this society, is hierarchically appraised and judged by jati fellows and by fellow villagers as superior or inferior to other families of its jati. Such judgments frequently differ in specific details but usually agree on the general ranking of a family, whether landowner or sweeper, as being among the more eminent or among the more negligible in its sector of the community. There are some villagers who may not be particularly concerned, in the ordinary round, with their family's status, but they can scarcely avoid some such concern when a marriage is to be arranged. A comparative weighing of status factors is built into the process. Even when a marriage takes place within the close circle of kin, as when a man in south India marries his sister's daughter, the family elders must consider the relative advantage of strengthening the family by inner reinforcement as against bolstering its status by external connection.

In the marriage negotiations, the achievements of each family's forebears are weighed as are the current assets, in wealth and personal charm, of its members. Temporal assets do not automatically bestow higher status. They must be used in ways that confer status and one of the main avenues is through establishing a marriage alliance with a family of unquestioned higher standing. The alliance does not at once make the lower family the absolute equal of the higher, certainly not in those parts of north India where inequality is stipulated through the formal inferiority of every bride's family to that of her groom.

What an advantageous marriage accomplishes for a status-ambitious family is to put its members into the same bracket of rank as the higher family. If previously that higher family had not deigned to take brides from the lower family because it was too poor or undistinguished—though being of the same jati they could have done so—the marriage demonstrates for all its world to see that the lowlier family has risen far enough for the higher to accept one of its daughters. The higher family, in north India, gains by this match through the lavish gifts which the lower gives to its daughter in her married home. The bride's family, in a Muslim village of Punjab where this gift flow has been closely studied, gives about ten times as much in gifts to the groom's family as they receive from them (Eglar 1960 : *108 - 15*; Marriott 1962 : *265*). Every marriage involves the affinal families in some common status. They place themselves in the same bracket of rank even in those parts of north India where, by definition, the family of a bride is inferior to the family of her groom.

In other parts of the land, no such formal disparity is required and the two families are expected to be of about the same status. There is still close examination of the respective status of each during the negotiations to assure that they are really on equal footing. Thus, in Ramkheri in Madhya Pradesh marriages are arranged between families which are about equal in reputation and wealth. Gift-giving is not heavily one-sided; the groom's family has somewhat greater expenses at the wedding although after the marriage they receive more from the bride's kin. As in most of village India, a wedding involves great expenditure, much gift-giving, large attendance by kin and allies of the two families (Mayer 1960 : *227 - 35*). The sides must be able to contribute to the occasion an amount appropriate to their mutual status; a family's status is tested when a child is married.

Throughout village India status mobility, for a family as for a jati, requires a solid economic base. Wealth is not a sufficient condition for attaining a higher rating, but it is usually a necessary precondition. A very poor family cannot begin to indulge in fancies about raising its status; its members can only marry off a child as best they can. Because economic considerations are so fundamental, marriage alliances may be arranged as much for mutual economic benefit as for direct status gain. This has been a major factor in recent marriages in Dalena, the Myrose village whose lands were not irrigated while those of surrounding villages were enriched by the introduction of irrigation. Dalena men have bestirred themselves and have prospered through the purchase of irrigated lands and through work in a nearby town. They have at the same time increased their marriage alliances with families in nearby irrigated villages. "As Dalena farmers bought wet lands in neighbouring villages they wanted to strengthen their foothold in these villages by marriage ties." Dalena girls are, in turn, sought as wives by the men of these other villages because they like to establish affinal ties with the entrepreneurs and town workers of Dalena. Experience in the town is an asset for a prospective groom as was demonstrated when the daughter of a wealthy traditionalist of Dalena was married to a man of an inferior lineage and from a very poor household of that lineage, because the man is a factory worker and has acquired some of the town ways. When the girl's father appeared uncertain about the match, the suitor got his town friends to convince the father of the suitability of the marriage. For the young man it meant a marked rise in status. "He used his work in the factory to achieve higher prestige within the traditional social system of the village" (Epstein 1962 : 296 - 301; 1960 : 199). Affiliations with town and factory are becoming incorporated with the more traditional criteria of economic advantage.

The advantages for the two principals as well as for the two families are not ignored. A family will hesitate to give its daughter in marriage into a village in which there is much conflict or into a family in which the work will be extraordinarily hard. But the girl and the boy are not expected to take much part in the family deliberations because their youthful fancies are not very relevant to the serious, long-range considerations which have to be kept paramount in negotiating a marriage alliance.

The Explicit Structure of Marriage

Two kinds of rules are followed in marriage negotiations, the explicit structural rules of endogamy and exogamy, and the implicit rules of the game of maneuvering for family advantage. The structural rules require that the couple belong to the same endogamous group, the jati, and also that each spouse come from a different exogamous category within the jati. Each jati defines these categories in its own way and there are myriad elaborations on these rules, but in fundamental outline they are quite similar throughout the land.

Exogamy means that husband and wife may not be related to each other before marriage in ways which are prohibited, quite as incest is prohibited. Tabooed relationships are of two kinds; certain specific kin positions, for example a man and his mother's sister, and certain kin groupings, such as all who are patrilineally descended from the same ancestor, real or mythical. In jatis which follow Sanskritic scripture usage, the prohibited kin positions are collectively known as the Sapinda relations and are traced through both father and mother. And the patrilineal class of kin, related by patrilineal descent from a legendary forebear, is usually called "gotra"[3] (Kane 1941 : 452 - 500; Kapadia 1958 : 124 - 30). In a jati of the lower echelons other terms for the exogamous categories and different principles for establishing them may be used. But people of all jatis observe some exogamy by kin position and, commonly, by kin grouping also (see Srinivas 1942 : 32 - 49, 57 - 65).

Exogamy by locality as well as by kinship is observed in some regions. Over a large part of northern India, husband and wife must not come from the same village or cluster of villages. This local exogamy is found from West Bengal to eastern Punjab, in Rajasthan, Gujarat, and into Madhya Pradesh. It does not hold for some of the Himalayan hill people (Berreman 1962) and its southward limit is reached in the Malwa region of Madhya Pradesh where marriage within the village is allowed but is uncommon and is not very well regarded (Mayer 1960 : 209). The rationale is that a boy and girl who were born and raised in the same village are somehow related and should not marry even though no kin or clan connections are known. This is a valid reason when all in a jati-group of a village belong to the same lineage or clan (Gould 1960 : 478 - 83; 1961), but usually there are several clans of the same jati in one of these villages and yet marriages within the village are barred.

It may well be, as Berreman suggests, that the structural reason for village exogamy is the desire to isolate the bride as much as possible from her natal family and thereby to keep affines at a safe distance (Berreman 1962 : 57 - 58). If so, this isolation is increased in those parts of north India where village hypergamy is added to village exogamy. This means that if *any* family of village A has taken a bride from village B, then a daughter of village A, of *any* jati, must not be given in marriage to village B. Since reciprocal exchange of brides is forbidden, a family of village B can have no bridal hostage from village A through whom they might possibly induce favorable treatment for the girl they have given to village A. The bride is thus all the more cut off from the influence of her natal home and village. This is an augmented instance of the general tendency in north India to favor marriage alliances at a farther remove both in space and in kin relations than is preferred in Dravidian-speaking areas (Karve 1953 : 228 - 29 *passim,* Dumont and Pocock 1957 : 62 - 63).

Endogamy, the other part of the explicit structural rules of marriage, means that the couple must stem from two families which have historically belonged, because of their common attributes, to the same set of intermarrying families. That historical nexus is accounted for in myth, is bolstered by ritual, is manifest in daily practice, and is maintined by forces within and outside the jati. Yet there are ways of reinterpreting the history and of readjusting the boundaries of the endogamous group.

The Implicit Structure of Marriage Negotiations

Within each jati's code of exogamy and endogamy, marriage negotiations follow certain implicit rules through a complex series of stylized maneuvers and spontaneous manipulations. Among very poor families the preliminaries are brief, the matter quickly settled. But with families of any jati who have something to bargain about, who can afford to aspire to better place, or strive to maintain their traditional position, the negotiations are typically intricate. They follow an unwritten game theory which is well understood by the participants, certainly by the adept specialists in the game, the marriage brokers and go-betweens. Each family attempts to maximize its gain through the marriage and to minimize any loss, either in status, wealth, or the welfare of its child. Each brings to bear whatever resources it has; if it is deficient in one kind of resource it plays up its other strengths. The family of a patently defective son uses its wealth and influence to secure a passable bride for him. A family whose son has a research degree and a foot in the higher civil service can arrange a match that bejewels the family with dowry, prestige, and the comely person of the bride.

The fact that each side in the negotiations is alert to its own advantage and the family's long-run gain does not at all mean that one side must lose in the transaction. The mutually desired outcome is that both sides should feel that they have gained. To advance this end there are ritual devices by which, once the collective bargaining is over and agreement reached, the two sides ritually signify their present and future amity (see Epstein 1960 : 204). Ordinarily both sides do gain, though not the same things. When a family's wealth and its status in the jati are markedly unequal, its members will usually try to make an alliance with a family which needs the wealth and can impart better status. A family's status, like the ritual purity of its members and the ranking of its jati, requires continual revalidation. But family prestige can, in some degree, be transmitted through a marriage alliance, unlike ritual purity and jati rank which cannot be imparted across families. Families which have no great imbalance between resources and respectability, tend to seek alliances with families that are about equal, or under hypergamy, as nearly equal as the hypergamic rules permit.

A marriage alliance always entails some redistribution of wealth as well as of persons. In a good many jatis of south and central India, the family of the groom pays bridewealth at marriage to the family of the bride (Karve 1953 : 162 - 63, Srinivas 1942 : 14 - 21). After marriage, however, the woman's family keep giving gifts to her and her children. In most of north India it is the family of the bride which gives to the groom and his family with little or no return from them. Both kinds of giving serve to stabilize the marriage.

The redistribution of wealth affects many more people than the two principal families. A wedding is often taken as an opportunity to activate a network of gift giving with families of different jatis as well as among kin. A prospering villager can give generous gifts at a wedding to people with whom he could not previously have afforded to exchange gifts or favors (Karve 1953 : *125 - 26*). Establishing a wider range of gift-giving brings returns in power as well as in prestige to a magnanimous donor. The recipients are more apt to support the gift-givers in the perennial contentions of village life.

The whole wealth distribution, like the alliance itself, entails both explicit and implicit rules. Which family gives more, what kinds of gifts are given and to whom, are explicitly stipulated by jati consensus. But how much is given, in what proportions and under what circumstances, is finally determined only after playing the serious game of negotiating a match.

Reducing Uncertainties in Marriage Arrangements

So momentous is the occasion that several kinds of precautions are taken to allay the uncertainties involved in the decision. Astrology is one such means; arranging prepuberty marriages is another. Widening the radius of search for a possible spouse is yet another way of assuring that the best possible choice will be made.

All marriage plans must reckon with the supernatural forces which affect the course of every critical venture—auspicious and inauspicious days, favorable and unfavorable omens, the horoscopes of the couple and their astrological congruence. Through astrology man's uncertainty about his personal fate is made more tolerable because his fate is seen as linked into a grand mechanism of astral spheres which move in preordained and predictable cycles across the firmament of time. In conformity with the celestial cycles move the fortunes of persons and societies. Each person—better, each soul—becomes geared into the cosmic movement at the moment of birth. The nature of his entrainment is forever determined at that moment when his personal fate latches into the grand apparatus. One's horoscope reveals how his life fits into the celestial progression to which all life attaches. The fate so ordained for one person may be forecast as being utterly incompatable with that of another, and if the two join their lives in marriage only disaster for them can ensue, so any plans for their union must be abandoned. Yet astrology is a flexible art, not entirely impervious to manipulation. It is always possible for determined matchmakers to seek another, more favorable reading from a different astrologer. Conversely, should one side want to withdraw tactfully from a proposal, it is sometimes possible to locate an astrologer whose examination of the two horoscopes will find an insuperable bar to the match.

Astrology, as part of the Sanskrit tradition, must be used in planning marriages in those jatis which guide their rituals by Sanskrit scripture. In the middle and lower social ranges, especially in south India, there are many who make no use of astrology. But peoples of all jatis believe in auspicious and inauspicious days and in favorable and unfavorable omens. These beliefs postulate a similar, though simpler, view of some grand, impersonal mechanisms which affect each life and through which each person must thread his fate. There is a certain parallel between these beliefs and the people's theory of caste. In both cases the universal structure, of fate and of society, is seen as absolutely decreed and, in the large, immutable. Yet, within both these fixed frames men try hard to better their position and that of their kin.

Another way of reducing the uncertainties of a complex marriage negotiation is to make a definite agreement before the prospective bride reaches puberty. Then all can proceed according to a clear schedule without pressure of the problem of the girl's sexuality. She begins full marital life immediately after menarche. In some jatis the exact interval is prescribed, thus for certain Brahmans the nuptial rites which mark the start of sexual relations must take place sixteen days after the onset of first menstruation. This firm calendar is not the only advantage of celebrating the formal wedding before the bride's—or even the groom's—puberty. Another advantage is that each family can immediately benefit by whatever advantages it has achieved through the alliance. This status capital can then be used to push its ranking still higher in other negotiations.

A family with both ambition and means is likely to search as far afield for a prospective spouse as it can, because a wider radius of search produces more alternatives from which to select the best alliance. Higher and wealthier jatis usually bring brides in from a wider territory than do lower groups. Thus the average distance of the bride's village is 37.5 miles in the highest jatis of a village in Faizabad District (U.P.) while the average distance for the next lower jati blocs is 6.4 and 7.5 miles (Gould 1960 : 486). Similar spread occurs within a jati, as among the Noniyas, traditionally lower-ranking earthworkers, of Senapur in U.P. In that village the average distance of Noniya marriage alliances is 12 miles, the nearest affinal link being 3 miles and the farthest 55 miles. But among those of the jati who have acquired western education and live in towns as professional men or government officials, there is a different marriage network, mainly with similarly wealthy and elite families. This net has a much broader range, extending in a few cases to as much as 300 miles. But for families whose wedding parties and visitors must come by oxcart or local bus no such extensive and expensive range is possible; the bulk of their marriage alliances are made within a quite compact territory. The shape of that territory is defined as much by the main travel routes and by the existence of previous alliances as it is by physical distance alone (cf. Gould 1960 : 481 - 82; Miller 1954).

Jati demography and history also affect the radius of matrimonial alliance. In Rampur, near Delhi, the more common circumstance is reversed in that two of the lower jatis have a much greater average distance for matrimonial alliance than do the two highest jatis. The dominant Jats and the Brahmans bring brides from an average of about 12.5 miles while the low Chamars average 20 miles and the Nais, barbers, average about 24 miles. Barbers have only a few families in any one village and so must sometimes reach far to find an eligible bride; the Chamars have long struggled against the overlord Jats and have recently found good jobs away from the village. With more resources and rekindled hope they are probably seeking a broader base of power beyond the close neighborhood of their village.

Marriage and Cultural Communication

One great outcome of this seeking for family and jati advantage in marriage is that every person is tied into a network of social relations extending across many villages and each person's network of social relations extending across many villages and each person's network is linked to innumerable other networks. For all the social avoidance and segregation with a local caste system, there is no sharp break in communications and relations among the local systems of Indian culture and society.

"This small village of 150 households," Lewis says of Rampur, "may therefore be seen as forming the locus of affinal kinship ties with over four hundred other villages. . . . This rural cosmopolitanism provides a striking contrast with the characteristic village isolation found in rural Mexico" (1958 : *161 - 62*). And it is a salient fact of Indian society, that the people of one village are in touch with kin in scores, often hundreds, of other villages (see Rowe 1960 : 299; Mayer 1962; Cohn and Marriott 1958). The multiple interlacing of villages is primarily a function, not of polity or economy, but of jati and of family. In their totality these lively networks profoundly influence the whole culture and society, but each link is fashioned with an eye to the welfare of a little domestic group, its status, its economic advantage, and by no means the least, the future well-being of its child.

Rural cosmopolitanism prevails even where marriages within a village are permitted, as they are in Wangala in Mysore. In 85 per cent of recorded marriages in the dominant Peasant Jati, traced over four generations, the bride and groom came from different villages. In recent years there has been an increase in marriages within this village because of a special economic influence. The whole range of the villagers' social relations has been narrowed because their energies are concentrated on growing sugar cane and under the quite exceptional local conditions of sugar production, in which a state-owned factory takes care of marketing and managerial functions, they do not need wide social contacts. Hence when only the currently existing marriages are tabulated, 42 per cent are within the village and 58 per cent between villages.

A different trend has occurred in the nearby village of Dalena. As noted above, their lands did not get irrigation as did the villages all about them and Dalena people had to enlarge their social relations if they were to benefit from the prosperity of the region. Hence the proportion of intervillage marriages rose from 44 per cent in the four-generation record to 69 per cent in existing marriages (Epstein 1962 : 167-69, 296-97). The comparison not only reflects the play of economic interests on the forming of marital alliances, it also shows that in both these villages, where marriage within the village is permitted as it is throughout South India, there was nonetheless a considerable outreach of affinal ties. A village is far from an isolated and insulated community, and the way of life in a village, in every part of this civilization, has long been subject to multiple influences from beyond the village bounds. Not the least of these outside influences are brought in by the wives.

The Wedding

After the negotiations are completed, the wedding is solemnized and enjoyed. The wedding not only symbolizes the couple's union, it also proclaims the alliance so that all people in each family's social orbit may know of it. The importance attached to weddings throughout village India is exemplified in the tabulation of wedding expenditures in the two Mysore villages just mentioned.

A wedding is the largest single expense which most families in these villages have to bear. Weddings in Wangala, Mrs. Epstein notes, provide a principal step in the "struggle for status." The groom's family here carries most of the wedding costs and typical budgets of these expenditures show how costly this status struggle is at every income level. A family in the very poorest group spends about Rs. 272 to marry a son, a relatively poor farmer family Rs. 1,218, a richer farmer Rs. 2,110, and one of the very richest, magnate families Rs. 2,866. The very poorest family, with exceedingly little to spare, still manages to pour out three or four months' income on the marriage rites. The relatively rich families devote close to a year's total income to marry each son.[4] Of the total expenditures in cash by everyone in Wangala, 5 per cent was spent on weddings in 1955, a normal year in this respect. Savings in this prospering place came to 16 per cent of the average monthly budget. "Most of the savings are spent on weddings when economic differentiation displays itself in lavish feasts" (Epstein 1962 : *101, 108, 110*). That is, when family wealth is translated into family prestige.

In the contrasting village, whose people have been impelled to turn outward while the Wangala villagers were turning inward, the "struggle for prestige among middle-farmers in Dalena is differently expressed." They think it more important to have a bicycle or a watch and similar possessions than give a lavish wedding feast. Such personal possessions bring prestige both in town and village while wedding expenditures impress mainly one's fellow villagers. Hence weddings are less expensive in Dalena than in Wangala and are one-day affairs rather than being three-day celebrations as is normal in Wangala. For all that, Dalena people still spend a very sizable sum on weddings. A typical wedding expenditure budget for one of the poorest families is Rs. 225, for a poor farmer Rs. 712, for a rich farmer Rs. 895, and for a magnate Rs. 2,402. Despite the partial eclipse of weddings as occasions for prestige-gain, the chief moneylender in Dalena tried to improve his social status by staging a very costly wedding for his son. And Dalena farmers, whether of the richer or the poorer class, still lay out a good part of a year's income on the wedding of a son (Epstein 1962 : 263 - 66).

Among the vast majority of India's people, a wedding is at once a culmination and a beginning, a demonstration and a test, a stage and a theater, an affirmation and a consolidation. It is the climax of the negotiations and the formal beginning of the new relationship. It is the grand occasion for demonstrating the family's social worth through the participation of kin, jati fellows, village neighbors, and prestigious friends. Certain measures of their esteem are quite precise, as when the size of each gift and the name of its donor are loudly announced to the assembled guests. As it is a demonstration so also is it a test of status. Here, best of all, can a family's claims to eminence be gauged by the wealth, power, and purity which its members can mobilize for the event. Also tested and demonstrated in the festivities are the relative standings of the guests. Who is accorded precedence by the hosts, who sits near whom, what courtesies are extended to which guests, all these proclaim relative rank among individuals of a jati as they do among jatis. For this reason a wedding in a village of strongly contentious factions can be shot through with bickering and can become a scene of high tension.

For the principal actors the wedding provides the stage for a supreme pageant. It is an exalted occasion for the bride and groom; both are temporarily transfigured into a regal or divine pair and "the aura which shines around them also touches the members of their families" (Dumont 1959 : 519). It is a theater for aesthetic enjoyment of many kinds, of the quality of the musicians, of the munificence of the bride's jewels and costumes, even to the elegance of the groom's equipage. And a counterpoint of humor often sparkles through the solemnities, as in the chorus of bawdy songs sung by neighbor women and in the more private but equally ribald jokes made by other participants and guests.

All major rites affirm, in a kind of metalanguage, a people's leading values: weddings are principal nodes of social life in India and are used to affirm a number of values, some affirmations are in the ritual itself, others in what appears as byplay. Through all the vast variation in ritual detail among jatis and regions, there are certain ritual constants by which the hopes for the marriage are acted out. Typically there are some symbolic expressions of the couple's unity (as in taking steps together), some ritual action to show their new relation to each other and to their respective families, some ritual acts done together before the deities to invoke divine blessings and at the same time to proclaim the new social fact before society.

In addition to such avowals, other assertions may crop up at a wedding. Just as tensions about disputed rank or village factions often intrude into the occasion, so do the tensions between the newly allied families appear. Thus Mrs. Tilak in describing her wedding in a Maharashtra village about 1880 notes that "On those occasions the bridegroom is encouraged to have a fit of the sulks." Her bridegroom was instructed to ask for the gift of a rug and to sulk until he was promised it. But he tired of the tactic quickly, joined the wedding party and so forced his family to come along with him to the wedding feast. "There was none of the usual quarrelling and ill-feeling from beginning to end" (1950 : *12*). Such trials of strength between the two families at the time of marriage are still not unusual; a main theme of village drama, as Beals notes for a Mysore village, concerns this tension (1962 : *24*).

Yet a wedding is a force for social consolidation as well. The alliance is formed; despite bickerings and other signs of tension the bond is sealed. Each family, in rallying its kin and supporters, revitalizes its ties with other families of jati and village. It also keeps going, through the wedding and all the rest of the marriage complex, the endless cycle of family life and thus of society itself.

As the family cycle in India takes certain characteristic forms because of the emphasis on filial and fraternal solidarity, so do patterns of marriage follow characteristic forms because of the importance of alliances in the struggle for status. Formal rules of exogamy and of endogamy are followed in most societies, the particular Indian phrasings of such rules are used throughout the Indian culture sphere. But the formal rules tell us little about common motivations which underlie a person's diverse roles within his society. One such integrating principle which we have noted here is the continuous quest for social status within a hierarchical social frame. It is a principle of culture and of personality in India which typically finds a main expression in the institution of marriage.

The close meshing of each villager with many others, the ramified, nonatomistic nature of village society are both reflected in and reinforced by marriage alliances. Through marriage cultural communication is widened and facilitated, making possible the wide sharing of cultural motifs, of which the motifs of marriage are part. Marriage practices have been changed in India from our earliest knowledge of them and will undoubtedly be changed in the future. The pace of change is not usually rapid in those principles which have emotional hold, as the relation between son and parents or a man's standards for judging himself. Leslie Spier pointed out that "It is largely in connection with unconscious segments of behavior that emotions reign and that there is greatest stability in culture" (1954 : *19*).

Still, large-scale changes are coming about in modern India; marriage forms and even underlying principles may well be in process of alteration. Whatever directions the changes take, to quote Spier again, "We have every reason to expect an orderly growth of cultures, orderly in the sense that new forms unfold from antecedent states without discontinuity" (1954 : *20*). To appraise the dynamics of Indian culture, it is necessary to grasp the fundamental forms and principles which the peoples of this subcontinental area use. Among the more basic forms and principles are those of marriage.

NOTES

1   The term jati means an endogamous group of the caste order as that order is recognized in a locality. It is used to avoid some of the ambiguities of the terms caste or subcaste.

2   Land economics can powerfully stimulate adoption. In one Mysore village where irrigation has made land far more remunerative and socially even more precious than before, the orderly transmittal of an estate is of high importance. In the preponderant jati of landowners 10 per cent of all the males had been adopted. But in a nearby village, its lands not irrigated and economic opportunities not so bound in with the land, only 2 per cent of the men of the jati had been adopted (Epstein 1962 : *179, 306*). But whatever may be the incidence of adoption, it is everywhere in India an approved method of maintaining family development when parturition fails.

3   Gotras bearing the same name and claiming the same progenitor may occur in different jatis, but this has no effect on marriage rules which apply only within the jati. The term gotra is used in some jatis for other kinds of groupings but when this occurs there is another term for the exogamic descent group (see Madan 1962 : *72 - 73*, Dumont and Pocock 1957 : 52).

4   Mrs. Epstein estimates the average monthly income per consumption unit in Wangala at Rs. 33. Men above fourteen years are counted as one consumption unit, women and children at given fractions of a consumption unit. The poorest households have a monthly expenditure per consumption unit of Rs. 10 to 15 (1962 : *342*). I have based the estimated proportion of income devoted to weddings on rough extrapolations from these figures. A similar estimate, that between six months' to more than a year's income is spent on a wedding, is given for weddings in Ramkheri in Madhya Pradesh (Mayer 1960 : *227*).

Culture Change
in a Navaho Community[1]

HARVEY C. MOORE

SURROUNDED by a large and complex Anglo-American society, not to mention other Indian societies, Navaho culture as
a whole is not today a self-contained system. External imperatives
alter the Navaho economy, social relations, curing practices, rear-
ing of the young, material culture, and many other aspects of the
Navaho way of life. Contemporary Navaho culture contains many
of the traditional goals but increasingly fewer of the traditional
means. The transmission of traditional Navaho culture to the very
young, insofar as it is achieved by the enculturative forces of
familial and kin groupings in a community context, tends to encourage the formation of a personality structure harmonious with
the goals of the culture when it was a more self-contained system.
Yet, in both the personal life and in the societal life of the older

HARVEY C. MOORE, presently Chairman of the Department of Anthropology at American University in Washington, D. C., has worked and
travelled in Africa, and has done ethnology in the American southwest.

youths and adults of the community there is often observable a pragmatically derived demonstration of newer techniques and newer goals. Furthermore, on the level of the tribal government, *i.e.,* the official, albeit nontraditional corporate symbol of the tribe, certain other important new practices appear. However, neither the changes in the personalities nor in community societal life nor in the official viewpoints of the Tribal Council provide a meaningful new synthesis that can give to the local community a new vitality and direction.

The student of the community and the influences that affect it readily sees two salient external macrocosms that make demands for change upon it. Both the Anglo-American culture and the Navaho tribal government make demands that may not be entirely ignored by those Navahos whose interests are still largely community oriented. The macrocosm of American culture is not only an influence for change in the Navaho community but also is an uncertain model, for it is changing in itself. Concurrently, but not consequently, the executive and legislative branches of the Navaho tribal government are changing in their methods, goals, and degree of interaction with the wider Anglo economic and political bodies.

This article concerns itself mainly with defining some cultural changes in a community. Interpretation is usually confined to the microcosm for which evidential data are presented. Changes in the macrocosms of American or Navaho cultures are considered only where necessary to an understanding of the particular community which is the subject of analysis. Data for a historic baseline, derived from the author's 1953 study of the community, a northern salient of the Navaho reservation, are compared with the data from his restudy of the community in 1961. The research was undertaken with particular interest in the hypothesis that as long as the people of the community continued to regard the herding economy as the economic ideal there would be resistance to culture change. There was also a wish to test the extent to which elements of the "core culture" resisted or did not resist change. In this study quantifiable data were collected where possible, not so much for statistical induction as to indicate directional trends toward new practices (cultural change) or to show enduring practices (cultural stability).

The findings of the 1953 study showed certain outstanding features. The community was little acculturated to Anglo culture. The extensive practice of peyotism was evidence of willingness to accept religious acculturation to practices of other Indians. Relations with whites had not always been harmonious. The community had a history of disputes with adjacent Anglos about grazing practices and settlement patterns. In some instances the disputes took the form of lengthy legal battles. Accumulated historic grievances made the community rather hostile to whites. Also many members of the community felt neglected or mistreated by and alienated from, if not hostile to, the Navaho corporate entity symbolized by distant Window Rock Headquarters.

Between 1953 and 1961 large oil and natural gas fields were developed, primarily in the western and southern part of the community. They considerably altered the face of the range and resulted in a network of intracommunity and access roads. Thus while in 1953 the community was relatively isolated, in 1961, the tripling of access roads and the new internal roads, replacing earlier trails, increased community interaction. Activities connected with building and, to a less extent, maintaining the fields brought to the community technological, social, ecological, and economic aspects of Anglo culture. The oil revenues going to the Navaho tribal government caused increased attention to the community where the wells were located. Individual economic aspirations greatly increased in the members of the community although few had lands in severalty and consequently few received royalties.

In the farflung community north of the San Juan River the author, in 1953, collected school and other census data, prepared his own census of adults, and then engaged in formal interviews, informal interviews and observations.[2] In 1961 the same techniques were used but the 1953 interview schedule was revised to include subsequent events.[3] Twenty-six respondents, called the

Panel Group, were selected by random sample in 1953. It was possible to reinterview twenty-one of the Panel Group in 1961 and to interview sixteen additional persons using a formal interview schedule. The additional sixteen composed a stratified sample particularly relevant to understanding reactions to the oil-gas development. In 1953 the Panel Group plus one interpreter was interviewed. These twenty-seven are called the Total Group (TG) for 1953. The Total Group consisted of 37 persons in 1961. Percentages were computed for both Panel and Total Groups for both years in preparation for a longer study of community organization. In this article readability will be facilitated by using mainly percentages for the Total Groups only.

The discussion presented here focuses upon change as expressed in interactions and change as expressed in awareness. These two facets of change will be reviewed with respect to political matters, livelihood, curative practices, and education.

Political

The people in general were more active politically in the community and had more extra-community political awareness in 1961. More looked to the Tribal Council than to the Indian Service as a primary source of help, a reverse of viewpoint from 1953. More expressed unqualified approval of the Tribal Council and fewer unqualified disapproval. In 1961, unqualified disapproval was expressed by 16 per cent whereas 33 per cent had expressed unqualified disapproval in 1953. Interestingly enough, unqualified approval was expressed by 16 per cent also. (Approves, unqualified: 1953: PG, 0.0 per cent; TG, 0.0 per cent; 1961: PG, 19 per cent; TG, 16.2 per cent. Disapproves, unqualified: 1953 PG, 38 per cent; TG 33.3 per cent; 1961: PG, 4.7 per cent; TG, 16.2 per cent). An independent analyst studying the field data[4] noted an increase in knowledge of the Tribal Council. By 1961, a few might actually be called well informed. Even so, about a third had very little comprehension of it.

In 1961 the people felt it was the responsibility of the Tribal Council to provide employment within the community. A third of the respondents regarded it as the source from which other forms of economic help should come also. No other source was mentioned with anything approaching this frequency. In 1953 about half the respondents felt help was the responsibility of the Federal Government. This change of attitude reflects not only the greater awareness of the Council in 1961 but also the knowledge that oil and gas wells in the community's area had greatly increased tribal revenues.

National political awareness, as distinguished from awareness of the Indian Service, had increased. Also there was more voting activity. In 1953 none of the respondents had voted in the preceding presidential election; in 1961 27 per cent had so voted, with preference for the Democratic Party about four to one.

The people in 1961 were much more aware of the state of Utah. The federal law that originally had added to the Reservation that half of the community in which oil was found later had stipulated that 37.5 per cent of net profits from all mineral rights would accrue to the state of Utah to be used for the benefit of the people in the land added. The complexities of administering the oil royalties were not problems of which the people were knowledgeable, but they disapproved of the handling of funds and regarded the state with either indifference or animosity. Only four respondents found anything favorable to say. People felt the state was depriving them of the benefits of the accrued funds. Federal litigation was regarded by some as the way to correct the situation. Recourse to litigation is partly attributable to a history of lawsuits between some persons in the community and neighboring Anglos. Many Navahos were enthusiastic about past decisions of the federal courts and sanguine about future ones. Some were willing to contribute from their meager funds to support litigations although previous suits had led some to take financial risks from which they did not successfully emerge.

In summary, the people were feeling increasingly aware of

and alienated from the state of Utah. They were rather ambivalent in their approval of the Tribal Council but felt increasingly dependent upon it. As the Council took over responsibilities formerly belonging to the Bureau of Indian Affairs, it assumed a scapegoat function. For instance, the people felt the tribal funds, although heavily derived from oil and gas revenues produced by the land of the community, were not used to help this community as much as some other communities. Contributing to the ambivalence were not only the Council's acts of omission and commission but also generalized resentments deriving from the past history of the area. The area to an extent had had a separate history since before the Ft. Sumner period (1864 - 68). Most Navahos had been interned there, but a portion of this community had not been. There was a tendency to exaggerate the number of ancestors who had remained free and unconquered in spirit. The old historical reality of feeling different had been reinforced by a more recent history that made the people feel that prior to the discovery of oil they had been neglected and ignored by, first, the Bureau of Indian Affairs, and second, the Tribal Council.

Economic

Between 1953 and 1961 there were considerable economic changes. The traditional idealogical attachment to herding and farming declined. For example, herding was recognized as the primary source of livelihood by only about 40 per cent of the respondents in 1953, but 85 per cent of the respondents said the need for more stock was their primary economic concern. In 1961, only 32 per cent said their primary economic concern was a need for more stock, a drop of over 50 per cent, unaccompanied by any perceptible increase in herds.

Wage work decreased as a primary source of income during the eight year interval. Some of the decrease was caused by aging of some respondents and/or by an increase in social security and welfare benefits. More importantly, the decrease reflected a shift in the pattern of employment. Wage work among males decreased and wage work among females increased slightly, the latter largely because in 1961 women could work in the community not only for the Bureau of Indian Affairs but also on temporary Tribal Work Projects not previously available. Off-reservation seasonal agricultural employment in areas contiguous to the community stayed at about the same level. However in 1953 about 40 per cent of the men in the respondent households had worked in non-agricultural employment at some distance away during the preceding five year period. In 1961, no respondent had been so employed. In part this decline is connected with the reduced job opportunities for unskilled labor in the general American economy. More particularly, however, prior to 1953 about 37 per cent of the males had done some railroad work and none had been so employed in the five year period including 1961 reflecting new railroad maintenance practices. The relative scarcity of off-reservation wage earning opportunities is underlined when it is seen that employment on the infrequent Tribal Work Projects (which lasted an average of about ten days) afforded a primary source of income to 13.5 per cent of all respondents and a supplemental source to another 35.1 per cent.

The oil and gas fields employed only two respondents. This is related to the small number of Navahos who had the qualifications of formal education of an eighth grade minimum or a suitable work history. Nevertheless, there is a strong feeling that employment in the local community is a right and that it is the responsibility of the Tribal Council to provide a solution. Not only did they feel it was the responsibility of the Tribal Council to provide employment within the community, but in 1961 a third of both the Panel Group and of the Total Group regarded it as the source from which other forms of economic help should come. No other source was mentioned with anything approaching this frequency. This was in contrast to the situation in 1953 when around half the respondents felt that help was the responsibility of the Federal Government. This reorientation stemmed not only from an awareness of the Tribal Council, but also from an awareness that oil and gas wells in their area had greatly increased the revenues administered by the Council.

Where and how income is expended is also relevant to the economic analysis of a community. There were four trading posts in the general area under study, but the one located in the center of the community apparently was the one most used. It was estimated that in 1961, considerably more than half the lambs, sheep, goats, wool, and mohair traded was handled through this post. Credit was an important aspect of trading post operation, and was extended to those who were considered good risks, either in terms of herding operation or in terms of other regular income. Almost half of the 1961 respondents who had checks to cash (and all but three said that they did cash checks) usually cashed them at this trading post. The trading post therefore obviously continued to be the major point of commodity exchange and supply.

On the other hand, there was evidence that some of those who had cash income were shopping off-reservation. Slightly more than half of the respondents who cashed checks said that they usually cashed them at banks or stores in adjoining towns—principally in Cortez, Colorado. The supermarket in Cortez was mentioned by a number of respondents in 1961, and several said that they shopped off-reservation because the prices at the trading post were too high.

In 1961 respondents were asked about principal items of expenditure. As would be anticipated, all respondents (except one, for whom no budgetary data were secured) listed food as the major item. Over 85 per cent also included clothing. One might derive a number of inferences from the fact that the third most frequently listed item of expenditure was either automotive repair (35.1 per cent) or payment for automotive purchase (18.9 per cent). Purchase of jewelry (the traditional form of saving) was mentioned by somewhat over 15 per cent. Other items of expenditure mentioned, but by three individuals or less, were home improvement, purchase of winter fodder for stock, and income tax.

In both periods the traditional economy was inadequate for

the needs of the people. In 1953 about 70 per cent of all respondents reported having less than seventy-five stock units in the family. About the same situation was reported in 1961 with the further statement that the respondents regarded the oil and gas development as a detriment to the traditional economy. Compensation for damage to stock was not believed to offset the detriment, although compensation ranging from a reported under $100 to over $1,000, had been received by about 48.6 per cent.

Worthy of note is what appeared to be a lessened dependence on the young for herding, especially in the wintertime when school is in session. Data were not collected on this point in 1953 because the writer assumed a heavy dependence on the young at all seasons. There was no evidence to cause this assumption to be questioned. By 1961 he suspected attitudes had changed, and he discovered that only 10.8 per cent of the respondents depended primarily on a family member under sixteen years of age to be responsible for the herd.

Curative Practices

Let us now turn to curing practices and preferences. Curing is a focus of Navaho culture and choice of curing practices sometimes reflects a traditional pragmatic attitude. In 1953 many would use three kinds of cures: traditional Navaho ceremonies (96.2 per cent), peyote rites (85.1 per cent), and the hospital (92.5 per cent). In addition, those who at some time had gone to other tribes for sucking cures numbered over 40 per cent. Stated first preferences for curing in 1953 were one, traditional Navaho medicine (48.1 per cent) and two, peyote (14.8 per cent). Those who said they preferred equally Navaho, peyote, or Western medicine numbered 25.9 per cent; but Western medicine as a clear first choice was mentioned by only 3.7 per cent. In 1961, those who said their first choice went to Western medicine numbered 56.7 per cent and those who liked best Navaho medicine numbered 24.3 per cent. Peyote as a first choice was 5.4 per cent. Those who preferred all three equally were 5.4 per cent. Impressively, in 1961, private Western facilities were used by 62.1 per cent, although they had to pay for those facilities; and free Public Health facilities were used by 35.1 per cent. Clearly this is a change of behavior connected with a core element of Navaho culture. Navaho sings, of course, continued to be used and in 1961 were used by 83.7 per cent of the respondents (cf. 94.5 per cent who used the hospital). Sings continued to be not only genuinely popular but to have a competitive advantage because they often could be conducted in a familiar milieu.

Let us look briefly at social roles connected with curing. In 1961 people performing none of the curative roles of singer, diviner, or peyote priest were 64.8 per cent of the respondents, almost 10 per cent more than in 1953. The writer knows of only two men in the community who were studying to be singers. Both were middleaged.

Education

By 1961 there was a tremendous increase of children in school, although all pupils beyond the first grade had to live out of the community. About 50 per cent more children were in school, composing 88.6 per cent of all children between the ages of six and eighteen years. There was a decrease of 40.8 per cent in those who had never attended. In the age category of six to eighteen only 5.7 per cent had never attended school. Not only were more children in school, but they were starting younger and staying longer. This change must be considered in the light of an increase in the number of seats made available by the Indian Service school system. However, it does not reflect compulsion resulting from a more vigorous enforcement of a truancy system. There was an increase in level of educational aspiration of parents for children and a decrease of negative expression concerning schooling. In 1961 education was regarded as "very important" by 43.2 per cent, or by four times as many people as in 1953. There was a decrease of over 50 per cent in the heretofore traditional "It's up to them" answer concerning the level of education children should attain. Traditionally children's wishes concerning educational decisions would quickly have been mentioned. In 1961 the remark "It's up to them" was made by only 13.5 per cent (cf. 37 per cent in 1953).

In 1953 respondents tended to define lack of formal education in terms of disadvantage in securing and holding a job off-reservation. In 1961 there was no longer this tendency; and when respondents spoke of the importance of education for their children, the orientation seemed to be toward job opportunities within the reservation.

Summary and Final Remarks

Clearly culture change occurred in the community between 1953 and 1961. Not all of it need be elaborated upon here. For instance, in 1961, there were more radios and fewer persons lived only in hogans (43 per cent; the rest had houses as well and these had tripled in number). The Tribal Council had built a fine new chapter house. The central trading post was much enlarged and had a greater variety of goods. Pickup trucks were in good condition, and there were other evidences of the increased amount of money which had come into the community in the past eight years.

The new roads and bridges had expanded the number of people coming to the trading post and attending chapter meetings. There was a schism in the community over how the oil revenues should be spent, and the community was split into two groups. The less revolutionary group wanted present handling of funds by the Council and Utah to be improved. The other wanted the control of the funds to be given to certain people of the community. The second group was smaller but had a more educated leadership, including a white rancher and a Salt Lake City lawyer, as well as the tribal councilman.

Any real testing of the role of the continuing ideal of a native subsistence economy has to take into account not only the changes in that ideal but also the historical factor of unspent millions of dollars which the people wished could be spent or invested to their profit. Desire to participate in the off-reservation wage economy was slight. Relocation was of no interest. While interaction with the outside was increasing in such things as awareness of the Tribal Council, awareness of welfare benefits, voting, seeking Western medicine, sending children away for an education, and shopping outside, the individual Navaho of this community became less and less a worker in the outside economy. Some of the changes were largely in social relations, but some involved new cultural goals for society and personality. Despite the fact that the traditional economy is not self-sufficient and most of the livelihood must come either from outside the community or through non-Navaho technological patterns being practiced by the non-Navahos in the community, the changes, some chosen and some unavoidable, were not always ones that would further adjustment to the Anglo technology and economy.

Changes in what might be considered core features of Navaho culture (*e.g.,* herds, decentralized authority, individualization, and sings) include a marked trend away from an ideal which focuses its hopes on an increase in the herds as the primary economic solution and more emphasis upon a livelihood with a return in money rather than kind. Until the 1920's there was no central political body. It came into existence then largely because of Indian Service persuasion and had little autonomy, nor was there any considerable popular Navaho interest in it. By the early 1950's, with Indian Service encouragement, it was becoming more independent but it was much less in popular awareness than was the Indian Service itself. By 1961, the Tribal Council was central to much of the people's thinking. In 1961 parents were acting as if individualism could sometimes be breached in that they were more willing to state opinions about what is desirable for children instead of saying children should decide for themselves. Nontraditional curing methods have attained higher priority when compared with sings. Some of the change is compartmentalized, *e.g.,* education for Western culture is left to the schools. Some of the change is fusional, *e.g.,* behavior at chapter meetings is neither like leader-led discussion of a secular problem in the group gathered for a squaw dance nor like an open discussion in a New England town meeting but is a new synthesis reminiscent of some features of both. Some of the change is incorporative, that is, borrowed elements are fitted into place and elaborated upon in terms of pre-existing patterns.[5] The Navaho goals are no longer purely traditional nor are they largely Western. They reflect some new realities or perceptions of reality, and they reflect retention of older values even after their functional potential is gone. The changes toward greater belief in education and somewhat greater political activity appear to be changes that will help them cope better with the reality of the outside world. The kind and direction of economic changes indicate that a socially satisfactory solution of the livelihood problem is still far distant.

The various changes, small and large, indicate that the student of contemporary Navaho culture change must increasingly be a student of the several models which are both resisted and accepted. An understanding of behavior in its various dimensions among the Navahos requires study and understanding of events and ideas impinging upon the Navaho from neighboring states, the nation, and even at times the world of international relations. Navaho conscious reactions to these events vary with the level of the society involved.

The roots of the logic used in many of the interpretations of the various models are deep in the history of the Navaho culture. An analytic study of and understanding of contemporary Navaho change requires one to be forearmed with a knowledge of the historic base. As the ramifications of change are pursued, it becomes increasingly imperative for Navahos and anthropologists studying the Navaho to have a knowledge of the wider context of which the Navaho are a part.

NOTES

[1]   An earlier version of this paper was read at the 1962 Annual Meeting, American Anthropological Association, Chicago, Illinois.

[2]   The 1953 field work was done by the writer but was part of a project headed by Dr. David F. Aberle. The support for the writer's work on Aberle's project came from the Social Science Research Council and the National Institutes of Health. Aberle counselled the writer before his 1953 summer research as he had done for other research in the summers of 1951 and 1952. Aberle's leadership and initiative were primarily the source of the 1953 interview schedule. He has given permission to use the 1953 community data collected by this writer; he has no responsibility for their formulation and interpretation. Other valuable assistance to the writer's field work has been given by Sarah Moore, who accompanied him to the field; numerous officials of the Bureau of Indian Affairs, but especially Walter Olson and Robert Young; and hundreds of Navahos. Ruth H. Landman kindly read the manuscript and gave advice. Obviously none of the foregoing is to be blamed for this chapter.

[3]   Funds for the 1961 study and its analysis were made possible by grant number M-4428 from the National Institute of Mental Health.

[4]   Mr. James E. Gardner, to whom acknowledgment is made of my considerable indebtedness for his tabulations and excellent advice.

[5]   Many concepts used in this summary are borrowed from the writings of Edward Dozier, Edward Spicer, and Evon Z. Vogt. See especially their articles in Spicer, E. H., ed., *Perspectives in American Indian Culture Change,* University of Chicago Press, 1961.

Ceramic Technology and Trade in the Palenque Region, Mexico

ROBERT L. RANDS

TECHNOLOGICAL analysis constitutes a useful but little-utilized approach to the investigation of prehistoric pottery. Archaeologists, too often lacking the necessary training and laboratory equipment to conduct detailed mineralogical studies, have understandably been discouraged from following out the potentials of this specialized approach. Ceramic technologists, few in number and overworked, have rarely been available to integrate their findings with systematically conceived archaeological programs. The present paper will outline methodology, current findings, and theoretical significance of an attempt to utilize ceramic technology as a means of tracing trade relationships. Focus of the investigation is the major Maya ceremonial center of Palenque and outlying sites in northeastern Chiapas and adjacent Tabasco (Figure).

ROBERT L. RANDS is Associate Professor of Anthropology at the University of North Carolina, Chapel Hill. He has done extensive research in the archaeology of the Maya and the southeastern United States.

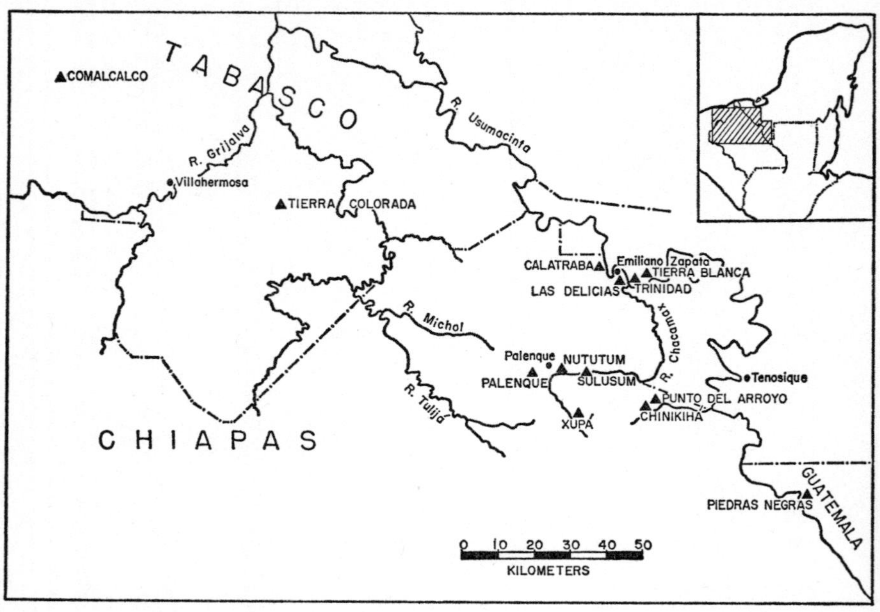

The Palenque survey area in relation to certain western Maya sites. Pottery from all archaeological sites except Piedras Negras and Comalcalco has been sampled technologically as part of the Palenque ceramic project

Prior to middle Classic times Palenque had apparently been a small, unimportant community, partially bypassed by the major streams of diffusion in the Maya area. Following a comparatively brief period of Petén-oriented ceramic influences, Palenque pottery diverged notably from the better-known Maya patterns. By contrast, this was a time when the site flourished, architecturally and artistically. Toward the close of the Palenque occupation, near the end of the Late Classic period, ceramic connections were primarily toward the Tabasco-Chiapas plains. More striking than any of these influences is the localized nature of the bulk of Palenque pottery (Rands and Rands 1957; Rands 1961).

The role of trade in the ebb and flow of Palenque's contacts with other parts of the Maya area is a fascinating problem, to which ceramic technology should ultimately make a contribution.

Our present concern, however, is with an essentially different sort of trade. This may be characterized as short-range, intensive, and domestic, rather than far-flung, exotic, and foreign. It is the kind of trade which may not be too revealing in terms of cultural affiliations within the Maya area as a whole, but, properly understood, it can shed valuable light on the nature of Classic Maya society.

Palenque pottery is unusually difficult to work with, because of the excessive weathering and highly fragmentary condition. Surface finish, so important a guide in standard archaeological investigation, is all too often destroyed beyond recognition. This is a practical reason why we were early attracted to technological analysis, as a means of making some sense out of this recalcitrant material. As time went on, however, and the investigation was expanded by a limited ceramic reconnaissance of adjacent sites (Ruz 1959 : 270-76; Rands and Rands 1961), we began to appreciate the potentials of this approach as a means of tracing places of manufacture and patterns of subsequent trade.

Adequate technological investigation of an area of intensive trade includes not only analysis of pottery, recovered through survey and excavation, but a study of raw materials readily available to the potters of different locations. If particular raw materials, such as clay and temper from a definite location, can be shown to have been utilized in certain pottery types, a major breakthrough will have been achieved. Even negative evidence, which eliminates potential natural deposits as the materials from which a given body of pottery was made, will result in a better understanding of the problem. More meaningful questions can then be asked about locale of manufacture and routes of ceramic exchange. My wife, Barbara C. Rands, and I have been developing a technological approach along these lines for several years, aided especially by Anna O. Shepard, who examined a large sample of Palenque pottery and provided insights for the ordering and understanding of this complex body of material. A systematic and expanded investigation is now being carried out at the Research

Laboratories of Anthropology of the University of North Carolina.[1]

How to obtain an adequate sampling of technologically analyzed pottery is a major problem. Examination with the binocular microscope, which constitutes only a first, though fundamental, step, is in itself a time-consuming task. Our sampling has been standardized to include all sherds showing any of the following culturally significant features: rims, bases, supports, appendages, and other modes of shape, slip and painting (when observable), and plastic decoration. At this writing, more than 4,700 sherds, from Palenque and ten adajcent sites, have been processed in this way. Also analyzed are some 350 figurine fragments. Microscopic examination has taken two directions: *1]* the establishment of temper-textural classes; and *2]* the determination of mineral particles which are apparently natural inclusions within the clay from which the pottery was made. Of these two approaches, the first has been more widely used, both in standard archaeological and technological investigations (cf. Shepard 1956: *156-58*). The fact that natural inclusions are without direct cultural significance has, understandably, dissuaded the archaeologist, as a student of culture, from dealing with them. If sufficiently diagnostic, however, such inclusions hold a great deal of promise in an attempt to localize centers of manufacture, for one would normally expect basic clay for the pots, as distinct from special clay for slips, to have been obtained from relatively nearby beds.

It is planned to supplement this phase of the investigation by systematically carrying forward approaches which to date we have employed only occasionally. Reference is to the collection in the field and subsequent analysis of clay samples; preparation of thin sections and spectrographic analysis; refiring; X-ray diffraction studies; and a search for trace elements. Our aims are: *1]* to find where possible the same combination of diagnostic technological features in pottery from different sites; *2]* to determine whether clay from the location of these sites has the same technological properties as the pottery present at the sites; and *3]* to correlate these findings with attributes of style, shape, and (where possible) surface finish and function.

Excavation and survey of smaller sites has, to date, been carried out largely to the north and east of Palenque. By the time one passes some twenty-five or thirty miles from Palenque, most of the ceramic assemblages are basically and profoundly different from pottery of the same period at Palenque. Nevertheless, a few items are shared, although in significantly different percentages. Technological data suggest that noteworthy correspondences in these distinct ceramic zones may be due to the presence of trade goods rather than resulting simply from common cultural patterns. As to be expected, however, pottery at sites only six to eight miles away is virtually identical in a number of respects to that of Palenque. Even so, surprising differences exist at nearby sites in apparently contemporaneous ceramic assemblages, particularly in the rarity at the small sites of the smoothly-finished, quartz-tempered Red-brown pottery which formed so important a ceramic class throughout the Palenque occupation.

Completed analyses for temper and texture reveal the following major distributional patterns through time and space. Along the limestone escarpment that rises sharply at the south of the alluvial plain of Chiapas and Tabasco, a shift from carbonate temper (calcite or dolomite) to quartz sand is evident, especially in the utility jars and basins (Palenque, Chinikihá). At Palenque, which occupies the very edge of the escarpment, sand-tempered Red-brown pottery was always popular, but the presumably imported gloss ware, as well as utilitarian pottery, tended to be carbonate tempered in Early Classic times. At Chinikihá, the Early Classic commitment to carbonate temper was more complete. Sites yielding only terminal Late Classic pottery, which lie at the foot of the escarpment (Nututum, Sulusum), or only a short distance south into limestone country (Xupá), have an almost exclusive use of quartz sand in their tempered pottery. In addition, at all these sites—Palenque, Nututum, Sulusum, Xupá, Chinikihá— silty-textured to fine paste pottery occurred in moderate amounts in advanced Late Classic times. On this level of analysis, therefore, the escarpment region, at the south of the survey area, showed considerable homogeneity but underwent pronounced shifts through time. At Chinikihá, however, volcanic ash temper—occurring on a Late Classic level—was more common than at the other sites. Also, carbonate is of crystalline structure in the pottery of Chinikihá, but only rarely so at Palenque.

Some twenty miles to the north, along the Usumacinta River, lie the sites of Tierra Blanca, Trinidad, Las Delicias, and Calatraba. Sequences extend from Preclassic times. In this region, to judge from samples which have been analyzed, temper consisted largely of volcanic ash. The end of the Late Classic witnessed the rise of Balancan (z) Fine Orange, while other fine paste types preceded Fine Orange and were better represented than in the escarpment sites to the south. In spite of these textural changes, the sharp temporal shifts in tempering materials noted to the south are not evident. What was the source of the volcanic ash in these alluvial sites? Thick-walled utility pottery sometimes contains pumice fragments along with the ash, and it is possible that floating pumice from the river was ground up to produce the temper. (Pieces of pumice occur from archaeological levels along the Usumacinta.)

Inclusions in the clay form a more complex distributional pattern than do the temper and textural classes. The inclusions, as has been noted, are in themselves lacking any cultural significance, often being microscopic in size, but in certain cases should prove to be important in recognizing tradepieces and locating centers of manufacture. It has become apparent, at Palenque and the survey sites, that much of the pottery—roughly 60 per cent [2]—bears one or more natural inclusions in the clay. Not included in this figure is the almost ubiquitous clear silt or sand. Examples of inclusions are ferruginous lumps, carbonate particles, volcanic dust, and phytoliths—the latter consisting of opal, derived from silica-accumulator plants. In addition, some of the ceramic pastes are highly micaceous. A distinctive rose quartz occurs (usually in pottery which is tempered with volcanic ash), and a "dirty sand" complex is characterized by biotite, white and gray quartz, and dark slate or siltstone. Abundant opal and volcanic dust in fine paste, cream pottery constitutes a striking association, which occurs on a Late Classic horizon at many of the sites. Inspection would have raised the possibility that this was tradeware, but technological analysis provides a new dimension of probability. A northern origin, perhaps not too far from the survey area, is suggested for this opal-and dust-bearing pottery, on the basis of distributional evidence. Further remarks will largely be confined to a single inclusion, the opaline phytolith.

At Palenque and the survey sites, approximately 35 per cent of the pottery which has been analyzed contains phytoliths. Opal, abundant in the pastes of much of the Fine Cream, Fine Black, and Fine Gray pottery, is conspicuously absent in Fine Orange, including at least the Balancan (z) and Matillas (v) Ceramic Groups. This points to a different source for the Fine Orange as opposed to the other fine paste wares. Carbonate-tempered pottery is also largely lacking in opal, as is the sand-tempered Red-brown pottery. The latter is abundantly represented at Palenque, constituting almost 50 per cent of the pottery and occurring with little change in frequency throughout the ceramic sequence. Forms include tripod plates and allied everted-rim bowls, cylinders, cache vessels, and incense burners. Some 98 per cent of the figurines and figurine molds so far analyzed at Palenque are also of Red-brown.

We have regarded Red-brown as indigenous in the sense that it was a basic ware, being manufactured at or close to the site. Its negative association with opal is shown by the presence of this inclusion in only about 5 per cent of the Red-brown pottery, whereas phytoliths occur in approximately 25 per cent of the remainder of the pottery at the site. This is one of several indications that different sources of clay were used in the manufacture of the ceramics which are found at Palenque. A half dozen samples of raw clay from the proximity of Palenque, two from the foot of the ruins, have been analyzed and found to be without opal inclusions. Some of the clay fires to a reddish-brown color, approximating that of the Red-brown pottery. Therefore, the technological data, as currently understood, are consistent with the belief that the Red-brown pottery (or at least some of it) is of local manufacture.

In contrast, ceramics from the survey sites nearest to Palenque show a preponderance of opal inclusions. At Nututum and Sulusum, a few miles to the east on the Chacamax River, more than 70 per cent of the analyzed pottery contains phytoliths. At Xupá, lying a short distance to the south, the occurrence of opal drops to 30 per cent. Unslipped, sand-tempered jars and basins, which usually bear opal inclusions, are heavily represented at Nututum and Sulusum, to a great degree accounting for the high occurrence of opal at these sites. Stylistically similar quartz-tempered utility is also common on late horizons at Palenque but does not begin to approach its abundance, greater than 75 per cent, at Nututum. This could be interpreted to mean that Palenque was abandoned before the maximum occurrence of sand-tempered utility but that occupations at Nututum and Sulusum continued until a greater popularity was achieved. Another possibility is that functionally-differentiated classes of pottery (service and utilitarian) were appropriate to an elite ceremonial center such as Palenque and to a secondary center on the order of Nututum. On the other hand, the data may well indicate that the Chacamax sites of Nututum and Sulusum lay at or close to the center of manufacture of the quartz-tempered utility, trading it to Palenque, but receiving in return a significantly smaller amount of the Red-brown service and ceremonial pottery of Palenque. We favor the latter interpretation but, regardless of these varied possibilities, some selective factor involving trade is indicated.

The nearest sizable ceremonial center to Palenque is Xupá, about ten air miles distant. Fairly close affiliations in vessel shape exist to late pottery at Palenque. However, much of the general class of pottery at Xupá which most closely resembles Red-brown of Palenque is exceptionally micaceous, and this would appear to rule out a common source for these sherds. Does all of this mean that Nututum and Sulusum at the foot of the escarpment formed part of an economic zone which sustained Palenque, but that Xupá had its own relatively independent economic sphere, at least so far as service pottery was concerned? Even if this position can be maintained for the pottery, is it permissible to generalize in this way from the ceramic data to the myriad activities which leave no direct stamp on the archaeological record?

The role of trade in Maya culture is poorly known, especially as one probes back beyond the protohistoric period.[3] Nevertheless, speculation is profitable, providing it can be subjected to testing. The following reconstruction is an extension of certain commonly held ideas about the nature of Classic Maya settlements.[4] It is offered as a working hypothesis which appears to fit the findings of our investigations and calls attention to certain problem areas. Modifications may be required, either in our interpretation of the technological data or in the hypothesis. It is to be hoped, however, that as sampling becomes greater through field work in hitherto untouched parts of the Palenque region, a firm basis will be established on which to test these ideas.

Central to the thinking of many Mayanists are concepts which may be termed the *ceremonial center,* the *tributary* or *satellite community* and the *sustaining area.* A more closely calibrated typology of units of settlement (Bullard 1960) consists of the Cluster (or small hamlet), Zone (group of some fifty to one hundred houses associated with a Minor Ceremonial Center), and District (grouping of Zones with a Major Ceremonial Center as its nucleus). In the discussion that follows, the ceremonial center equates best with Bullard's Major Ceremonial Center, his Minor Ceremonial Centers being included among the satellite communities. Palenque, for example, would clearly be a Major Ceremonial Center, Nututum and Sulusum qualifying as Minor Centers, and Palenque's *sustaining area* would apparently correspond to the District.

The ceremonial center, apart from priests, rulers, administrators, and retainers, is frequently believed to have lacked a significant resident population. No doubt, during times of architectural activity, many workmen were to be found in the center, perhaps spending the night there (or on its outskirts), perhaps returning daily to nearby homes. Also, the center must have held many people during public ceremonial observances in the religious calendar. While we do not know the degree of freedom or coercion of the peasant class (Willey 1956*b*), it seems fair to speculate that the same people (and their families) who labored most often on the public works of a particular ceremonial center returned most frequently to that same center to watch the ceremonies, or possibly to participate in them. We do not know whether a particular individual would normally labor on public works of more than a single major center or whether his services would be divided between two or more centers of comparable size. I would suspect, however, that his primary allegiance was to one principal center, although he might also work on smaller "neighborhood" projects.

All of this is to say that a single major ceremonial center, such as Palenque, probably exerted an effective political control over the manpower of a more or less definitely recognized area, having the primary call on the services of the people residing in this region. If this is so, it seems reasonable that these people attended the public ceremonies of "their" center more frequently than they attended those of other centers of equal importance—though we cannot be sure that the peasant-laborers did not also engage in widespread pilgrimages.[5]

If the bulk of the population resided away from the ceremonial center in satellite communities, it would seem to follow that many of the craft activities took place in these settlements. It is possible, however, that certain of the more specialized craftsmen lived at or close to the ceremonial center. On the basis of present-day Highland Maya practices, considerable craft specialization in the various communities is to be inferred, the products of one being distinct from the next either in the general class of objects which were manufactured (such as pottery or textiles) or in their detail (*e.g.,* form or function of the pottery). On the other hand, sixteenth-century and contemporary economic institutions of a specialized sort show a comparatively weak development among the Yucatecan Maya (Sanders 1963 : 233 - 34; Tax 1952).

A dispersed, amorphous pattern of settlement, in which one community merged by imperceptible degrees with the next, is sometimes assumed for the Classic Maya (Type B in Willey 1956*a*). This could have lessened feelings of community separation and, accordingly, have minimized the "appropriateness" for each community to specialize in its own craft productions. However, in urbanized settings such as Tenochtitlán, wards, barrios, or the calpulli maintained economic specializations, in spite of their spatial proximity.

How would specialized products have been exchanged under the dispersed conditions assumed for the Classic Maya? Itinerant merchants could have carried goods widely, far beyond the zone of effective political control of a particular ceremonial center. In addition, many products were probably exchanged through the marketplace. Possibly centers such as Palenque, in addition to functioning as places of religious and administrative activities, served as marketplaces, especially on important dates in the ceremonial calendar. The concurrence of large markets and principal fiestas is, in any event, an important pattern in Highland Guatemalan communities today. The small Classic settlements, whose laboring forces were directed primarily to a particular ceremonial center, may also have tended to channel their craft productions through the market located in the same center. To the extent that this was true, the smaller satellite communities formed a sustaining area for a single major ceremonial center, these units being integrated along political, religious, and economic lines.

If this reconstruction is substantially correct, and pottery was produced in one or more of the tributary sites within a single sustaining area, what distributional patterning of the ceramics would one expect to find? The principal marketplace, located at the ceremonial center and attended most consistently by people having sociopolitical and ceremonial allegiance to that center, would apparently funnel the pottery primarily to the various satellite communities within the sustaining area. People from outside the district, who attended the market less frequently, would take home significantly smaller quantities of the pottery. To be sure, if the pottery had some special appeal due to its hardness or unusual aesthetic properties, it might be prized by outsiders and obtained in large quantities. Unattractive pottery holding valued contents might also pass widely in trade. In most cases, however, and especially when dealing with plain utilitarian pottery, the archaeologist should find a sharply reduced amount of the pottery in question as he passed to sites beyond the border of the sustaining area. If this is correct, the sharp dropping off of the pottery produced at a particular time would indicate approximately the boundaries of the sustaining area for that period.

Suppose, however, that although the preceding sociopolitical reconstruction is basically correct, no pottery was produced within a given sustaining area. All ceramic goods would then be imported from outside the area, and the suggested model clearly could not hold true. This is just one of a great many modifications of the working hypothesis which, if correct, would necessarily alter the archaeological findings. If the market, rather than a wide-ranging merchant class, functioned as the primary mechanism for distributing the pottery, it is possible that politically-independent though economically-linked regions of intensive trade might still be discernible. However, one would expect the boundaries of such regions to be blurred, lacking the relatively sharp definition of sustaining areas which were based on coinciding economic as well as social, political, and ceremonial activities.

Still another hypothesis would grant that pottery was produced locally, within a given sustaining area, but hold that the source of sizable quantities of the ceramics lay outside the area.[6] Special problems are introduced if later Meso-American patterns are taken as rigorous models for the market economy of the Classic Maya. Such present-day institutions would include market regionalism (expressed in Pre-Columbian times as the alternation of market days within either a single sustaining area or in adjacent districts) and a system of daily local markets onto which was superimposed special periodic markets, the latter serving to attract people from afar.

It would be fruitless at this time to pose a full series of alternate reconstructions, for the detailed data on which to evaluate them are not yet available. However, a few additional factors are relevant to the possibility that no pottery-producing centers existed within a given sustaining area. Bullard (1964 : 281), on the basis of his survey of house mounds in northern Petén, concluded that sustaining areas of the Classic period averaged no more than one hundred square kilometers (thirty-eight square miles) of habitable upland, "small enough so that most Maya farmers living within the area could walk either to the ceremonial center or to their fields and return home again in the same day." Yet McBryde (1947 : 80) found that only fifteen centers supply almost all the pottery now used in southwestern Guatemala. This is certainly a comparatively widespread type of trade, far exceeding the supposed limits of the Classic sustaining area, and other ethnographic data point in the same direction (La Farge and Byers 1931 : 66, *Fig.* 20). On the other hand, the geologically recent mantle of volcanic ash which covers parts of southwestern Guatemala may have made it difficult to locate suitable clay (McBryde 1947 : 54), a factor which would not have been operative to limit the number of pottery-making communities in the Palenque region. Indeed, as has been seen, clay with excellent plastic qualities occurs at the foot of the Palenque ceremonial center and may have served as a source for the Red-brown pottery found so abundantly at the site.

Among our major aims in the present investigation is to see which of the possible models that might be constructed along these lines best fits the combined archaeological-technological data. Does a specific assemblage of pottery, characterizing Palenque's sustaining area, have abrupt boundaries, in keeping with the hypothesis which was presented first, or do the ceramics merge imperceptibly with assemblages characteristic of other major centers? If boundaries can be defined, were they relatively static or changing through time, and how extensive were they? A related set of problems deals with the interplay of style and technology: to what extent do distributions of culturally-shared ceramic traits correspond to areas of actual trade in pottery? On the basis of present information, it appears that fairly sudden spatial breaks in ceramic trade were not unknown in the region surrounding Palenque, although stylistic patterns were somewhat more widely shared. Whether this holds true generally is one of the questions that a combined archaeological and geological approach should help to answer.

NOTES

[1]   The present program of research is supported by a grant from the National Science Foundation. Dr. Roy L. Ingram, a clay mineralogist, is my research associate; Paul H. Benson, III, and Edward B. Sisson, graduate students in geology and anthropology, respectively, are research assistants. A great deal of the burden of technological analysis has fallen on Benson. The aid during previous years of Drs. Robert H. Shaver and Anthony R. Cariani of the Department of Geology, University of Mississippi, is gratefully acknowledged, as well as support in other phases of the Palenque project by the Wenner-Gren Foundation for Anthropological Research, Institute of Andean Research, John Simon Guggenheim Memorial Foundation, American Philosophical Society, and Faculty Research Committee of the University of Mississippi.

[2]   It is to be understood that the percentages used here are preliminary as of May, 1964, and may be amended by further laboratory analysis and field work.

[3]   Ethnohistoric data on Lowland Maya trade are summarized in Scholes and Roys (1948), Roys (1943), Tozzer (1941), and Blom (1932). Analyzing sixteenth-century Aztec and Maya institutions, Chapman (1957) makes a sharp distinction between the market and long-distance trade. Most attempts to reconstruct pre-Spanish trading relationships among the Maya have dealt with comparatively widespread commerce (*e.g.*, Smith 1955 : 7 - 8; Thompson 1964).

[4]   See Brainerd (1956), Willey (1956*a*), Willey, Bullard and Glass (1955), Coe (1962), Sanders (1963), and Bullard (1964) for recent

studies of Lowland Maya settlement patterns. Thompson (1954 : 57 - 61) reconstructs the ceremonial center, as it functioned during Classic times among the Lowland Maya, along lines of the present-day concourse or "vacant" town of the Guatemalan Highlands. However, additional community types occur among the Highland Maya, and somewhat differing interpretations exist as to the nature of the Lowland civic center (Borhegyi 1956; Shook and Proskouriakoff 1956; Miles 1957).

Coe and Haviland (n.d.) depart even farther from the model of the concourse or ceremonial center, estimating Late Classic Tikal to have had a resident population of at least ten thousand persons, consisting mostly of occupational specialists. However, a sustaining farming population of equivalent size is postulated by these writers. Vital to the present discussion are the related questions: would such an outlying population have included a pool of unskilled labor, devoting a significant part of its time to public works at Tikal, and would its commerce in pottery have been channeled primarily through this center?

5   Pilgrims from distant points referred to in sixteenth-century accounts are believed by Scholes and Roys (1948 : 33 - 34) to have consisted mostly of wide-ranging merchants.

6   Support for such a reconstruction may be found in contemporary Guatemala, where ceramics are known to have been channeled into a single market from five distinct pottery-producing centers, located at varying distances from the market place (McBryde, 1947 : 56, Map 15).

Seriation in Archaeology

IRVING ROUSE

This manuscript was read in first draft by Michael D. Coe, Roy Hodson, and William J. Mayer-Oakes; and I wish to acknowledge the help I have received from them, particularly in matters of bibliography.

So MANY articles have recently been written on seriation that I hesitated when the editors of this volume asked me to prepare another one. Upon reviewing the previous articles, however, I found that they differ significantly. Moreover, none fully covers the subject, since each is written from the standpoint of the author's own experiences. There seemed to be room for another article discussing the potentialities of the technique, the assumptions behind it, and attempting to reconcile the differences in the literature. These are my aims here. I shall not go into the details of applying the technique, since they have been well covered in the previous articles (Ascher 1959, 1963; Brainerd 1951; Cowgill 1963; Ford 1962; Jelinek 1962; Meighan 1959; Robinson 1951; Rowe 1959, 1961, 1962).

IRVING ROUSE is Professor of Anthropology at Yale University in New Haven, Connecticut. He has done archaeological research in Connecticut and in the Caribbean area and was formerly president of the Society for American Archaeology and editor of *American Antiquity*.

History of Seriation

So far as I am aware, Christian J. Thomsen was the first to use the technique when, in 1816 - 19, he organized the collections of the Danish National Museum into a series of three groups on the assumption that the local culture had developed through the Stone, Bronze, and Iron ages respectively (Daniel 1950 : *41*). Jens J. A. Worsaae confirmed this sequence in 1839 - 41 by excavating a series of Danish burial mounds and arranging them in the order in which their grave goods appeared to have developed (Rowe 1962 : *130 - 31*). Rowe (1961 : *326*) has referred to this approach as "evolutionary seriation."

Thomsen also proposed another approach to seriation, although he did not have enough data to do much with it: "investigation of the FORMS of the objects and of the ORNAMENTS with which they were decorated, with a view that by a careful comparison and by accurately noting what sorts are generally found together, we may ascertain the order in which the successive changes took place, and thus determine the periods to which a mere inspection of the ornaments will authorize us to assign the object" (Ellesmere 1848 : *69*). John Evans (1850 : *132 - 34*) made use of this approach to seriate prehistoric British coins. He assumed that the more similar the coins were, the closer in age they were likely to be or, as Fox (1875 : *308*) subsequently put it, that "like fits on like." Rowe (1961 : *326*) has proposed that this approach be called "similary seriation."

Both the evolutionary and similary approaches were employed by Flinders Petrie (1899, 1901, 1904) in his studies of prehistoric Egyptian burials. Petrie arranged a series of nine hundred graves in chronological order by use of the following five criteria: *1*] actual superimposition of graves or [their constituent] burials . . . ;   *2*] development or degradation of form . . . ;   *3*] statistical grouping by proportionate resemblance . . . ;   *4*] grouping of similar types, and judgement by style . . . ; and

5] minimum dispersion of each type, concentrating the extreme examples" (Petrie 1899 : 297). So far as I am aware, Petrie was the first to use the criteria of frequencies of occurrence   [3] and overlapping distribution of artifact types   [5]. His work has led to the use of these criteria for the dating of a great variety of grave lots in both Old and New Worlds, *e.g.,* Kroeber and Strong (1924).

Franz Boas seems to have been the first to seriate refuse deposits. In 1910, he collected potsherds from the surfaces of sites in the valley of Mexico, arranged them in three successive groups, ending with the historic Aztec pottery, and encouraged Manuel Gamio to check the sequence by stratigraphic excavation (Adams 1960). Kroeber (1916) similarly seriated collections of pottery from the surfaces of Pueblo sites, working back in time from the historic to the prehistoric pueblos. Spier (1917) combined this approach with stratigraphic excavation in his classic study of Zuni ruins. This started a trend in American archaeology which has culminated in the graphic seriations of James A. Ford (1962) and the statistical studies of Robinson (1951) and Meighan (1959).

But the technique of seriation has not been limited to artifacts, burials, and collections. It has also been applied in recent years to structures (*e.g.,* Roberts 1939 : 253 - 59) and to components (*e.g.,* Rouse and Cruxent 1963 : 18). These extensions of the technique are frequently overlooked because of the current preoccupation with the seriation of refuse collections.

Definition of Seriation

If this paper is to accomplish its aim, we shall have to develop a definition of seriation which encompasses all the approaches that have just been reviewed. Let us begin by examining the definition in a recent publication of mine (Rouse and Cruxent 1963 : 18): "In its most general sense [seriation] means placing a number of components . . . in a logical order. For example, one may find [component] A at one end of a site and [component] B at the other end, with little or no admixture, in which case one may say that the people of [components] A and B occupied the site at different times. However, one will not know whether [component] A or B came first, unless and until one is able to relate them to another phenomenon that has been dated. If, for example, one finds European trade objects in association with [component] A but not with B, then one can say that component B preceded A at the site."

Further reflection, and review of the other papers under consideration, have convinced me that this definition is inadequate because it includes only two of the five elements essential to seriation, viz., the units [components] that are to be dated and the reasoning by means of which they are arranged in a series. Rowe (1961 : 326) adds a third element when he states that "the logical order on which seriation is based is found in the combination of features of style and inventory which characterize the units, rather than in the external relationships of the units themselves." By thus focusing on the content of the units, Rowe differentiates seriation from stratigraphy, which is the study of superimposition of units. His focus on content also serves to distinguish seriation from the procedure of dating units by correlating them with other chronological systems, such as geological sequences or the Christian calendar.

Rowe's statement, however, does not differentiate seriation from synchronization, *i.e.,* from the procedure of dating units of one area by correlating them with units of another area that have already been dated; for this, too, is done by studying features of the cultural inventory. To eliminate synchronization, we must add a fourth element to our definition of seriation by specifying that seriation is applicable only to the units of a single area. This is the position taken by Ford (1962 : 49).

Limitation to a single area improves the definition of seriation but is still not entirely adequate, since it fails to take into consideration the possibility that two ethnic groups may have lived side by side in the same area for a long period of time, as the Pueblo and Athapaskan peoples have done in the Southwest during the past five hundred years. Correlation of Pueblo and Athapaskan remains, for example, must be considered synchronization rather than seriation, since it involves two separate cultural traditions, rather than a single one, and the principles of logical ordering therefore do not apply. If units A and B belong to the same tradition, they can be seriated by fitting their artifactual content into a common stream of cultural development, but if A belongs to one tradition and B to another, their developments will run parallel and correlation of the two becomes a matter of synchronization rather than seriation.

The technique of seriation is not applicable, either, to remains which come from the same area but are far removed in time. Western Europe, for example, has yielded two groups of bifacially chipped projectile points, one characteristic of Solutrean culture, *ca.* 25,000 B.C., and the other, of various Neolithic cultures, some 20,000 years later. It would be absurd to think of including Solutrean and Neolithic points in the same seriation, since they belong to completely different traditions, yet we would admit the possibility of so doing if we were to limit seriation only in terms of area. To avoid this absurdity, we must recognize that the technique can only be applied to a single local tradition.

Seriation, then, may be defined as follows: *It is the procedure of working out a chronology by arranging local remains of the same cultural tradition in the order which produces the most consistent patterning of their cultural traits.* This definition contains all five of the elements that we have found necessary in order to distinguish seriation from other chronological techniques: *1]* the units seriated,   *2]* the traits which characterize those units and which serve as the criteria of seriation,   *3]* the cultural tradition to which the traits belong,   *4]* the area in which the tradition occurs, and   *5]* the historical pattern which is distinctive of the tradition and against which the traits are matched. Let us now consider each of these elements in turn.

The Units Seriated

The authors of the previous works on seriation differ considerably in their treatment of the units of seriation. Rowe (1961 : *326*) offers the broadest range of possibilities: "The units seriated may be individual specimens of a particular kind (pottery vessels, stone axes) or units of archaeological association, such as grave lots or single deposition units of refuse, such as might be found in a 'one period' site." Ford (1962 : *41*), on the other hand, specifies only "surface collections [and] excavated collections which are not in stratigraphic relationship to one another." Petrie (1899) deals only with graves, as already noted, and Rouse and Cruxent (1963 : *18*) with components.

How are we to reconcile these differing statements? The key, I think, is to recognize that we can only seriate the results of specific historic events, *i.e.,* of actions which have occurred at particular points in time. In effect, it is these events which we arrange in chronological order, though we actually do so by seriating the archaeological remains that have resulted from them. Rowe's phrase "individual specimens of a particular kind" provides a good example. The manufacture of an artifact is a specific event, occurring at only one point in time; and a series of artifacts therefore represents a number of points in time, which can be arranged in chronological order.

The procedure of seriating artifacts will be discussed later. Here, we need only note that it is done by comparing them in terms of their distinctive features. The method can be applied to artifacts of any kind, but it will be more successful if the artifacts have complex features, since these provide a better basis for seriation. Pottery vessels are most suitable, especially if decorated; potsherds not so much so (*e.g.,* Kroeber 1963 : *68-69*). Coins, such as were studied by Evans (1850, *Fig. opp. p. 127*), are likewise easy to seriate because of the complexity of their designs.

In my own work (Rouse 1939, *Chart 6*) I have found it

possible to seriate not only artifacts but also individual features of artifacts. For example, one may take a collection of pottery head lugs and arrange them in chronological order according to the attributes of each head; and one can do this regardless of whether the lugs have broken off the vessels or are still attached. If the lugs are still attached, of course, one will be dealing with the same artifacts as in seriating whole vessels but will be treating them in a different manner: instead of seriating them in their entirety, one will be seriating them as lugs, disregarding the other features of the vessels. Subsequently, if one desires, one can re-seriate the vessels in terms of another kind of feature, such as rim profiles or design motifs (*op. cit.*).

This approach works because, in the case of each kind of feature, one is dealing with the products of a single segment in the procedure of manufacturing artifacts. Each feature will have been produced at a single point in time, and it is these points which one arranges in chronological order. The approach will not be worthwhile, however, unless all the features under study are readily recognizable as products of the same procedural segment and are complex enough to provide a good basis for seriation. It would be useless to seriate the features of simple artifacts, such as stone axes, since this would only yield the same result as seriating them *in toto*. One is justified in seriating artifacts feature by feature only when they are complex enough in technology, shape, or decoration to justify breaking them down into their parts, or when one finds them actually broken into features, as in the case of the pottery lugs mentioned above.

Graves—better called tombs in the present context—may also be seriated, as Petrie (1899) was the first to demonstrate. Petrie's tombs were proper units of seriation because each was presumably the result of a single act of burial, *i.e.,* a particular historic event. If, on the other hand, his tombs had been constructed in several different stages, as was true of some of the burial mounds in the eastern United States, then he would have had to seriate each stage separately. The tombs must be sufficiently complex so that one is able to compare their architectural features and to arrange them in the order in which these features have developed.

Though none of the works under review says so, it is also possible to seriate structures of other kinds, such as houses, temples, and mounds. Here, more than in the case of tombs, one must look out for the possibility that there have been successive stages of construction, which would make it necessary to break the buildings down into parts. For example, Roberts (1939 : 253 - 59) has seriated Anasazi buildings in the Whitewater district of Arizona in the order of their development from single-room pit houses to multi-room, above-ground pueblos; and, in so doing, he found it necessary to subdivide certain pueblos into building stages.

Individual features of structures may also be seriated, so long as each is sufficiently complex and has resulted from a recognizable segment in the total procedure of erecting the structure. For example, Watson Smith (1952 : 317) has arranged the mural paintings of the pueblos of Jeddito Wash, Arizona in chronological order by studying, among other criteria, "certain associations of possibly chronological significance, inherent in the murals themselves." Masonry construction has been treated in a similar manner by Nelson (1920 : 388 - 89) and others.

Thus far, we have been discussing tombs, houses, and structures of other kinds as products, *i.e.,* in the same way in which we had previously dealt with artifacts. From this standpoint, we may consider both structures and artifacts to be fabrication units, since both are subject to seriation in terms of the qualities built into them by the artisans. Both structures and artifacts may also play another role in seriation, if they are containers: they may serve as repositories for smaller artifacts. If they do, they can be seriated as deposition units rather than as fabrication units.

Worsaae was looking at structures from this point of view when he seriated the Danish burial mounds in terms of their grave goods. In these mounds, he noted, "we can in general expect to find together those things that were originally used together at one time" (Rowe 1962 : 131). More important than the use of the artifacts, however, is the probability that all the artifacts of each grave lot were deposited at the same time. If they were, one is justified in arranging the lots in the order in which the acts of deposition took place. If, however, the people had reopened the graves for successive depositions, as the Megalithic inhabitants of western Europe were accustomed to do, then the method would not work. The same approach may be applied to artifacts found in houses or other structures. For example, Kidder (1962 : *134*) seriated the rooms of Pecos pueblo in terms of the pottery each contained and was thereby able to work out the order in which the pueblo grew.

Rowe (1961 : *326*) has also pointed out that it is possible to seriate "deposition units of refuse." I assume that by this he means the lots of artifacts obtained from units of refuse. My own work in seriating Haitian shell middens may be cited as an example (Rouse 1939, *Chart 3*). Refuse pits, strata, or any other clearly distinguishable natural division in the refuse may be treated in the same way. Alternatively, one may seriate the collections obtained from arbitrary units of refuse, such as blocks defined in terms of section and level, or areas of surface collection (*e.g.,* Goggin 1950).

Seriation works in these cases because it is concerned with the results of particular acts of deposition, occurring at points in time which can be arranged in their proper sequence. Ford (1962 : *41*) has expressed this as follows in discussing his own approach, which is based upon collection of potsherds from the surfaces of refuse deposits: "Each collection must represent a short period of time— the shorter the better. A sampling of the ceramic population representing an instant of time would be ideal but, of course, is never achieved. Sherd collections representing long spans of time are valuable as indicators of localities that might yield stratigraphy, but they cannot be used in seriation."

Ford's last sentence raises a question we have not yet considered. So far, we have assumed, as Ford does, that each act of producing an artifact, a structure, a grave lot, or the collection obtained from a unit of refuse has taken place at a point in time. In fact, however, each act will have required a length of time, and this will have varied from act to act. Even Ford's units are not instantaneous, as he points out; most have probably resulted from the dumping of refuse by a number of people over a period of days or weeks. The manufacture of an artifact will likewise have taken more than a moment of time, especially if the artifact is complex; and the construction of a temple will have required weeks or even months. One must therefore assume that some length of time is required to produce any unit of seriation. The real problem is not this, but to make sure that each of the items included in a single seriation has been produced in an equivalent length of time.

This problem has already been discussed in connection with the use of tombs and other structures as units of seriation, and we have noted that it is sometimes the practice to break structures down into construction units in order to equalize the length of time represented by each one. Alternatively, one may find it advisable to omit from one's seriation structures or refuse units those which have been produced in too long or too short a period of time. Arbitrary units of refuse have an advantage over natural units from this standpoint, because one can design them in such a manner that all will represent roughly equivalent periods of time. It is advisable, as Ford points out, to design them to represent the shortest period of time, but this is not necessary.

In reviewing Ford's publication, Cowgill (1963:697) has claimed that the idea of a component is implicit in Ford's approach. However, Ford's deposition units are not equivalent to a component, for the latter encompasses all the refuse deposited by one community at a particular site, and this will amount to much more than the refuse deposited in the shortest period of time. Moreover, it does not matter to Ford whether all his distribution units come from a single component, which has been deposited by one community, or whether he makes his collections from different components, so that a number of communities are involved. As he says, he is concerned that the collections "represent the entire span of occupation in the area under study," not the entire range of communities in the area (Ford 1962 : *41-42*).

Nevertheless, components are proper units and have been seriated, for example, by Cruxent and me in Venezuela (Rouse and Cruxent 1963 : *18*). When Rowe (1961 : *326*) refers to the seriation of "single deposition units of refuse, such as might be found in a 'one period' site," I assume that he means a component. The term refers either to a culturally homogeneous site or, if the site is heterogeneous, to a culturally homogeneous unit within it.

The particular event represented by a component is not an act of deposition—we have seen that it takes many such actions to produce a component—but the action of a community in occupying a particular site. Hence, we may refer to components as "occupation units," in contradistinction to the fabrication and deposition units discussed previously. In theory, the act of occupation subsumes many actions of both fabrication and deposition, since it includes all the activities that went on at a site. In practice, only refuse may have survived, especially if the community that inhabited the site was simple and carried out most of its activities with the aid of perishable materials. The components of advanced communities are much more likely to contain not only refuse but also the remains of burials, houses, temples, caches, votive offerings, etc. Such components will offer a greater variety of criteria for seriation than either fabrication or deposition units can offer.

The act of occupying a site is not only complex but also it takes longer than the acts of fabrication and deposition; and the problem of inequalities in the duration of the occupation units is correspondingly greater. The problem should not be exaggerated, however, for there are limits to the time which elapses during the occupation of a component. It will be kept within fairly close range, so far as any series of components is concerned, by the settlement patterns of the inhabitants. Moreover, if people stay at any one site for too long a period of time, they are bound to modify their culture, this will produce a new component, and as a result one will be seriating the site in terms of two components rather than one.

Not all sites, of course, are places of habitation. A common practice among the Woodland peoples of the eastern United States, for example, was to live in one place and bury the dead some distance away. Ideally, the resultant village and burial sites should be treated together as a single occupation unit, but this is not always possible. It may be necessary to seriate the habitation and burial sites separately. In such cases, each habitation and burial site has to be regarded as a separate occupation unit, unless there is only a single burial to a site, in which case the latter can be seriated as a fabrication or deposition unit.

Sites inhabited seasonally by the same community should also be treated together as a single occupation unit for purposes of seriation, but this is even more difficult to do. It may be more practicable to limit one's series to sites inhabited during a single season of the year. Thus, problems involving either the duration or the definition of components may make it impracticable to use them as units of seriation; but where they can be used, they are relatively reliable because, as already noted, the seriation can be based upon such a great variety of activities.

The units of seriation are summarized in Table 1. Two conclusions may be drawn from this table: archaeological remains of any kind can be seriated, providing only that they are clearly identifiable, readily divisible into units, and complex enough to provide a good basis for seriation; and most remains can be put into series of several different kinds. For example, individual artifacts may be arranged in series of whole artifacts or of individual features; structures may be seriated either as fabrication units or as deposition units; refuse collections can be seriated either in terms of natural divisions, such as middens, or in terms of arbitrary divisions, such as sections and levels or areas of surface collection; and, in the happy event that artifacts, graves, buildings, refuse, and traces of other activities occur together, they may be seriated *in toto* as occupation units.

1. Units of seriation

General Categories	*Activity Involved*	*Resultant Units*
Fabrication units	Manufacture	Individual artifacts
	Segment in the manufacturing procedure	Individual features of artifacts
	Construction	Graves, monuments, or buildings
	Stages of construction	Building units
	Segments in the procedure of construction	Individual features of buildings
Deposition units	Burial	Grave lots
	Use of buildings	Associated artifacts
	Dumping of refuse	Refuse collections (according to natural or arbitrary units)
	Other kinds of deposition	Caches, votive offerings, etc.
Occupation units	Habitation by one community	Habitation sites
	Habitation by successive communities	Components
	Burials by a community	Cemeteries
	Separate religious activities	Sacred places
	Seasonal habitation	Seasonal sites

The archaeologist who is about to undertake seriation will do well to consider the total range of possible kinds of units and to select the ones which best fit the available data and are most likely to achieve maximum results. Too often, it has been the practice blindly to select the kind of unit that is fashionable in an area. For example, archaeologists in the California bay area concentrated for many years on the study of refuse with poor results, so far as cultural chronology was concerned; and then it was found that the study of burials yielded much better results (Beardsley 1948 : *3*).

The Criteria of Seriation

The previous works vary as much in their treatment of the criteria of seriation as in dealing with the units of seriation. Petrie (1899 : 297) has listed five different kinds of criteria, which have already been quoted. Rowe (1961 : *326*), on the other hand, refers only to the "features of style or inventory which characterize the units" of seriation. Ford (1962 : *41*) insists that "types" of pottery are the proper basis for seriation, though he concedes that my alternative use of "modes" is also possible. Rouse and Cruxent (1963 : *18*) seriate instead in terms of "complexes or styles."

Despite the diversity of these statements, all are underlaid by the same general principle. We have seen that the units of seriation are products of particular actions, it being the times of these actions that we arrange in series. The criteria of seriation, on the other hand, must be recurrent qualities, which are shared by several units and which therefore enable us to relate the units to each other. Criteria limited to single units cannot be used, since they do not provide a practicable means of relating the units.

Let us look at the recurrent qualities in terms of artifacts. When an artisan makes an artifact, he will be influenced by the standards of the culture to which he belongs, and will build into the artifacts attributes which conform to those standards. When he or a colleague makes a second artifact for the same purpose, he will be subject to the same influences and as a result the second artifact will share many of the attributes of the first artifact. This process will be repeated again and again, with the result that the same attributes will recur on a large number of artifacts. It is these recurrent attributes which serve as the criteria for seriating artifacts.

One way for the archaeologist to get at the recurrent attributes is to sort out a collection of artifacts into classes of like objects (*e.g.,* Rouse 1960 : *315 - 16*). Then he may compare the artifacts in each class and work out the complex of attributes which characterizes them, either intuitively (Ford 1962 : *14 - 16*) or statistically (Spaulding 1960). This complex of attributes is termed a type, is given a name or a number, and all the artifacts of the class are said to belong to that type.

A type, then, is a complex of attributes which distinguish the artifacts of a class. Since its constituent attributes are recurrent, it, too, is a recurrent phenomena and may therefore be used as a criterion of seriation. For this purpose, it may be studied in various ways, either in terms of its frequencies of occurrence, association with other types, or development through time; these need not concern us at the present stage in our discussion.

Types are not the only possible criteria of seriation. One may also seriate artifacts, for example, in terms of modes. To explain this kind of criterion, we shall have to return to the artisan's procedure. We discussed it previously as the total succession of acts which has led to the production of artifacts. Now, let us consider only that segment of the total procedure which leads to the production of a single feature of an artifact, such as a lug. The artisan will have conformed to the standards of his community in performing this segment and therefore the feature he produces will, like the total artifact, bear attributes which are shared with the corresponding features of other artifacts. For example, a pottery head lug will have the same kinds of eyes, mouth, and headdress as a number of other lugs. By grouping all these head lugs into a class—whether they are attached to the pots or broken off—and abstracting the distinctive attributes from them, one may arrive at a type of feature, which will bear the same relationship to the features within its class that a type of pottery bears to the pots within its class. One may say, for example, that a certain lug is of lug type 1; and at the same time one may find that the pot to which the lug is attached is of pottery type 1.

Types of features are easy to confuse with types of artifacts. especially when, as in the example given, numerical designations are used. In order to avoid such confusion, I have proposed that the term type be restricted to types of artifacts and that the term mode be used instead for types of features, referring to either parts or aspects of the artifacts (Rouse 1939 : *42 - 56,* 1960 : *313*). This proposal has been accepted by a number of archaeologists (*e.g.,* Ford 1962 : *16*). On the other hand, Rowe has used a different terminology; he refers to types of features as "features of style" or simply as "features" (Rowe 1961 : *326,* 1959 : *320*).

Since my term mode has priority, I shall use it here in preference to Rowe's term feature. I shall also continue to contrast mode with feature, using the former word to refer to recurrent attributes and the latter, to the particular features upon which the attributes occur. Rowe did not make this distinction, but it is important that we do so, in order to avoid confusing criteria of seriation—modes—with units of seriation— features.

A mode, then, consists of a series of attributes which recur on the corresponding features of a number of artifacts; and it bears the same relationship to those features that a type bears to its corresponding artifacts. One may say that any particular feature exemplifies, belongs to, or represents its mode in the same way that an artifact exemplifies, belongs to, or represents its type. And one may derive a mode from the features that exemplify it in the same way that one may derive a type from the artifacts that exemplify it, either by intuitive inspection of features that have been classed together or by statistical manipulation of the attributes shared by those features. A mode, finally, is just as appropriate a criterion for seriation as a type, because it, too, is a recurrent phenomenon rather than a feature resulting from a particular action of the artisan in making a specific artifact.

Types and modes need not be restricted to artifacts. One can also form types by classifying structures; and modes, by classifying features of the structures. Types and/or modes of structure can then be used for seriation, as in Petrie's (1899 : *297*) studies of grave "forms" and Smith's (1952 : *317*) work with mural paintings. Indeed, any of the kinds of fabrication units listed in Table 1 can be seriated in terms of either types or modes.

Since deposition units are composed of artifacts, they, too, can be seriated in terms of types or modes. Occupation units pose a different problem. In seriating these, we are not concerned with the actions of individuals leading to the manufacture or deposition of remains but rather with the act of a community in occupying sites. As a result, the criteria of seriation cannot be types or modes, which refer to the activities of individuals; each must be something which refers to its community as a whole, viz., the total culture of the community. Each must include not only types and modes, which are in effect the material culture of the community, but also its customs and beliefs, *i.e.,* its nonmaterial culture, insofar as these can be inferred from the remains.

The literature contains a number of words referring to the total cultures of communities. English archaeologists frequently call them cultures (*e.g.,* Childe 1956 : *111 - 12*), but American archaeologists have preferred more technical terms, such as phase or focus (*e.g.,* Willey and Phillips 1958 : *21 - 24*). Some of us have instead used descriptive terms, such as industry, complex (of types), or style (of features), the effect of which is to indicate the kinds of criteria we have emphasized in defining cultures (*e.g.,* Rouse and Cruxent 1963). I shall here use the term phase, because it is more consistent with the technical terms type and mode I am using for the other kinds of criteria of seriation.

Phases are obtained by taking a number of components and grouping them into classes (Rouse 1955 : *713 - 14*). If one does this properly, one will find that the components in each class share most of their types, modes, customs, and beliefs (insofar as the last two can be inferred from the remains), in which case one is justified in saying that all the components belong to the same phase. It is customary to give the phase the name of a typical component and to define it by listing its characteristic types, modes, customs, and beliefs.

A phase is thus comparable to a type or a mode, though on a

higher level of abstraction. Just as a type, for example, consists of a complex of attributes characteristic of a class of artifacts, so a phase may be defined as a complex of types, modes, customs, and beliefs characteristic of a class of components. And just as a type recurs in all the artifacts of its class, so a phase may be said to recur in all the components of its class. It is this recurrent quality which gives phases their utility as criteria of seriation.

The relationship of modes and types to phases is diagrammed in Table 2. Some modes are shown there as subdivisions of types

2. Criteria of seriation

Mode 1
Mode 2   } Type 1
Mode 3

Mode 4
Mode 5   } Type 2   } Phase 1
Mode 6

Mode 7
Mode 8
Mode 9
Inferences concerning
nonmaterial culture

for the following reason. Each mode consists of the attributes distinctive of one feature, each type consists of the attributes distinctive of all the features of an artifact, and therefore one might expect the attributes of all the modes to coincide with the attributes of the type. They will do so, however, only if the artifact is extremely simple, for otherwise the classifier will have had to make a selection of the most diagnostic attributes and his type will subsume only the modes containing those attributes (Ford 1962 : *48 - 49*). The modes excluded from the type have to be considered independent variables, forming separate elements of the phase, equivalent to the type. Modes *7 - 9* in Table 2 are intended to illustrate this point.

Let us now consider how modes, types, and phases can best be used to seriate the different kinds of units listed in Table 1. I shall limit the present discussion to theoretical considerations, leaving the practical values of modes, types, and phases to be treated in the subsequent section on the role of patterns in seriation.

In my opinion, Rowe (1959) is correct in stating that modes are the best criteria to use in seriating individual artifacts. They are also the best to use in seriating features or any of the other kinds of fabrication unit listed in Table 1. The reason is that we seriate these units in terms of changes in the way they were fabricated; the procedure of fabrication is governed by modes; and hence modes are accurate indicators of the changes. Types can also be used, but are not so sensitive indicators of the changes since each refers to the total procedure of making an artifact, for example, and therefore does not reflect changes in segments of that procedure, as modes do.

On the other hand, Ford (1962 : 16) is in my opinion correct when he states that types are the best kind of criterion to use in seriating surface collections or other deposition units. Here, one is dealing with completed artifacts, after they have been used and deposited in the ground, rather than with the procedure of manufacture. By definition, a type includes all the distinctive attributes of its artifacts; and hence changes in types accurately reflect the changes in the artifacts themselves. Each mode, on the contrary, contains only the attributes distinctive of a part of each artifact, and therefore it is not so good an indicator of changes in the artifact as a whole. To be sure, I have seriated my own West Indian collections in terms of modes (Rouse 1939, *Chart 3*), but I did so only because it was not practicable to use types. West Indian potsherds are found broken into more or less separate features, these features appear to have varied independently, and so it is difficult to identify types (Rouse n.d.). But wherever types can easily be identified, they are preferable to modes for the seriation of deposition units.

Turning now to the seriation of occupation units, I need only reiterate that neither modes nor types will be of any use per se, since they refer to individual actions and not to occupation by a whole community. Phases, being the cultures of the communities, are the sole criteria that can be used for seriating components and the other kinds of sites listed in Table 1.

We may conclude, then, that fabrication, deposition, and occupation units can best be handled in terms of different kinds of criteria. Individual artifacts, features, and other fabrication units ideally should be studied in terms of their modes, though seriation in terms of their types is also possible. Surface collections and other deposition units are most satisfactorily handled in terms of types, more poorly in terms of modes. Components and other occupation units can only be seriated in terms of phases.

In my opinion, much of the disagreement among previous authors about the criteria of seriation stems from their preference for the criteria best suited to the units they are accustomed to seriate. Rowe, for example, prefers the units here called modes because he is seriating artifacts per se, following the precedent set by Kroeber in Peruvian archaeology. Ford favors types because, as he says, they are best suited to the seriation of collections, in the manner pioneered by Kroeber and Spier in Southwestern archaeology. Cruxent and I used the criteria here called phases because we were seriating whole components. There is nothing wrong with any of these approaches; one goes wrong only by attempting to apply one kind of criterion, such as types, to units for which it is not suited, such as components.

It must be admitted, though, that Rowe (1959) is correct when he states that seriation in terms of modes produces finer temporal discrimination than seriation in terms of types. Similarly, seriation in terms of types will produce finer discrimination than seriation in terms of phases. The reason is that modes, being the smallest of the three kinds of criteria, can change more rapidly than types, though, of course, not all of them do; and types, being intermediate in size between modes and phases, can change more rapidly than phases. If, therefore, one is interested in establishing subperiods of time within a single site, one will be well advised to use modes as the criteria of seriation. If, on the other hand, one proposes to work out the succession of periods in a local area, one will do better to seriate in terms of types. But if one wants instead to set up a regional chronology, encompassing a number of local areas, as Cruxent and I did in Venezuela, then it is more appropriate to work in terms of phases. It is advisable, in other words, to select not only the units but also the criteria of seriation in terms of one's research objectives (Lathrop, 1964).

Traditions

Only Rowe (1961 : 326 - 27), of all the previous authors, has discussed the need to limit seriation to a single cultural tradition. However, this is implicit in the work of the others. Indeed, the very term seriation implies continuity. Let us now inquire into the nature of this continuity. The units of deposition do not, in themselves, provide any continuity, for each is the product of a unique event. We might think of them as a series of dots, which we arrange in temporal order by means of seriation (Fig. *1*, A). Our present problem is to find out the continuities between these dots.

The obvious place to look is at the criteria of seriation, *i.e.*, the modes, types, and phases. Since these are recurrent phenomena, they have some persistence through time and serve to link the dots together, as in Figure *1*, B, where several different modes, types, or phases are shown in the form of lines placed side-by-side, in order to indicate the fact (originally pointed out by Petrie, 1899 : 297) that modes, types, and phases tend to overlap in distribution.

But this does not completely resolve the problem, for there is more to the continuity of culture than the simple persistence shown in Figure *1*, B. Each mode, type, or phase is normally succeeded, after the period of overlap shown in Figure *1*, B, by a new mode, type, or phase which retains some of the characteristics of its predecessor, thereby making it clear that the new mode, type,

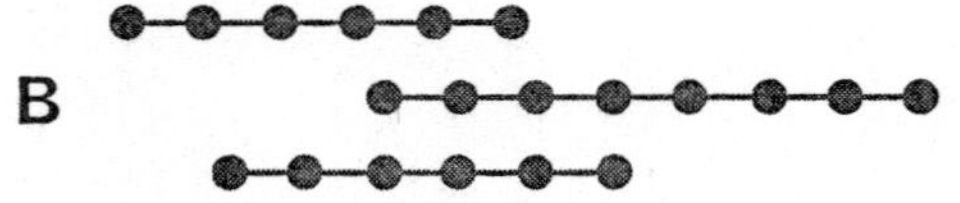

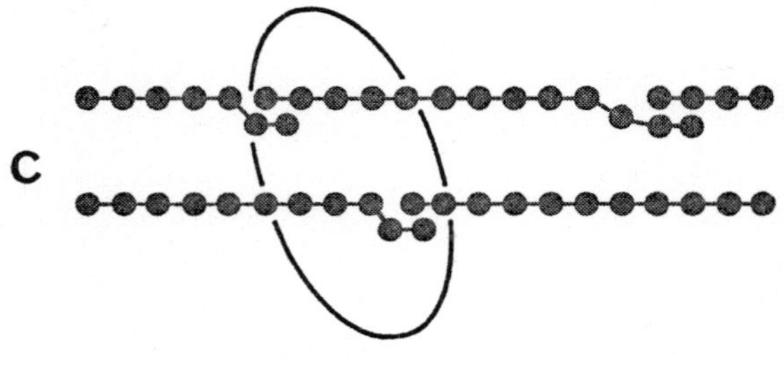

1. Temporal distribution of the units of seriation [A], the criteria of seriation [B], and traditions [C]. The circle symbolizes the area in which the traditions occur

or phase has developed out of the old one. This process is repeated again and again, and produces a tradition of modes, types, or phases, which have developed one from another. Such traditions may be symbolized by jointed lines, as in Figure *1*, C, where each segment refers to a single mode, type, or phase and the joints are overlapped to indicate that the original mode, type, or phase has persisted alongside its successor for some time before finally giving way to it.

For example, when a certain mode of lug is succeeded by a new one, the lugs of the new mode will retain some of the attributes of the original lugs, such as their eyes and mouth, while also having new attributes, such as a different form of headdress.

Repetition of this process will produce a succession of linked modes, *i.e.,* a continuity in the ways of making lugs. We may refer to this as a modal tradition. The same process operates on the level of types and that of phases, producing typological and cultural traditions respectively. A typological tradition consists of a series of types which have given rise to one another; and a cultural tradition of phases which likewise make up a single line of development. (For examples of typological traditions, see Willey 1945; and of cultural traditions, Rouse and Cruxent 1963. They are called series in the latter book, but this is not good usage in the present context because of the possibility of confusion with the kind of series shown in Figure *1,* A.)

It is important to note that the development which takes place within a tradition is as often regressive as progressive. A tradition is simply a measure of continuity in cultural change, and does not imply any particular kind of cultural change. Ford (1962 : 6-7) has emphasized the fact that cultural change goes on continuously. Why, then, is a tradition not a continuous thing, which never stops—a perpetual stream of cultural development, so to speak? It would be if it existed in isolation, but it does not. Any tradition is bound, sooner or later, to come into contact with a different tradition which has intruded from another region as the result of diffusion or migration. When this happens, it is likely to have one of three results: either tradition 1 will die out, leaving only tradition 2; tradition 2 will die out leaving only tradition 1; or the two will somehow fuse to form a new tradition 3. In all three of these cases, at least one of the two traditions will have come to an end.

There is also a fourth possibility. Traditions 1 and 2 may retain their separate identities and go on as before. For example, a new tradition of making lugs may become alternative to the original one; or the potters may begin to make alternative types belonging to distinct traditions, using one perhaps for cooking pots and the other for grave furniture. Similarly, two phases belonging to different traditions may exist side by side in separate ecological niches, as the Norse and Eskimo did in medieval Greenland (Willey *et al.* 1956 : *10 - 11*).

The continuity of traditions may also be broken by archaism, as Rowe (1961 : *326 - 27*) has pointed out. Artisans may for some reason decide to imitate an earlier mode or type. It is not so likely that they would go back to a former phase, though this has frequently been the aim of revivalist cults. Finally, it is reasonable to suppose that revolutions have taken place during prehistory, as they have in history. For example, potters may have abruptly stopped making lugs; or they may have abruptly shifted to new types of artifacts. A revolution on the level of phases, leading to the appearance of a completely new cultural tradition, is more difficult to envisage but is, for example, what Childe (1936 : *74 - 117*) had in mind in writing about the Neolithic revolution.

Traditions, then, are finite entities, like their constituent modes, types, and phases; and have both beginnings and ends, as illustrated in Figure *1*, C. We need not go into the question whether they can be grouped into larger units, such as co-traditions (Rouse 1957), since this is beyond the scope of the present study.

The role of traditions in seriation is a limiting one. They cannot in themselves serve as units, and they have too long a duration to be of any practical value as criteria; but they are needed as a device to eliminate remains which do not belong in the seriation. We have seen that remains of different cultural traditions should not be included in the same seriation because, if they are, the process of dating becomes synchronization rather than seriation. Cruxent and I made this mistake in our seriation of Venezuelan components (Rouse and Cruxent 1963 : *18*). We seriated the components indiscriminately, without paying any attention to whether they belonged to the same tradition, and as a result much of what we did was synchronization rather than seriation.

This may seem like splitting hairs, but it is a point of some importance. If all of our Venezuelan components had belonged to the same tradition, so that we really could have seriated them, we would have been able to place them in an inherent order, thereby obtaining positive evidence of their age. As it was, we had to rely upon negative data; we compared the components, found no evidence of mutual influence, took this to mean that the components could not have coexisted, and consequently placed them in a sequence. We may well have been right, but our conclusion was not so reliable as if we had been able to use the technique of seriation.

For another, hypothetical example, let us consider the seriation of surface collections in terms of type frequencies. If all the collections belong to the same tradition, we are able to proceed by matching the frequencies of the types in each collection against the pattern of frequency changes for the tradition as a whole. But if some of them belong to a different tradition, we will have to match the frequencies in these collections against a different pattern, that of the second tradition. Kluckhohn (1962 : *83 - 84*) has suggested how this might have happened in the Southwest. Outlying Pueblo peoples, with a less advanced culture, might have been attracted to the centers of Pueblo development and have settled down there alongside the more advanced peoples. The two groups would have shared many types of artifacts, but these would have existed in different contexts and therefore would have changed differently. In such a situation, one would either have to separate the collections by tradition and seriate them separately or, if this was impossible, abandon seriation entirely.

In studying the archaeology of more complex societies, one is even more likely to be faced with the necessity of distinguishing between several coexistent traditions. Urban and rural settlements or upper and lower classes may well have had somewhat different forms of culture and, if so, their remains will have to be treated separately for purposes of seriation (Mayer-Oakes 1963 : *58 - 59*).

Areas

Ford (1962 : *41*) is the only previous author to state explicitly that seriation must be restricted to a local area. He explains that this is necessary in order to eliminate the geographical factor. Elaborating on Ford's explanation, we may theorize, with Spaulding (1960), that culture history has three dimensions, time, space, and the form of the culture. Changes in culture can take place along any of these dimensions: they may happen in one place with the passage of time; they may occur as the culture spreads from one place to another; or they may consist of a sudden discontinuity in the form of the culture at one point in time and space. The aim of seriation is to derive the dimension of time from changes in culture; and for this purpose we must eliminate all changes which have taken place in the other two dimensions, so as to seriate only in terms of changes in time.

In the previous section, we considered how to eliminate changes due to discontinuity in form by use of the concept of tradition. Our problem now is to eliminate changes that have taken place in space. Willey and Phillips (1958 : 29 - 40) have defined traditions as continuities in time, and have contrasted them with horizons, which they define as continuities through space. Why, then, cannot we simply limit seriation to single traditions, as defined by Willey and Phillips, and thereby eliminate both discontinuity and space at the same time? It would be nice if we could, but unfortunately traditions and horizons are not so regular phenomena as Willey and Phillips thought. Most have a two-dimensional distribution in both time and space, as Cruxent and I have showed in our Venezuelan study (Rouse and Cruxent, 1963). It is therefore necessary to specify that the units seriated be limited not only to a single tradition but also to a single area. Such an area may be defined as a clustering of sites within which it is reasonable to suppose that there has been little, if any, geographical variation in culture, though several traditions may be present (Fig. *1*, C). The clustering will frequently be delimited by geographical factors; for example, Pueblo sites in the Southwest are clustered in areas suitable for farming and these are separated by expanses of wasteland in which few, if any, Pueblo sites occur. Other clusters may have to be delimited culturally; along the east coast of Florida, for example, I found that the frequencies of pottery types vary as much from the northern to the southern end of the Indian River as they do through time at any one point on the river (Rouse 1951 : *254*). If I had seriated my collections in terms of the frequencies of pottery types, I would have had to divide the river into at least two areas and seriate separately for each one. No general rule can be given for distinguishing areas — any more than for distinguishing traditions. It would be beyond the scope of the present paper to go into the various ways in which these two kinds of units are worked out.

Patterns

Three of the previous authors have discussed the patterns involved in seriation: Rouse (1939 : *83 - 92*), Rowe (1959 : *320 - 22*), and Ford (1962 : *39 - 40*). Though none of these authors shows any awareness of the work of his predecessors, they come to gratifyingly similar results, which form the basis for the following discussion.

Let us begin with an analogy. One of the most successful chronological techniques is that of dendrochronology. In this technique, one takes a series of borings from trees and matches them ring by ring, equating the rings which have the same sequences of widths, on the assumption that all trees have followed the same pattern of growth in their rings from year to year. Gradually, one builds up a master pattern of rings, consisting of the sequence of widths that has prevailed over a long period of time. Once this master pattern has been established, one may take any new boring, match the pattern of its rings against the master pattern, and thereby arrive at the relative age of the boring. This is possible, however, only if the boring comes from the same region as the master pattern, since the patterns of change in tree rings vary considerably from region to region.

Seriation is the same kind of procedure. One selects a series of archaeological units, such as artifacts, surface collections, or components; arranges them in their probable order; and studies the changes in their criteria—modes, types, or phases—through the sequence thus established. After one has repeated this process with several series of artifacts, collections, or components, overlapping in age like the borings from trees, one should be able to build up a master pattern of changes in either modes, types, or phases, which will hold true for the entire tradition and area under study. This master pattern can then be used to date new artifacts, collections, or components as they are found, simply by matching their modes, types, or phases against the master pattern of changes in these criteria.

Dendrochronology has one great advantage over seriation. In dendrochronology, much of the order of one's units—the rings—is directly observable in the borings, and one has only to reconstruct the order at those points where one boring ends and another begins. In seriation, on the contrary, no part of the order is observable; it must be completely reconstructed. To be sure, one can frequently get at it by other techniques, such as stratigraphic excavation, which will yield part of the order in the form of a superimposition of levels or layers (cf. Cook 1960 : *261 - 70*). For the moment, however, let us consider only pure seriation, in which no part of the order is known. The supplemental use of stratigraphy and other chronological techniques will be discussed in the next section.

When Petrie (*1899*) seriated his Egyptian graves, one of the things he did was to arrange them in terms of the permutations in their types of artifacts. He assumed that there had been an overlapping of types of the kind shown in Figure 2,A, in which each line symbolizes the temporal distribution of a single type; and he put his grave lots in the order which caused the distribution of their types to conform to this model. In effect, he worked out a master pattern for the distribution of artifact types in the Predynastic graves of upper Egypt. When, therefore, a new grave is dug, its relative age can be determined by fitting the particular combination of artifact types it contains into this master pattern; it may,

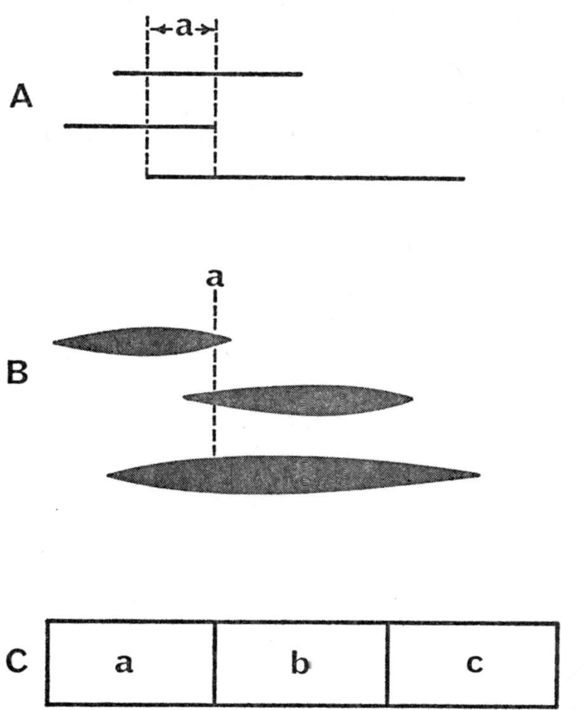

2. *Occurrence* [A], *frequency* [B], *and development* [C] *patterns*

for example, belong in period *a*, because it has the complex of types present during that period.

Petrie also seriated his graves in terms of the frequencies of the types they contained. In so doing, he implicitly assumed a pattern of change like that shown in Figure 2,B, where variations in the widths of the lines indicate changes in the popularities of the types. In effect, he put his grave lots in the order which best conformed to this model, *i.e.*, which made the changes in frequency most gradual. In this way, had he desired, he could have worked out a master pattern for the changes in frequency of artifact types in the Predynastic graves of upper Egypt. When, thereafter, a new grave was dug, it could have been dated by fitting the frequencies of its types into the master pattern; it might, for example, fit at point *a* because its types have the frequencies shown there.

Petrie also arranged his graves in the order of their development. In effect, he established types of graves and arranged those types in the order in which they seemed to have developed in accordance with the model shown in Figure 2,C, where each rectangle represents a successive grave type. Once he had done this, he could take a newly dug grave, match its type with one in the master sequence, and thereby determine the relative age of the grave. If the grave were of type *a*, for example, it would fit in period *a* in the sequence.

These three examples illustrate the three main kinds of patterns that have been used in seriation. Petrie and his successors have found it possible to seriate in terms of the pattern of occurrences of modes, types, or phases; in terms of their changes in frequency; or in terms of their pattern of development. We shall refer to these as occurrence, frequency, and development patterns respectively; and shall consider each in turn.

Occurrence patterns consist, as we have seen (*Fig.* 2,A), of a number of overlapping persistences through time. I worked out the model for this kind of pattern in my Haitian study by plotting the distribution of both modes and types against a vertical time scale consisting of four periods (Rouse 1939, *Chart* 6). More recently, Rowe (1959 : 320 - 22) has devised the same model, though he prefers to draw his lines horizontally and limits them to modes (his "features").

Since overlapping is the key to occurrence seriation, one must be able to use more than one criterion. This rules out the occurrence seriation of occupation units, since a component, for example, can only belong to a single phase. To be sure, one can seriate components in terms of their constitutent modes or types, but when one does so, one is in effect converting occupation units into deposition units and into poor ones at that, since, as we have seen, it is better to seriate deposition units of shorter duration.

Occurrence seriation of artifacts and other fabrication units is also difficult, if not impossible, because so many alternatives are normally available to the artisan. If the artifacts are highly complex and variable, there will be no way to determine whether a certain mode is lacking because it had gone out of existence or simply because the artisan had chosen another alternative.

We are left with deposition units as the only kind of remains suitable for occurrence seriation. The criteria used can be modes and/or types, both of which are present in all deposition units. If one must make a choice between these, it is better, with Rowe (1959 : 328), to concentrate on modes, since they are more numerous, than types. One may be able to identify as many as one or two hundred modes in a single grave lot, whereas there will be no more than ten to twenty types. Within this range of modes, one can make a better selection of criteria; and one can also employ more criteria, thereby increasing the validity of the seriation.

Let us look at the procedure of seriating grave lots in terms of the occurrence pattern of their modes. The first thing to be done is to select those modes which are most likely to be chronologically significant from among the total range of modes (Deetz 1965 : 45 - 54). There is no point in trying to use the modes shared by all the grave lots, for such modes will not yield chronological distinctions. The best modes are those which occur in the fewest lots and which are therefore likely to have been limited to the shortest periods of time, as in the model (*Fig. 2,*A).

One way of proceeding is to prepare a strip of graph paper for each grave lot. Each strip is divided into segments, one for each of the selected modes. If the mode is present in a certain grave lot, its segment is darkened on the strip for that lot; if not, the segment is left blank. Then the strips are laid out horizontally, one above the other, and moved up and down until the order is reached which most closely approximates that shown in Figure 2,B, *i.e.,* until as many of the segments as possible take on the form of solid, vertical lines. These lines are drawn up on a sheet of graph paper, they become one's master pattern, and one can obtain the relative age of any new grave lot simply by preparing a strip for it and moving this strip up and down the master pattern until it fits in some place such as *a* on the model (*Fig. 2,*B).

Alternatively, one may prepare a card for each grave lot and list or punch the lot's modes on the card. Then the cards are arranged in order by grouping them in terms of the modes they have in common; this can be done either by inspection, with a needle, or in a computer. The aim should be to group the cards in such a way that all occurrences of each mode are closest together. The master pattern can then be drawn up from the cards.

The assumption underlying these procedures is that each mode has been invested only once and hence must have a continuous persistence through time. It is for this reason that collections are arranged in the sequence which causes the fewest breaks in the continuities of the modes (Rowe 1961 : *328*). There are, of course, exceptions to the rule of no reinvention, especially in the case of modes, which are by nature simpler than types and therefore more likely to be revived or reinvented (Rands 1961). This should not seriously affect the validity of the seriation, however, since it depends upon the overall pattern of distribution rather than upon what has happened to an individual mode.

A more likely source of error rests in the assumption that one's deposition units are all homogeneous. It is always possible that artifacts have intruded into the units since they were originally laid down, in which case they would disrupt the fit between the rest of the artifacts and their pattern of change. From this standpoint, it is better to apply occurrence seriation to grave lots than to refuse collections, since there are less likely to be intrusive artifacts in graves than in refuse deposits (unless, as already noted, it was customary to reopen graves at a later date to deposit additional material).

Turning now to frequency patterns, we shift from continuities of occurrences to changes in the numbers of occurrences within those continuities. The earlier workers expressed such changes by constructing graphs of different kinds (*e.g.,* Spier 1917, *Fig. 6*). Some recent authors have preferred a topographic approach (Brainerd 1951, *Figs. 93-99*). The current trend, however, is to portray the frequency changes by varying the widths of the lines of occurrence (*e.g.,* Rouse 1939, *Chart 6*). This trend has reached its peak in the "battleship curves" popularized by Ford (1962). Since I am not competent to evaluate these approaches. I shall arbitrarily limit myself in the following discussion to Ford's model, which has the advantage that it is consistent with the model we have discussed for occurrence seriation (cf. *Fig.* 2,A and B).

Deposition units are the only kind that can be used in frequency seriation. Fabrication units are impossible because a single artifact or building unit normally has only a one-to-one relationship with its modes. (There are, however, exceptions, as when a vessel is decorated with a pair of identical lugs.) Occupation units must also be ruled out because they bear a one-to-one relationship with their phases. By contrast, each deposition unit normally contains several artifacts belonging to the same mode or type. The number is largest in the case of refuse collections, and they therefore provide the best basis for working out frequency patterns. Grave lots do not work so well, since the number of examples of each mode or type is small; for this reason, as Rowe (1961 : *319-20*) has pointed out, it is better to seriate grave lots in terms of occurrence patterns.

Ford (1962) has discussed the procedure of frequency seriation with such clarity that I can add little here. As he says, surface collections have the advantage over excavated collections—whether from refuse or from buildings—that they represent the shortest periods of time. Let us therefore discuss the procedure as it is applied to them. Surface collections may be seriated in terms of modes, types, or a combination of the two. Neither has the advantage, so far as numbers of occurrences are concerned, since each normally occurs only once on an artifact. However, types tend to vary more in frequency because of their greater complexity, and this also makes them less subject to reinvention, as we have seen. Hence, if one must make a choice between the two, types are preferable to modes for use in frequency seriation.

Ford's procedure, using only pottery types, is to prepare a strip of graph paper for each surface collection. He divides this strip into segments, one for each type, and marks the frequency of the type on this segment in the form of a bar graph. Then he lays the strips out horizontally, one above the other, and moves them up and down until he finds the order which corresponds best to the theoretical model shown in Figure 2,B. Once this order has been established, he transfers the bars to a separate sheet of graph paper, connects them vertically, and thus produces a series of curves like those in the model. These are his master pattern; whenever he obtains a new collection, he can graph it on a strip to the same scale, move the strip up and down the master pattern until it fits the curve, and read off its relative age. If, for example, the frequencies in the new collection conform to those at point *a* on the curve, then it may be said that the collection dates from point *a*.

Two assumptions underlie this procedure. One is that all the potsherds in each surface collection were deposited at the same time. This, of course, will not be true if the inhabitants deposited their refuse haphazardly in different parts of the site or if the deposit was subsequently disturbed, for example by plowing. It is desirable, if possible, to eliminate from one's seriation all samples which have become mixed in either of these ways. This can be done by the use of cumulative graphs, as Jelinek (1962) has pointed out.

The second assumption is that types will have had the same relative popularity in all neighboring communities at any given point in time, such as *a* in Figure 2,B. Several authors, notably Goggin (n.d.) and Jope (1961), have checked this assumption by seriating collections of historic artifacts or buildings, the ages of which are known from documentary sources, and have shown it to be correct. The assumption will hold true, however, only if one is dealing with a single cultural tradition and a single cultural area. For example, having successfully applied the technique in the Ft. Liberté region of Haiti, I tried to use it in Puerto Rico and failed because, as I discovered later, Puerto Rico consists of at least two distinct areas and, in the final period of its prehistory, contained two separate ceramic traditions (cf. Rouse 1939 and 1952). The validity of a frequency seriation therefore depends upon the investigator's ability to limit himself to one tradition and area.

Occurrence seriation does not suffer so strongly from this liability because changes in occurrence vary so much less rapidly than changes in frequency (cf. Fig. 2,A and B). On the other hand, seriation in terms of frequency patterns has the advantage of eliminating the effects of intrusion of artifacts into the deposition units. We have seen that these may bias the results of occurrence seriation, but their effect upon frequency seriation will be negligible because of the larger number of examples of each type that are involved.

Frequency patterns also have the advantage over occurrence patterns in that they give more precise results. They place a collection at a point in time, whereas occurrence patterns place it only within a period of time, as may be seen by comparing Figure 2,A and B. On the other hand, if one's purpose is not to date a particular collection but rather to establish a chronology, *i.e.,* to set up cultural periods, then the two approaches will work equally well since in both cases one places the beginnings and ends of one's periods at the points where the greatest number of modes and/or types begin and come to an end (*e.g.,* Ford 1962 : 54 - 55).

Turning now to development patterns, we may note that they have the form shown in Figure 2,C. There is a single line of development, *i.e.,* a tradition, which is symbolized by the overall rectangle. This may be either modal, typological, or cultural. Depending upon which it is, it will be composed of modes, types, or phases, as indicated by the segments *a, b,* and c within the rectangle. Mode *a,* for example, will have given rise to mode *b,* and *b* to *c.*

Rowe (1961 : 326 - 27) has made a distinction between two kinds of patterns, evolutionary and similar. If I understand him correctly, an evolutionary pattern is a special kind of development pattern, while all other kinds of patterns fall within the similary category. To be evolutionary, a pattern must proceed from simple to complex, *i.e.,* in a progressive direction. Some development patterns do this but others proceed in a reverse direction and are regressive (Petrie 1899 : *297*). Still others vary in theme or in pattern of features without being noticeably progressive or regressive (Rowe 1959 : *322 - 33,* 1961 : *328 - 29*).

Rowe (1961 : *326*) argues that one must avoid seriating in terms of evolutionary patterns. This is not so; one need only avoid the assumption that all development patterns are evolutionary. For example, Thomsen's original seriation of Danish antiquities in terms of their development through the Stone, Bronze, and Iron phases (he called them "ages") is evolutionary, yet it worked (Daniel 1950 : *41*). It did so because Thomsen was concerned with what had happened in Denmark and succeeded in arranging the artifacts according to the actual pattern of development of the local tradition. Subsequent authors made the mistake of assuming that the same pattern would hold true for different traditions in other parts of the world, but this does not negate Thomsen's own seriation.

Development seriation is based upon the fact that, within any tradition, the constituent modes, types, or phases have an inherent order. Once one has found out this order, one need only take a feature, artifact, or component; identify the mode, type, or phase to which it belongs; and date it by attributing to it the order which its mode, type, or phase has within the corresponding tradition. In order to do this, one must be able to establish a one-to-one relationship between the units and criteria of seriation. Deposition units do not have such a relationship, since each contains diverse features and artifacts, representing different modes and types; but fabrication and occupation units do. Hence, development seriation is limited to units of these two kinds.

The other prerequisite of development seriation is that one must be able to isolate the remains of a single modal tradition, if

one is seriating features in terms of their modes; a single typological tradition, if one is seriating artifacts in terms of their types; or a
single cultural tradition, if one is seriating components in terms of
their phases. It would be beyond the scope of the present paper to
discuss how to do this (see, *e.g.* Rouse 1955 : *718 - 20*); suffice it
to say that traditions are identified in the first instance by noting
resemblances between their constituent modes, types, or phases. To
be sure of the identifications, one must be able to check them by
determining that the constituent modes, types, or phases do in fact
occur in sequence. Since this is what one is trying to find out by
means of seriation, the reasoning is circular, but only partially so.
In effect, one assumes that a given tradition is valid in order to test
whether it actually is.

In a previous section, I noted that modes, types, and phases
tend to have a partially overlapping distribution within their
traditions (*Fig. 1,C*). It is a weakness of development seriation
that it cannot discriminate overlapping. This problem is most
serious on the level of modes because so many alternatives are
available to the artisan in performing different parts of the procedure of manufacture. The problem can be largely overcome by
selecting modes which are nonalternative. General stylistic trends
are the best. For example, students of Greek archaeology have
seriated Attic red-figured vases in terms of "a constant progression
from conventionalized to naturalistic painting." Even here, Richter
(1946 : 23) has observed that "it is quite possible that some
people lagged behind and during their maturity painted in the
style current in their youth. [Nevertheless] we must date their
works in the period in which their style was generally practiced;
for it is the author's style not his individual propensities that
concern us."

The problem is not so great on the level of types, since fashion
dictates that, once a new type has come into existence, its predecessor will quickly lose popularity. There will be some overlapping,
but a new type should not persist alongside an old one for any
great length of time unless they belong to different typological

traditions, in which case it would be impossible to seriate them in terms of the same development pattern.

Rowe (1961 : 328 - 29) has suggested seriating artifacts successively in terms of different modal traditions. This would have the advantage of reducing the amount of overlap between modes, but I doubt that the reduction would be any greater than in a single seriation in terms of the typological tradition. A type, as we have seen, may be regarded as a complex of modes, and therefore a typological tradition is the sum total of a number of modal traditions (Rouse 1960 : 315 - 16). This being the case, seriation of a number of artifacts in terms of the development within their typological tradition should yield the same result as seriation in terms of the developments within several modal traditions. To be sure, some modal traditions may have varied independently of the typological tradition, but if so, they cannot be included in the same seriation anyway, because they will have different patterns of development.

On the level of phases, I do not believe that the problem of overlapping is significant. Here, it will take the form of survival of an earlier phase alongside its successor in a peripheral region. The investigator should be able to draw the boundaries of his local area in such a manner as to eliminate peripheral overlapping of this kind. I do not think there is much possibility of an earlier phase surviving alongside a later one in a closely defined area unless the two belong to different traditions, in which case it will be impossible to seriate them together anyway.

There are, then, two practicable ways of doing development seriation, by seriating artifacts (or structures) in terms of their types and by seriating components in terms of their phases. In dealing with artifacts, one begins by hypothesizing that a series of types all belong to the same typological tradition. Then, one selects artifacts typical of each type, lays them out on a table, and moves them around until they appear to be in the most gradual order of development. This should be the sequence of one's types, and therefore it may be used as a master pattern by means of which to date new artifacts: as these are found, they need only be matched against the typical artifacts in the sequence in order to determine their age relative to the sequence.

Alternatively, one may proceed in terms of cards rather than typical artifacts. One prepares a card for each type, listing or punching on it the attributes (modes) indicative of that type. Then one arranges the cards in the order which produces the most gradual change in the attributes. One may do this either by inspection, with a needle, or in a computer.

Cards or slips must be used in seriating components. First, one isolated a group of phases which seem to belong to the same tradition. Then one selects components which are typical of each phase; makes a list of the modes, types, and inferences about non-material culture that are distinctive of these components; and writes or punches these traits on a card. There will be a card for each phase. The cards are arranged in the presumed order of development of the phases either by inspection, by use of a needle, or in a computer.

If cards have been used, either on the level of types or phases, they constitute a master file, by means of which to date new artifacts or components as they are found. One need only match the distinctive traits of a new artifact or component against those on the cards in the file in order to determine the relative position of the artifact or component within the file and hence within its typological or cultural tradition.

The assumption behind this approach is that the complex of attributes (modes) comprising a type, or the complex of traits comprising a phase, varies gradually within a single tradition. One's aim, therefore, is to place the complexes in the order which provides the most gradual transition from one to another. This assumption has been confirmed in the classical Greek field, where vessels that can be dated historically show a gradual progression in both shape (Bloesch 1951) and design (Richter 1946).

Supplemental Use of Other Chronological Techniques

Inspection of the three kinds of patterns diagramed in Figure 2 will demonstrate that all three are reversible. The figure could be turned upside down and would still be valid. This reversibility is just as true of development patterns as it is of the other two kinds for, as we have seen, development can be either progressive or regressive. By itself, therefore, seriation gives only the order of arrangement of one's units; it does not tell the direction.

It is occasionally possible to determine the direction of a seriation from internal evidence. For example, Evans (1850 : *132 - 34*) discovered that the molds in which his prehistoric British coins had been cast had continued in use after their edges had broken down. It followed from this that the coins with complete designs were earlier than those from which the edges of the designs were missing.

Such an inevitable sequence from one type to another is rare, however, and ordinarily the investigator must have recourse to outside data in determining the direction of seriation, *i.e.,* he must turn to other chronological techniques. Rowe (1961 : 327) has suggested that this may be done either by beginning one's seriation at a known point in time or, preferably, by seriating between two known points. One known point will not be enough, though, for the seriation can proceed in either direction from that point. Two known points are the absolute minimum, and three or more are preferable.

It does not matter whether the known points are all at one end of the seriation, at both ends, or in the middle. For example, Kroeber (1916) was able to seriate back from several adjacent points, the modern Pueblo of Zuni and its historic predecessors, using the so-called direct historic approach. On the other hand, in Peru, where a succession of horizon styles is known, one can seriate between two of them, such as the Tiahuanaco and Inca horizons (Kroeber 1944). In Venezuela, Cruxent and I were able to use radiocarbon dates, scattered irregularly through our seriations (Rouse and Cruxent 1963).

Stratigraphic excavation is one of the best ways to determine the direction of a seriation, as Spier (1917) so ably showed. By choosing deep refuse deposits and dividing them into arbitrary levels, he was able to find out the trends of change in the frequencies of pottery types from the bottoms to the tops of the deposits. He then arranged his seriation of surface collections in the direction of those trends. This approach need not be limited to deposition units and to frequency patterns. For example, Petrie (1899) used the superimposition of graves as a means of determining the direction of his occurrence seriation. Cruxent and I have similarly relied upon the superimposition of components as a means of determining the direction of our development seriation.

Indeed, stratigraphy and seriation make an ideal combination. From stratigraphy can be obtained the trends of change but few stratigraphies are long enough to reveal the overall pattern of change. (Olduvai Gorge in Tanganyika is the exception.) By contrast, seriation does reveal the overall pattern, if properly carried out, *i.e.,* if one goes beyond the limitations of stratigraphic research to make excavations and/or surface collections in the places most suitable for documenting the total pattern.

Summary and Conclusions

The five elements essential to the process of seriation have been discussed in some detail. Two of these are limiting factors: the local area from which one's remains must be taken and the tradition to which they must belong (*Fig. 1,C*). We have considered all possible variations in the other three elements, viz., the units seriated, the criteria present in the units, and the pattern of change in the criteria, by means of which the dating is actually done. The units may be of three alternate kinds, fabrication, deposition, or occupation units (Table 1); the criteria, likewise of three kinds, modes, types, or phases (Table 2); and the patterns, of three kinds, occurrence, frequency, or development patterns (*Fig. 2*). By combining these variants, we arrive at twenty-seven alternative ways of doing seriation.

We have discussed all of these alternatives and have found that many of them are impossible because of incompatibilities in the elements involved. Other alternatives are difficult to use for one reason or another. The most practicable alternatives seem to be the following.

1] Seriation of small deposition units, such as grave lots, in terms of the pattern of occurrence of their modes.

2] Seriation of large deposition units, such as surface collections, in terms of the pattern of frequency of their types.

3] Seriation of artifacts or other fabrication units in terms of the patterns of development within their modal and/or typological tradition.

4] Seriation of components or other occupation units in terms of the pattern of development within their cultural tradition.

One's choice among these alternative approaches to seriation will depend upon several factors. Foremost among these is the nature of the available material, whether it consists of individual artifacts, collections from deposition units, or data about components. It is also important to pick the kind of material that happens to be most complex and tends to vary most through time: in some cases, this will be refuse; in others, structures; and in still others, grave furniture.

The interests of the investigator must also be taken into consideration in choosing from among the four alternatives. For example, he may be interested in dating a particular group of specimens, as many amateur archaeologists are, in which case [*3*] is the proper procedure to use. If he wants to date sites rather than artifacts, then he should choose [*4*]. Strictly speaking, alternatives [*1*] and [*2*] do not date either sites or artifacts but only the collections being studied.

The investigator may be more interested in the pattern of change represented in his units than in the units themselves. He may aim to establish a master pattern, by means of which to date new artifacts, components, or collections as they are found. Alternatively, he may want to use the pattern as a basis for setting up cultural periods, *i.e.,* for establishing divisions of time comparable to cultural areas in space. In this event, he should plan his work so as to produce the desired kind of periods. If, like Rowe, he is interested in distinguishing subperiods, *e.g.,* within the occupation of a single site, then [1] is the approach to use. If, with Ford, he aims to establish the chronology of a local area, then [2] and [3] are preferable. But if he is primarily interested in building up a broad regional chronology, as Cruxent and I were in Venezuela, then [4] is most suitable.

Whatever his objective, he must be sure to supplement seriation with another chronological technique, since seriation by itself gives only the order and not the direction of change. Indeed, the more kinds of approach one can bring to bear upon problems of dating, the more reliable one's results will be. It is for this reason that Petrie's and Spier's works stand out as major landmarks in the history of seriation, Petrie's (1899) because he was the first to combine several different kinds of seriation with stratigraphy and Spier's (1917) because he was the first to supplement seriation of surface collections both with stratigraphy and with the direct historical approach.

Work Habits, Postures, and Fixtures

ROBERT F. G. SPIER

Introduction

Man is a creature of habits which ease his way through life. To the extent that these habits are learned, and shared with other members of the same group, they are termed cultural. These habits, found in all realms of human activity, extend to habits of work, including both motor habits directly related to the use of tools and postural habits displayed while using these tools. Closely related to both are the work auxiliaries, here called fixtures, which include workbenches, vises, other work holding devices, and, by extension, some simple machines.

Though the existence of motor habit patterns has long been recognized they have rarely been the subject of explicit study.

ROBERT F. G. SPIER has done fieldwork in the western part of the United States and Europe in the areas of ethnology and material culture analysis. He is Associate Professor of Anthropology at the University of Missouri in Columbia.

Anthropologists have tended to ignore motor habits even while describing the technical processes in which they are involved. Despite the unspecific and diffuse nature of these observations, it is, of course, thanks to them that we have become aware of gross differences in manual habits between cultures of major areas, such as the Occidental-Oriental contrast in push- and pull-tools.

Beyond any question of interest in the subject, which must be answered by each investigator for himself, there may have been a technical reason for the general failure to record the motor aspect of technical operations. With one position of hands or feet, of arms or legs, or of the body rapidly following another, the observer finds it difficult to keep pace with a descriptive longhand record. While cinematography may seem the obvious answer to the problem, it raises others in its turn, such as expense, interference with the process, and the difficulties of subsequent analysis. Some interested and willing souls have overcome these, fortunately, to present us with excellent records on film. However, the development of some form of abbreviated note-taking, perhaps comparable to dance notation, which involved no special equipment beyond a pencil and paper, would greatly facilitate the observational process and increase the likelihood of such records being taken as adjuncts to other investigations.

Work postures, likewise a significant part of the process, are also often inadequately recorded. However, the lack here may not be as serious as with direct manipulative habits. Gross bodily postures are longer sustained, perhaps for hours, than are the fleeting positions or movements of fingers, hands, or arms. Therefore, in a given time span, there occur fewer bodily postures than manipulative positions with attendant ease of recording. Further, these gross postures are often evident in photographs or sketches of people at work. Timed sequence pictures can provide an adequate record, while even general views of the work scene can be quite revealing on this score.

Related to both motor habits and postural habits, but decidedly more static, are the fixtures pertinent to a given work situation. The recording of these is comparatively easy and may even be conducted after the fact by utilizing museum specimens as the basis for study. It must be admitted, however, that this latter mode is far from ideal; still, it is possible in a way that motor habit and postural studies are not.

The Problem

It has been generally assumed that the bodily postures of adult humans are culturally conditioned, viz., of all the postures anatomically possible a selected few are frequently assumed and sanctioned as proper in a given circumstance. It has been shown that the occurrence of a particular bodily posture may have an areal, or cross-cultural, distribution comparable to the distribution of other more commonly recognized cultural elements. In brief, the occurrence of conventional bodily postures possesses certain characteristics which lead us to believe the postures to be directly or indirectly influenced by cultural factors. For example, a person may be taught to sit while eating, but, additionally, tight clothing or standards of modesty may prohibit certain anatomically possible sitting positions. Few anthropological studies have been devoted to the question of demonstrating this commonly-held assumption. We are greatly indebted to Hewes (1955, 1957) for having contributed to the subject.

The bodily postures examined by Hewes were those primarily of repose, but also under a variety of other conditions. He comments on the sample underlying his study, "I have recorded information on about one hundred of the commonest postures, chiefly of the sitting, kneeling, crouching, and squatting varieties. . . . Sleeping or reclining postures have been entirely omitted. . . . Dance positions have also been excluded, perhaps arbitrarily; . . . the attitudes dealt with here are maintained for minutes, at least" (Hewes 1955 : 234). One is tempted to assume that conditions which characterize the whole are also characteristic of one of its parts, namely that work postures have been influenced by some of the same factors which have borne upon other postures. If this is so, then work postures should also be consistent within a culture and show similarities to general bodily postures of that culture.

It must be admitted that the procedure of comparing work postures with the bodily postures noted by Hewes is somewhat circular. Hewes's data on bodily postures include those on work. However, considering the difficulty of finding adequate pictures and records of work postures, it may be surmised that this category of information did not contribute heavily to Hewes's conclusions.

In addition to the effects on work postures of the general postural training received by the individual, there may also be found the effects of the task and tools in hand. Certain operations and the handling of certain tools are perhaps more easily performed while standing, or while sitting, but other tasks may be performed equally well in either position. If these ambipositional tasks are found to be consistently performed in one position rather than the other, we may suspect the influence of a cultural standard. Much the same may be said of associations between postures and the use of certain machines, such as grinding wheels or lathes, or the use of certain fixtures, such as workbenches. This paper proposes to discuss some aspects of the relationships between general bodily postures, work postures, tools, and work fixtures. No extensive survey is attempted and examples will be drawn from Old World cultures.

Observed Work Postures

The data for work postures were derived from published sources, with attention given to works devoted to craft or industrial pursuits, such as carpentry, joinery, and smithing. Of over two hundred individuals recorded from these pictures, half were Europeans between the fourteenth and nineteenth centuries. The remainder was divided on a three to two ratio between Far Easterners (Japanese and Chinese of the nineteenth and twentieth centuries) and ancient Egyptians. As most of the operations illustrated are those of full-time practitioners, men predominated in the pictures. Therefore, women, appearing in only a few instances, were eliminated from the sample in order to make it sexually homogeneous; consequently all comparisons with general bodily postures must be with those of males.

Europeans have for centuries been noted for their chair-sitting habit. Lacking a chair, they will sit on stools, benches, blocks, and similar supports, but rarely on the ground. By contrast with some world areas, Europe has not notably linked elevated seating and social status. While the precise form of seating may vary with the status of the occupant, we find persons of all classes sitting upon something. Under these circumstances, we can expect European workmen to sit or stand optionally at appropriate tasks unless there exists some overriding tradition to the contrary.

The European work posture records were sorted into those tasks, such as hoeing or chopping with an ax, which are evidently best accomplished standing, and those tasks which optionally may be performed either standing or sitting. In this latter category were placed those tasks known to be performed, in any culture, either standing or sitting, though not necessarily in both positions in the same culture.

Among Europeans in the exclusively standing posture category were twenty-one individuals of whom ten were standing evenly with both feet on the ground, ten were standing but leaning into their work (as a man forcing a shovel into the ground), and one was standing while holding down his work with his foot (a wheelwright boring the hub of a wheel). In the optionally standing or sitting group were ninety-eight individuals of whom fifty-six were standing, four were seated astride their work or a bench, thirty-two were sitting on elevated seats (chairs, stools, etc.), three were sitting on the ground, and three were kneeling.

The ancient Egyptian sample was similarily sorted, with the following results. Six persons employed the exclusively standing

Work postures	EUROPEAN				EGYPTIAN			
	Number Group	Number Total	Percentage Group	Percentage Total	Number Group	Number Total	Percentage Group	Percentage Total
Exclusively standing		21		18		6		11
Optionally standing or sitting:		98		82		50		89
Standing	56		57		9		18	
Elevated sitting	36		37		23		46	
Ground sitting	3		3		3		6	
Kneeling	3		3		15		30	
Total		119		100		56		100

position. In the optionally standing or sitting group were fifty individuals of whom nine were standing, fifteen kneeling, three sitting on the ground, and twenty-three sitting on elevated seats (mostly stools).

The Japanese sample yielded the following results. Nine persons stood at exclusively standing tasks. Twenty-five, in optionally standing or sitting pursuits, were distributed with five standing, two seated on elevated seats, twelve seated on the ground or floor, and six kneeling.

The Chinese sample, the smallest, had one person standing at an exclusively standing task, with his foot holding down the work. Thirteen individuals were in the optionally standing or sitting group with two standing, nine seated on elevated seats, one seated on the ground, and one kneeling.

The result of this cross-cultural sample are summarized in Table 1, with percentages calculated to the nearest per cent. While the sample size makes any refined statistical analysis subject to question, certain gross differences in percentage of occurrence are apparent, especially when categories are combined. The European sample had 57 per cent standing and 37 per cent sitting on elevated seats. Two of the three sitting on the ground were Flemings engaged in shearing sheep, while the third was an Italian assayer hammering in a cupel. Three persons were kneeling.

Although the Europeans have been lumped together in the

| | JAPANESE | | | | CHINESE | | |
| Number | | Percentage | | Number | | Percentage | |
Group	Total	Group	Total	Group	Total	Group	Total
9		26		1		7	
	25		74		13		93
5		20		2		15	
2		8		9		69	
12		48		1		8	
6		24		1		8	
	34		100		14		100

1. Summary of Posture Sample

foregoing, we are aware that these people are not homogeneous in habits. This awareness is heightened by observing the differences between pavers in various countries. A Flemish paver of the fifteenth century uses a low, four-legged stool, while a German paver of the same date uses a one-legged stool of similar height (Singer 1956: II, 525, 526). Beyond the question of choice of seating, a difference existed in the direction of work. R. J. Forbes has commented, "Incidentally the French and Flemish paviours seem to have sat on four-legged stools and to have moved forward as they laid the cobbles. The German paviours had the well known one-legged stool and moved backwards as they paved" (Singer 1956: 526). This same one-legged stool, and backward work direction, may be observed among twentieth-century Dutch pavers; Dutch stone cutters use the same stool, in varying heights. The English paver may not have used a stool at all and have worked backwards. An illustration of an English paver shows the man, on his feet, bent sharply from the waist with right foot advanced and knee deeply bent, and the left foot somewhat behind the level of the hips and the knee slightly bent (Singer 1956: 545). The posture, excepting possibly the bent knees, is reminiscent of some primitive peoples who use a short-handled hoe.

By contrast with the Europeans the ancient Egyptian sample had only 18 per cent standing, while 46 per cent used elevated seats. Six per cent sat on the ground and 30 per cent knelt. This is the highest incident of kneeling noted in any of the four groups. It is possible that the Egyptian sample, taken mostly from tomb decorations, is not a true reflection of workmen's postural practices due to artistic license; the figures and their postures may be highly stylized. Nonetheless the artists must have taken some cognizance of postural standards to have produced credible and acceptable results. In the absence of direct evidence to the contrary, these postures must be accepted as normal.

The Japanese sample shows 20 per cent standing at work. Almost half, 48 per cent, were seated on the ground or floor, and two persons (8 per cent) used an elevated seat. The remaining 24 per cent were kneeling. When combining the figures for all non-standing postures, the Japanese sample shows almost the same proportions of standing to nonstanding (20 : 80) as does the Egyptian (18 : 82), but the percentages of those using elevated seating and those sitting on the ground are almost reversed (Japanese 8 : 48 and Egyptian 46 : 6).

The very small Chinese sample shows a marked predominance of elevated sitting positions, 69 per cent, over standing positions, 15 per cent. The difference is accentuated if one contrasts standing positions with nonstanding positions.

Postural Comparisons

Comparisons of specific postures in the several samples were made with those illustrated by Hewes (1957). As he had not dealt extensively with standing postures, of which he shows fewer than ten resting positions, the analysis was confined to sitting, kneeling, and related positions. Even with this exclusion it was not possible to apply the procedure to the entire remaining group; in some pictures the position of the legs was obscured, as by a workbench, or only vaguely depicted. However, this vagueness did not interfere with the earlier crude sorting into the various postures listed below. For purposes of this study certain liberties were taken with Hewes's classification. Attention, at this point, was focused on the legs, with some latitude allowed in position of torso, and no equivalence required of arm positions. Hewes's figures are shown at rest; my samples of work postures were of people in action.

Certain postures, frequently encountered in this study, are not fully represented in Hewes's published categories. For example, elevated sitting on very low stools or chairs produces leg positions which resemble, generally, those of various deep squats or ground-sitting positions; yet sitting, which involves a seat, and sitting on the ground, which involves no seat, should not be classed together. Similarly, there are variants, with both high and low seats, in which one foot is advanced while the other is tucked back at the line of the chair legs or even under the seat. When other criteria failed to produce adequate classification in these cases, primary attention was paid to the position of the thighs, whether parallel or spread apart, and in the latter instance how widely spread. Short of developing a new postural classification scheme, with attendant difficulties in making comparisons, these *ad hoc* modifications must be allowed.

In Table 2, which summarizes the result of comparisons with Hewes's published data, it will be seen that six of his eight sedentary postures are represented. Absent from the samples under discussion are postures having the legs folded to the side (Hewes's nos. 106 - 108) and asymmetrical floor-sitting postures (nos. 120 - 125). The apparent discrepancies in frequency between Tables 1 and 2 are a product of difference in classification systems. As mentioned above, some seated postures were classified as squatting when a low seat was in use. Floor-sitting, Hewes's term, and ground-sitting are considered to be the same in this analysis.

Elevated sitting (chair-sitting, Hewes's nos. 30 - 39.5) is dominant among the European workers, used by more than half of the Egyptian and Chinese workers, and markedly infrequent among the Japanese. This is in accord with expectations; for the Europeans, ancient Egyptians, and Chinese are all known as generally using chairs and stools in the time period covered by this survey. The Japanese, by contrast with their Chinese neighbors,

2. Nonstanding postural analysis

Postural type (numbers according to Hewes)		EURO-PEAN Number	EGYP-TIAN Number	JAPA-NESE Number	CHI-NESE Number
Chair-sitting					
(Nos. 30–39.5)	30	2	20	1	0
	31	11	0	0	2
	32	14	2	1	2
	38	2	0	0	0
Per cent of group		78	60	12.5	57
Floor-sitting					
(Nos. 41–75)	41	2	0	0	1
	42	1	0	0	0
	51	1	0	0	0
	52	1	0	1	1
	72	0	0	1	0
	73	0	0	1	0
Per cent of group		14	0	19	29
Cross-legged					
(Nos. 76–90)	80	0	0	4	0
	81	0	0	1	0
Per cent of group		0	0	31	0
Kneeling					
(Nos. 100–105)	100	0	0	1	0
	102	1	4	1	0
	104	0	0	1	0
Per cent of group		3	11	19	0
Deep squat					
(Nos. 110–116)	115	0	2	1	0
Per cent of group		0	5	6	0
Asymmetrical kneeling					
(Nos. 126–132)	126	1	1	0	1
	126.5	1	0	0	0
	127	0	4	0	0
	128	0	1	0	0
	129	0	0	1	0
	130	0	3	1	0
Per cent of group		5	24	12.5	14
Total		37 100	37 100	16 100	7 100

made little use of chairs. The process of Westernization in Japan, which had not proceeded far when Morse made his observations, may have produced some changes in Japanese postural habits (Morse 1904, 1917). It would be interesting to know what the results have been.

Floor-sitting (nos. 41 - 75) is comparatively infrequent among all four groups, but notably absent in the Egyptian sample. Its apparent higher incidence among the Chinese is likely attributable to sample size. The figures agree with expectations and those for the Japanese present no contradiction. Though the Japanese are described as floor-sitters (Hewes 1957 : *125*) this appelation is true only in contrast to chair-sitters and not literally true. In fact, Japanese floor-sitting is better described as cross-legged sitting, kneeling, or squatting, which Hewes makes clear in another context. "Sitting in what might be described as a 'deep kneel,' with the feet under the buttocks, dorsal surfaces down, is the normal Japanese sitting posture for both sexes" (Hewes 1955 : *240*). This deep kneel position (Hewes's nos. 102 - 104) differs noticeably from those in the floor-sitting category. At least half of the floor-sitting positions have one or both legs outstretched with the knee locked or only slightly flexed.

When one examines in detail the three Japanese cases which have been classified as floor-sitting, it is seen that these are marginal to the type. The first case is of a blacksmith, with buttocks resting on the floor, who is operating a box bellows with his extended left foot (as a Westerner might reach out with a hand). As the view is from the rear the right leg is not seen, but is presumed to be stretched in front, probably with knee slightly flexed, or else crossed in front of the body. The second case is of a wood-turner whose posture is discussed below in the section on lathes. The third case is of a joiner working at a very low bench, perhaps eight inches high. His buttocks rest on the floor, his right leg is crossed between his body and the end of the bench, and his left foot, with leg extended and bent, rests on the work on top of the bench. All three postures are highly specialized according to circumstances.

Cross-legged sitting (nos. 76-90) is absent in all groups except the Japanese, where it accounts for one-third of the sample. The cross-legged sitting is not a standard posture among Europeans or Chinese, but is noted from ancient sources for both sexes in Egypt (Hewes 1955: *239, map* 2). On closer inspection this Egyptian datum evidently refers to Hewes's posture no. 88, cross-legged sitting with knees somewhat raised, rather than nos. 80 and 81 in which the knees are essentially flat to the floor. Though in Japan cross-legged sitting is suggested as possessing religious links (Hewes 1955 : 240), its occurrence among these workmen can be related to the presence of work fixtures. Three tortoise-shell workers are sitting close to (*i.e.,* facing) workblocks; unless these blocks were straddled, no other sitting posture would bring the workman close enough. One potter is similarly seated at a lower block on which a vessel rests. A second potter is sitting cross-legged before a tournette holding a vessel. Saving a taboo on the posture because of its religious connotations, it could well be employed under these circumstances, being known as an established cultural trait in Japan.

Kneeling (nos. 100-105) is absent among the Chinese (sample size?), and virtually so among the Europeans. It occurs in about 10 per cent of the Egyptian sample and about 20 per cent of the Japanese sample. While Hewes does not note this position for ancient Egypt, he does mention its use in Islamic and European cultures as a prayer position (1955: *240;* 1957: *128*). In the three cases here, among ship carpenters, it may be an adaptation to a work situation; no stool or chair would be stable on the sloping surfaces where the men are at work. Among the Japanese kneeling postures require no further comment.

The deep squat (nos. 110-116) occurs infrequently in the Egyptian and Japanese samples and not at all in the European and Chinese series. This posture is widely distributed over the world except among European and derivative cultures (Hewes

1955 : 238). Possibly one would find its distribution to be complementary to that of chair-sitting.

Asymmetrical kneeling (nos. 126-132) includes a minor fraction of the Europeans, only modest numbers of the Japanese and Chinese, but about one-quarter of the Egyptians. The Egyptian workers in this postural group include three joiners (one polishing a cabinet, one sawing an upright plank, and one using a bow drill), two goldsmiths (one using a blowpipe, the other pounding on a low anvil), and two flint knappers.

General consideration of kneeling postures has appeared above, but an amalgamation of categories might be considered. When kneeling (nos. 100-105) and asymmetrical kneeling (nos. 126-132) groups are combined, it is found that no great change occurs in the European and Chinese samples. However, in the Egyptian series the joint group numbers 35 per cent and in the Japanese series the joint group numbers 31.5 per cent. This heightens the contrast between the two pairs of peoples and shows the Egyptian postures to be about two-thirds chair-sitting and one-third kneeling. The Japanese sample is not so lopsided in favor of one postural mode, being approximately one-third cross-legged sitting and one-third kneeling with the remaining third distributed in all other categories.

In summary, we find no group in our sample employing work postures which differ markedly in type or frequency of occurrence from those which have been noted as generally habitual in these same groups. These workmen are found to share in the habits of the groups of which they are a part and to differ, if at all, only in ways demanded by particular work situations.

Relations to Tools and Fixtures

Beyond the question of relationship between work postures and those employed in nonworking circumstances, we must consider the possible influence of tools and fixtures used. The use of certain tools presupposes a standing posture, and it was partially on this basis that the original sorting of standing activities from optionally standing or sitting activities was made. Yet some of the tools which we customarily associate with standing postures are capable of use while sitting. The saw presents a possible case in point.

European sawyers, both top man and pit man, customarily stand at their work, whether using a true pit or a trestle to support the timber being sawn. The European pit saw cuts on the down stroke. Chinese sawyers, whose timber is set at an upward slope across an X-frame, use mixed postures, the top man standing on the timber or a foot plank while the pit man sits, with legs extended though slightly flexed, or half kneels, on the ground beneath. The Chinese pit saw's teeth are raked from the center toward the ends to cut, for half its length, on the pull stroke. Each sawyer makes his maximum contribution to the operation at the beginning of his pull stroke with arms fully extended.

In other uses of the saw the Europeans, from the time of the Romans, are pictured as standing. Whether using an open saw or a framed pattern, the joiner usually has a foot or a knee on the board he is cutting. The saw, if it had a directional rake at all, probably cut on the push stroke. When two men are sawing veneers both stand facing each other on opposite sides of a verti-cally-clamped timber with the framed saw between them; the saw probably lacks a directional rake to the teeth.

A Chinese joiner, with a framed saw, is pictured using it in the European fashion, standing with his knee on the board. By contrast the Japanese carpenter is described by Morse in these terms, "the [Japanese] carpenter saws and planes on the floor, and it is an odd sight to see the carpenter's shop with no bench or vise" (Morse 1917 : I, 60). To a degree Morse later contradicts himself, but not with regard to sawing.

The use of the plane is another activity in which regional postural differences may be found. To a man the European carpenters and joiners are shown standing at the task of planing. This may be found in pictures covering two millenia in lands from

Greece to England. In all cases save one the working surface is substantially elevated either by having the work piece placed on a bench or table or by its own height, as would a door when placed on edge. The exception, and only partial at that, is an Italian joiner of the fourteenth century who has a small timber resting on a knee-high jointing bench. The man is standing, sharply bent from the waist.

There are no comparable Egyptian pictures, for the plane was lacking among them. However, a joiner is pictured smoothing a chair leg, presumably with a scraper, while holding the free leg in his lap and sitting on a low stool or block.

No Chinese pictures of carpenters or joiners using a plane are found in the sample.

The Japanese are described by Morse as planing while sitting on the floor, but he does not illustrate this operation. Instead we find sketches of two Japanese carpenters standing while using the plane. Of one instance he writes, "To plane a board they fasten it to uprights, and not a trace of a carpenter's bench or table of any kind is seen" (Morse 1917: 1, 379). The sketch accompanying this comment shows a broad board fastened, with its main surface vertical, across two posts. The board is at shoulder height to the carpenter who is holding his plane vertically and presumably drawing it downward.

In the second instance Morse writes, "Figure 301 shows the long plane of the carpenter resting at an angle on the ground, the other end propped up on a wooden horse. The wood to be planed is moved back and forth on the plane and is always drawn toward the carpenter. Here is one of those curious reversals of practice so often alluded to by travellers: the wood is moved instead of the plane and drawn toward the carpenter instead of the other way, and the plane is upside down" (Morse 1917: 1, 373). The figure shows a workman standing beside the upper end of the sloping plane which rises to about waist height. It is surprising that Morse, who was a man of great knowledge, was unfamiliar with the cooper's long jointer plane, also with the blade edge upward, which was still in use in his native New England in the late nineteenth century. This European-American tool and the Japanese plane in question have the same general form, the difference between them being primarily the angle of the blade. The Japanese plane evidently had its edge directed toward the lower end of the plane, while the European-American model has its blade edge pointed toward the upper end of the slope. In the latter case the wood is pushed away from the workman over the cutting edge.

It must be admitted that there exists between the European and Japanese planes a basic difference which may have forced the European carpenter to stand while permitting his Japanese counterpart to sit. The common European plane is customarily pushed to cut; the common Japanese plane is usually pulled to cut. Both planes have the blade edge directed downward. One is probably better braced while sitting, especially on the floor, to pull than to push a tool, but in the standing position either direction is equally possible. Furthermore, on occasion European woodworkers will draw a plane toward themselves and on very heavy work two men may move the plane, the senior pushing and guiding the plane while his helper pulls. A few special models used by Europeans, *e.g.,* a short, heavy cooper's plane, are intended only to be pulled. For many models of both European and Japanese planes, especially those either lacking handles or possessing only cross-handles, it makes no substantial difference in which direction they are used. The choice is entirely up to the operator and is then presumably governed by what he has learned from his fellows.

Turning from hand tools to a simple machine, the lathe, we find a parallel case of choice rather than necessity. In the Western tradition the operator of a lathe, and certain similar machines, customarily stands at his work. With a powered lathe, especially a machine lathe, this is not necessitated by any requirement of the tool. With some modern automatic lathes the operator's role may be more often that of an observer than an active manipulator.

In our postural sample are seven items involving the use of a lathe, five European, one Chinese, and one Japanese. Two Europeans, fourteenth-century French and seventeenth-century Netherlands, are using springpole lathes while standing; though one cannot be absolutely certain in the latter case in which the turner's figure is partly obscured by his lathe bed. A sixteenth-century French turner is standing at a lathe powered by descending weights. Two nineteenth-century artisans, a glass cutter and a potter, are standing at lathe-like machines which derive their power from some external source. The twentieth-century Chinese lathe operator is not pictured but is reported to sit on a seat while pressing alternately two suspended pedals to operate his reciprocating lathe. The nineteenth-century Japanese turner sits on the ground with legs extended. Having each foot through a loop in the end of the lathe-turning strap, he moves his feet down alternately to operate his lathe. Not included in the sample, but certainly relevant here, is seventeenth-century Dutch ivory-turner who sits on a stool while operating a spring-pole lathe (Netherlands Open-air Museum, Arnhem, Print Collection, no. 28).

Possibly it may be argued that a standing position is required to operate a spring-pole lathe, to have the body's weight above the pressing foot, but we have seen European turners both standing and sitting at this contrivance. The standing position appears, on the basis of a small sample and some general impressions, to be the norm. For in later lathe forms, having continuous unidirectional rotation and deriving their power either from a foot treadle or from a great wheel cranked by a helper, standing was modal, and the addition of extrahuman power sources did not alter the situation greatly.

Is the lathe, then, a machine requiring at least an elevated operator's position, either standing or sitting on a raised seat? Evidently not. Indian brass spinners are seated on the ground at their lathes. A Georgian turner, using a bow lathe, is seated on the floor with his tool in his left hand, the bow in his right hand, and his feet braced against the lathe bed (Buschan 1926: II, 2, *fig. 415*). A right-handed nineteenth-century Egyptian turner is working his bow lathe in essentially the same manner, the only difference being that the Egyptian is using his right foot to help steady the tool on a rolling rest (Mercer 1960: *fig. 187*). There are similar cases from Arabia and the East Indies. In all instances the axis of rotation of the work is parallel to the ground, as it is in the modern lathe. One is forced to conclude that the lathe, as a device, does not greatly restrict the operator's choice of position.

As with the lathe, the powered grindstone in the West seems to call for a standing posture more often than the direct circumstances of work warrant. Standing may give clearance for the work to be moved around a waist-high contact with the stone. However, one can find evidence that this is not universally true.

Saw grinders in nineteenth-century England, employed in the manufacture of saw blades, sat on a straddle block facing the edge of the wheel. As the near side of the wheel turned upward (a contrast with most modern grinding wheels) the grinder could profitably use his body weight to hold his work down against the rotation of the wheel, occasionally rising almost to his feet to do so. Very restricted space for the work was available between the wheel and the end of the block and the operator's knees; it was evidently sufficient (Jones and Simons 1961 : *46, 48*).

A bizarre grinder's work posture is shown for sword grinders and cutlers in eighteenth-century France. These workmen lie prone on planks reaching over the grinding face. Their work is held in front of them at a level below the worker's face (Diderot 1959 : *plates 179, 183*). Though no explanation is known to me for the use of this work position, it evidently is confined to cutlers and is very old. The Utrecht psalter (ninth century) shows a sword grinder sitting above his wheel on a high scaffold and leaning on his work (Singer 1956 : *651*). C. C. Gillespie, editor of this edition of Diderot's plates, has commented on the prone grinding position as "a posture so characteristic as to have been almost emblematic of the trade" (Diderot 1959 : *notes to plate 179*).

Straddling positions were utilized with several Western tools and fixtures. In the early twentieth century there was current in

America a form of grindstone turned by two pedals connected by rods to cranks on the axle. The operator of this slow-speed wheel, common in small workshops or on the farm, straddled a saddle facing the grinding face of the wheel. The pedal arrangement enabled the operator to dispense with the boy who had turned, with a crank, this grindstone's closely related form which lacked both pedals and saddle. With this latter variant the operator stood at his work.

Another widespread straddle fixture was the shaving horse. This specialized workbench had a foot-operated clamp or vise at one end and a seat for the worker at the other. The workman pressed forward or downward with both feet on a pivoted beam the upper end of which actuated the movable jaw of a clamp. With the piece held fast in the clamp, the operator had both hands free, commonly to pull a drawknife. The fixture was standard among northwestern European and American coopers, tubmakers, shinglemakers, and others who shaved slats to comparatively thin sections.

The use of the shaving horse did not preclude standing postures among the same workmen to use the same tool (the drawknife, or the related spokeshave). The work was then clamped in a workbench vise at waist height for the same operation. A twentieth-century Danish wheelwright, who used the shaving horse, also placed spokes in a jig which held them above bench level (at almost chest height) for finishing with a spokeshave. This jig consisted of two dead centers, each mounted on a standard, one fixed in the bench proper, the other set in the movable vise jaw, between which the spoke coul be clamped and revolved. Because the work could be turned without releasing it, the jig is not strictly comparable to the shaving horse in which the work was always stationary. The spoke jig acted, however, in no way like a lathe.

While evidence on this score is somewhat mixed, one is led to the general conclusion that many tools and fixtures do not dictate the work postures of their users, though certain tools, such as the ax and shovel, certainly control posture to a degree. As further evidence that work posture is not absolutely toolbound, attention is directed to the contorted postures assumed by workmen in cramped quarters, *e.g.,* miners, using many of the same tools. Efficiency is possibly reduced, but work is performed.

The theory is here submitted that instead of work fixtures inevitably determining postures the reverse is true. Under these circumstances workbenches, in the Western sense, would be absent among ground- or floor-sitting peoples; this generally seems to be the case. Vises and similar work-clamping devices face competition from the workman's foot, especially among unshod groups. When present the vise or clamp often operates at ground level, possibly to hold, in a vertical plane, a board being sawn by a sitting or kneeling workman.

Relations to Other Factors

Beyond the relationships of work postures to habitual non-work postures and to tools and fixtures, there remain several other possible contributing factors. First, is not a standing position necessary for exertion of maximum strength, in the same way that a sitting one is advantageous for delicate manipulations? Doubtless this relation between posture and exertion is true in many cases, with due regard to the direction of effort and the means (here, tools) by which it is brought to bear. However, it is doubtful that maximum exertion is required in many instances in which the standing position is employed.

Standing, of itself, does not necessarily place the workman at a positional advantage. The sitting position, either somewhat elevated or on the ground, is the most powerful pulling position available to a man with his feet braced. Users of fixtures such as the shaving horse would be greatly advantaged by such a posture, and the Japanese carpenter using a pull-saw and pull-plane does not lose efficiency by sitting on the floor.

It is likely that maximum muscular effort was rarely employed by the classes of workmen or in the types of work under discussion.

No worker can sustain for protracted periods his maximum muscular output; in fact, furious physical activity at work is considered by many to be the mark of an amateur. The experienced workman proceeds at a slower, but steadier, pace and produces more in the long run. If occasional periods of high muscular effort, in a standing position, were called for, the workman might literally rise to the occasion, otherwise assuming another posture.

Second, beyond the capacities of the men one may question the capacities of their tools. The tools of earlier ages were often lightly built, of weak materials, and could not withstand the abuse that vigorous use would bring. The tool could not be forced, but when properly sharp would do the job at its own pace. Time was probably not an important factor in many cases.

Third, is it not possible that the standing posture for workers in Western cultures possesses some moral overtones? Here we find, in the midst of many seats, persistence of the standing posture when neither work nor tool demand it. Perhaps a man who sits at his work is not deemed to be giving his best. How otherwise would we come by the expression "to sit down on the job," or the notion that sedentary occupations are somehow less virile, less valuable, and less productive? Possibly the Western workman, standing at his work, is partially motivated by the impression of industry the posture creates.

Conclusion

We have examined the relationship of work postures to a series of other factors in the work situation. These included habitual nonwork postures, hand tools, fixtures, simple machines, muscular strength, and connotations of industriousness.

On the basis of a small sample, drawn from four Old World cultures, we have found work postures to be congruent to the habitual nonworking postures of the group in question, though with some exceptions. These exceptions, such as the frequent standing position of Westerners, seem to be the product of nontechnical factors rather than the demands of the task in hand. In general, the workmen of those peoples who habitually sat on elevated seats or who habitually kneeled or who habitually sat on the ground likewise used elevated seats or kneeled or sat on the ground. We can conclude that, in this respect at least, workmen whose task permits them to do so will behave posturally like their fellows not so engaged.

The use of fixtures—workbenches, vises, and the like—is evidently dependent on the general postural habits of the culture. In those groups not making extensive use of standing or elevated sitting positions workbenches are rare, work usually being performed on the ground. Vises and other work holding devices tend to be simple or absent, and a foot often holds the work.

Though certain hand tools require of their users a particular posture, usually standing, it has been seen that postures are not inevitably the product of the use of a given tool. Hewes suggests that, instead of posture fitting the tool the reverse may be the case. "Nearly every new tool or machine must be adjusted to some body posture or sequence of postures" (Hewes 1955 : 232). Not all tools need to undergo this adjustment for identical or closely related forms of a tool may be used in a variety of positions at the option of the worker. In exercising this option he seems more guided by other considerations than those of his tools. The options chosen tend to fall into a restricted group of postural categories rather than showing a random distribution. The conclusion reached is that these postures are not solely the product of technical demands.

As hand tools may be shown to possess a varying relationship to workers' postures, so the same is true of some simple machines. In only a few instances is a particular posture necessarily associated with use of a given machine. More often this machine, in a particular form, can be used in more than one position, *e.g.,* standing or sitting, but is prevailingly used in one of these positions in a single cultural context. It has been shown, for example, that Westerners generally stand at their lathes no matter what power source is used, be it foot-powered or driven from a water wheel. Again nontechnical forces seem foremost in setting the postural patterns of the machine users.

No great argument may be made, in the circumstances with which we have dealt, for requirements of maximum muscular efficiency dictating workers' postures. Maximum strength seems rarely to have been employed routinely and, within broad limits, most workmen could choose freely their work postures without regard for this factor. Variations in form or use of tool can often compensate for any disadvantages which might potentially be suffered.

If tools, fixtures, and demands of the job are all only loosely linked, as causative factors, to work postures, what are we to consider the primary causes of these postures? Preeminent among those considered have been the postural standards of a culture. The workman is evidently not exempted from the influence of these standards by reason of his manually productive activities. He applies to the work situation the postures which he is accustomed to assume under other circumstances. For all that we often refer, in anthropological literature, to craftsmen such as those discussed as full time craft specialists, this is not literally true, but refers only to their economically productive activities. Presumably the bulk of their lives is spent as more generalized members of their societies and they would then conform to general cultural standards, including those pertaining to postures.

The possible derivations of the general postural habits have been discussed by Hewes. He mentions clothing and footgear, fear of genital exposure, artificial supports, architecture, terrain and vegetation, and ground moisture as possible contributors (Hewes 1955 : 231 - 32). It is not our task to explore again these matters; the postural habits are taken at face value as influences on the individual.

We are left without substantial explanation for exceptions, some rather major, which do not conform to expectations based on the postural habits of a culture. Most notable is the occurrence of evidently unnecessary standing positions among European work-ers. Two suggestions are tentatively put forward. First, the stand-ing posture may have been retained from a period when the tools with which it is associated took another form which necessitated standing. Conceivably the form was so radically different as to actually have been a different tool, though used for the same purpose. The postural association would then be with the task rather than with the tool. A possible support for this argument might exist if it could be shown that the carpenter's plane sup-planted as a smoothing tool one which had to be used in a standing position. The now obsolete slick, a large smoothing chisel, might be a candidate as just such a predecessor of the plane though its greater antiquity is doubtful.

Second, the standing position may be used, or may have been used, for the impression it is believed to create in the mind of the onlooker. It carries for many persons connotations of forcefulness, purposiveness, and industriousness, all of which may enhance the prestige of the worker with his fellows. While it may be shown that these connotations are dubiously rational, once a chance asso-ciation occurred, possibly in another context in which it made more sense, it could be readily perpetuated or transferred.

An attempt has been made to demonstrate that work postures and certain closely related circumstances of manual activity are a definite part of a culture. These are far from being idiosyncratic or even restricted to special situations, but show broad general char-acterizations of which we should become more fully aware. In an era when we seek to apply anthropological findings to improve-ment, generally, of man's way of life, these basic factors in his technical pursuits assume added importance.

The Sharing Criterion
and the Concept of Culture

WALTER W. TAYLOR

A NUMBER of years ago, in *A Study of Archeology,* I argued that for defining culture in the holistic sense, for identifying the *cultural* in contrast to, say, the chemical, or the geological, or the psychological, a sharing or social criterion is not pertinent. Traits of culture in the holistic sense, I said, "may be either shared or idiosyncratic . . . an object or bit of behavior may be cultural even if it is the only example of its kind in existence or ever to have been in existence" (1948 : *102*). I maintained that only for culture in the partitive sense, only when we wish to distinguish one culture from another, is the sharing criterion germane and necessary. In the present paper, I wish to reiterate what I said at that time and to present evidence of a different sort in support of my viewpoint.[1]

WALTER W. TAYLOR is Professor of Anthropology at Southern Illinois University in Carbondale and his work in the field of archaeology has been carried on in the southwestern part of the United States and in Mexico. He has also studied the Neolithic cultures of Western Europe.

Because *A Study of Archeology* appeared in 1948, it might seem that to bring this matter up again is beating a dead horse. But the horse is not dead: many anthropologists continue to act and write as if the phenomena with which they deal are to be categorized *either* as cultural (shared by several persons) *or* as idiosyncratic (pertinent to one person alone). In other words, they believe that what is cultural cannot be idiosyncratic. They proceed as if the cultural and the idiosyncratic were coordinates, *i.e.*, mutually

| | | | CATEGORIES OF MEANING OR FRAMES OF REFERENCE | | | | |
			CULT.	SOC.	PSYCH.	BIOL.	CH.–PH.
LEVELS OF ABSTRACTION	EXPLANATORY	SHARED					
		IDIOSYN.					
	REFERENTIAL OR CATEGORICAL	SHARED					
		IDIOSYN.					
	OBSERVATIONAL		PHENOMENA OF THE REAL WORLD				

1. A conceptual scheme for the analysis of difference

exclusive alternatives on a single level of abstraction or mutually exclusive alternatives within the same frame of reference.

It is my contention, on the other hand, that traits of culture in the holistic sense can be *both* cultural *and* idiosyncratic, that these two categories are not mutually exclusive in any sense. For culture-as-a-whole, when we are trying to distinguish what is culture (or cultural) from what is something else, the sharing criterion is neither practicable nor actually used by most anthropologists, however much they may claim to do so. Furthermore, I believe that the sharing criterion is fallacious from an epistemological point of view. It will be from this point of view that I shall be arguing in what I have to say below.

The figure is a graphic representation of the points I wish to make. There are several qualifications which could be made with regard to it, but I shall merely note that the named frames of reference are taken from Kroeber (1936: *317 f.*), although equally valid ones could have been derived from other sources or created *ad hoc*. In other words, the scheme is flexible and applicable to a wide range of topical fields. It is perhaps needless also to say that the chart itself is but a formal and somewhat rigid depiction of an epistemological scheme, the nuances of which are far more delicate and, I should hope, much more real and variable than any diagram can be expected to show. I ask that it be used to clarify, not cabin, crib, or confine.

The real world is the realm of the phenomenal, the experiential. It is completely heterogeneous and idiosyncratic. Its phenomena are never repeated or reproduced—and this is true if only because the factor of Time is ever present and ever changing. In addition to this, however, it is true to the best of our present knowledge that no two objects, acts, or relationships in the real world are ever identical. The real world is an on-going, varying continuum in which there is neither repetition nor turning back, in which change and therefore difference is the unexceptionable rule.

Human beings function within this real world by continuously making observational abstractions as an integral part of being alive, of being sentient creatures, of living. These abstractions are as nonrepetitive and heterogeneous as the phenomena of that real world from which they are drawn. Our physical senses are capable of abstracting only idiosyncratic impressions. Each observation, each primary neurological response pertains to a situation which can only be unique. Nature is not categorized, and therefore abstractions made directly from nature cannot be categorical.

Order is imposed upon this heterogeneous mass of primary observational abstractions by referring them, on the basis of what we recognize and refer to as likeness, to categories of previously made abstractions. These categories are second-level, being abstractions from abstractions. They are created or learned by the individual in the course of his experience of living. They are infinitely numerous, and their criteria are infinitely variable. They constitute the so-called frames of reference, the categories of meaning, which are used to make cultural sense, that is, human sense out of heterogeneous nature. Without them, the world would be an amorphous continuum, a jungle of unconnected sense impressions too multitudinous, too complex, too unorganized, and thus too meaningless for human beings to understand and to cope with.[2]

Here then, on this second or referential-categorical level of abstraction, is our first concern with likeness—and here are our first meaningful differences. This is to say that differences have meaning only in terms of their departure from some generic, categorical likeness: it is often said that the exception proves the rule, but it is even more true that the rule makes the exception! In the real world and on the first or observational level of abstraction, everything is different, everything is therefore alike (in being different), and no meaningful difference can be said to exist. This fact reminds me of a personal and very trenchant experience of mine: our old Greek master, a marvellous teacher but a curmudgeon of the classic stripe, was forever crying to the heavens that I was a fool, that all his pupils were fools, that everyone is a fool; one day I could stand it no longer and muttered something to the effect that "if everyone is a fool, then no one is a fool—and that lets me out!" Dr. Brown's reaction to that bit of adolescent sophistry is painful for me to remember. But the point is valid. Meaningful difference must be a departure from some category of generic likeness. If everyone is a fool, then the word *fool* no longer differentiates certain people from others and loses its meaning. When all is like, then there can be no differences, and when all is difference, there are no meaningful differences.

In other words, for a stated difference or likeness to be meaningful, we must know *from what* there is difference or *in what* there is likeness. We must know the category of meaning, the frame of reference, within which the comparison is made. It is only minimally meaningful to say that some little boy is different from his siblings. What we really need to know is wherein the difference lies: whether in his stature, his hair color, his scholastic record, his relationships with his father, or just what. Nor does it convey meaning to state that the boy is like, say, a Ford automobile, unless we can include them both within some category of likeness: weight, age, geographic location, or some such. If no such common frame of reference is mentioned or tacitly understood—or even possible—it is of little or no significance to speak of likeness—or of difference.

The fact that these categorizations are made rapidly, almost instantaneously it seems, gives the impression that they have been made directly from the real world with no intermediate step of observational abstraction.[3] This gives them a quality of givenness, and thus we sometimes forget that it is we ourselves, not nature, that have put observations into categories. This ability to make observations and to categorize them with apparent simultaneity is one of the prime characteristics of human cognition and probably stems from our long period of learning and our (resultant?) facility in attaching meaning to mental constructs of our own creation, *i.e.,* to our faculty of symboling.

But we must carry this analysis a bit further. Let us suppose that we observe a family and remark that one child is different. By this we mean that Georgie is the only blond in the group, all the rest having black hair. Thus, the frame of reference in this instance is hair color. But another factor has entered: there is a norm. That is to say, a majority of the family has black hair, against which Georgie's blondness stands out as a divergence. The concept of the norm includes the sharing criterion, since it means that more than one individual possesses the normal characteristic. The idiosyncratic characteristic, on the other hand, may be possessed by one individual or by several, even by a good many, just so long as their number is less than that of the norm. From this and from Figure *1,* it is obvious that the normative-idiosyncratic antithesis is on a completely different analytical axis from that of the frame of reference. Neither the normative nor the idiosyncratic is coordinate with, or a mutually exclusive alternative of, any frame of reference!

But let us continue. Let us suppose that our interest is not so generalized or amorphous as to lead us merely to note a norm and a divergence in hair color. Perhaps the observer is a physicist and views hair color as a matter of absorption and refraction of light, *i.e.,* within a chemico-physical frame of reference. He also regards the norm of black hair as a chemico-physical norm and Georgie's blond hair as a chemico-physical idiosyncrasy. Perhaps the observer is a geneticist and views black hair as a genetic norm within a biological frame of reference. In other words, he assumes a biological explanation. Perhaps the observer is an anthropologist and views the family's hair color as natural, while he suspects that Georgie's hair has been dyed as part of a recent puberty ceremony. But he also realizes that doing nothing to change the color of hair is a (negative) culture trait, particularly since he knows that neighboring tribes have the custom of dying red the black hair of all males. Thus, he views the norm and the idiosyncrasy within the same (cultural) frame of reference, and he explains Georgie's blond divergence in terms of cultural causation.

These explanatory or causal abstractions have been made from a referential abstraction (hair color) which in turn was made from observational abstractions. Hence, as abstractions from abstractions from abstractions, they are on a third level. It is obvious, as was also the case on the second or referential level, that the normative-idiosyncratic antithesis is found *within* the frame of reference and cannot therefore be considered a coordinate of, or an alternative to, that frame. Thus, the cultural and the idiosyncratic are on two different axes of analysis, and talking of them as if they were on a single axis is talking at cross purposes, literally at cross-axes. It follows that it is logically fallacious to say that a phenomenon is either cultural or idiosyncratic. Within the cultural frame of reference there can be both normative traits (shared) as well as divergent traits (idiosyncratic).

But there are other problems here. From the example given

above, it is apparent that neither the physicist, the geneticist, nor the anthropologist made an investigation of the actual causes of the family's hair color. They assumed, for reasons of their own, that the color was due to causes lying within certain frames of reference, in this case, within those of their own competences. What would have happened if the geneticist, for example, had conducted an investigation and found that Georgie's blondness was not due to aberrant genes but to an application of hydrogen peroxide to his otherwise quite normal black hair? His hair color would still be a divergence from a biological norm, but the causes of his idiosyncracy would lie within a cultural frame of reference. At this point the geneticist might be expected to lose interest, if only because the cultural would be outside his competence. The anthropologist, on the other hand, would find a cultural frame of reference on an explanatory level of abstraction exactly to his particular taste. In fact, he would probably be interested in further explanatory investigations regarding what caused Georgie to have culturally altered hair color: tribal custom, clan prescription, family trait, personal fancy—and in the latter case, was it to bolster his own ego, to establish his manhood, to retaliate for some injury? In other words, before the anthropologist can be satisfied with his explanation of Georgie's hair color, he has potentially a considerable number of frames of reference to investigate.

This is merely to say that culture is an emergent, taking its particular character from the interrelationships and interactions of factors which often are, by themselves, pertinent to other frames of reference. Thus the norms and idiosyncracies of the cultural world, while certainly not entirely explicable in terms of other frames of reference, still derive considerable substance from noncultural factors. Culture is often responsive to reductionist explanation, if one but remembers that as a totality it is indeed an emergent, something *sui generis*—if not, perhaps, as much so as Leslie White would have us believe.

From all of the above, it is apparent that a number of rather explicit and detailed explanatory investigations have to be made if we are to go beyond a relatively simple (and thus often misleading) referential level of abstraction and arrive at a meaningful understanding of similarities and differences. It is also obvious that such investigations will have to be made both upon the norm and upon the divergence. Unless both are considered from the standpoint of a single frame of reference, we run the risk of falling into the fallacy of misplaced concreteness (Whitehead 1925 : *Chap.* III). Furthermore, we must be sure not to assume that likenesses on one level of abstraction necessarily have validity on other levels, particularly an explanatory one.

In archaeological terms, this means that we must not assume that similarities of chemico-physical specifications, quantity, provenience, or affinities, which are the only empirical data available to the archaeologist (Taylor 1948 : *113 - 14, 145*), permits us to classify objects together within a cultural frame of reference. As I have pointed out elsewhere (1948 : *115 ff.*), the archaeologist can attain the cultural frame of reference only by inference, and it follows that his cultural and culture classifications should therefore be groupings of inferences, not of empirical facts. But it is also true that the archaeologist must prove the validity of his inferential classifications by explicit reasoning from empirical facts which often fall within other frames of reference. This is to say that he must employ a reductionist approach, at least of a sort.

It is unfortunate that many archaeologists do not keep these distinctions clear in their thinking and writing. They often fall into serious error because they believe that classifications developed on the basis of likeness (as well as the treatment of divergences from those likenesses) should be based only on empirical facts, rather than upon inferences specifically and explicitly derived therefrom. If the archaeologist says that certain stone objects represent cultural similarity or, as a group, had cultural validity for their aboriginal makers because those objects have likeness within some noncultural frame of reference, he is guilty of the fallacy of misplaced concreteness. On the other hand, if he infers that the stone objects are similar in chemico-physical specifications or other empirical attributes because they represent the results of similar culture ideas, needs, motivations, etc., then he is on secure epistemological ground. Of course, there is always the possibility that it will eventually be shown that his data and/or his reasoning will not support such an inference. If this happens, it does not make his theory or his method fallacious. It merely makes his results unacceptable.

This analysis could go on at considerable length. Here, however, space does not permit more elaboration of the theoretical leads nor the following of them to their logical and practical conclusions. I wish only to point out that anthropologists (and this includes the archaeological subvariety) who specifically eliminate the individual, the idiosyncratic, the unshared from their definition of culture make two serious errors: they eliminate from their compass the actuality of cultural variation, and they talk at cross purposes. Furthermore, to jump ahead of the point at which we have left the present argument, they are also equating, and shifting back and forth between, the referential and the explanatory levels of abstraction. This leads them to a false conception of the relationship between what is cultural and what is noncultural—and often to the fallacy of misplaced concreteness.

Finally, I should like to point out that if, as I believe is true, both specific likeness and specific difference have meaning only in terms of already existing frames of reference based on generic likeness, then specific likeness and thus the sharing criterion cannot be a critical and necessary condition of any one frame of reference. For one thing, to insist upon the sharing criterion for any frame of reference, including the cultural, is to deny the significance, even the existence, of variation within that frame. Anthropologists do not deny the significance of variation for their studies within a cultural frame of reference, and thus, to be logically sound, they cannot insist upon the sharing criterion in their definitions of culture or the cultural frame of reference.

Someday, when the anthropologists have investigated the vital problem of "how like is like" and when they have come to some conclusion as to what the concept of sharing really means to them, then and only then can they properly open the discussion of the sharing criterion vis-à-vis the concept of culture and its definition.

NOTES

[1] A part of this paper in preliminary draft was read, as a sort of trial balloon, at the XXXVI International Congress of Americanists held in Madrid during September, 1964. It is expected that that version will be published in the *Actas y Memorias of the Congress.* The present paper is an edited version of the original plus an exposition of some further and consequent ideas. Anthony Wallace (1961 : *10 ff.*) has had something to say on this topic. His viewpoint, however, is somewhat at variance with mine and seems to me to be inconsistent with other points which he himself makes.

[2] "Classification is, in short, a device whereby we are enabled to simplify tremendously an environment which would otherwise be too complex for any finite intelligence" (Bode 1910 : *8*).

[3] "In order to understand the development of ideas and language, it is necessary to realize that a resemblance may be 'felt' before we know wherein it consists" (Bode 1910 : *12*).

BIBLIOGRAPHY

BIBLIOGRAPHY

ADAMS, RICHARD E.
1960   Manuel Gamio and stratigraphic excavation. American Antiq-
       uity 26 : 99.

ANDERSON, FRANK G.
1955   The Pueblo Kachina Cult: a historical reconstruction. South-
       western Journal of Anthropology 11 : *404-19.*

ASCHER, MARCIA
1959   A mathematical rationale for graphical seriation. American
       Antiquity 25 : *212 - 14.*

ASCHER, MARCIA AND ROBERT
1963   Chronological ordering by computer. American Anthropolo-
       gist 65 : *1045 - 52.*

BACON, ELIZABETH
1951   An inquiry into the history of the Hazara Mongols of Afghan-
       istan. Southwestern Journal of Anthropology 7 : *230 - 47.*

BANDELIER, ADOLPH F.
1890 - 92 Final report of investigations among the Indians of the
       southwestern United States. 2 vols. Cambridge: J. Wilson &
       Son.

BARNETT, HOMER G.
1953   Innovation: the basis of cultural change. New York:
       McGraw-Hill.

BEALS, ALAN
1962   Gopalpur. New York: Holt, Rinehart, Winston.

BEARDSLEY, RICHARD K.

1948　Culture sequences in central California archaeology. American Antiquity 14 : *1 - 29*.

BENNETT, WENDELL C.

1948　The Peruvian co-tradition. *In* A reappraisal of Peruvian archaeology. American Antiquity 13 : *1 - 7*.

BERREMAN, GERALD D.

1962　Village exogamy in northernmost India. Southwestern Journal of Anthropology 18 : *55 - 58*.

BLOESCH, HANSJORG

1951　Stout and slender in the late Archaic period. Journal of Hellenic Studies 71 : *29 - 39*.

BLOM, FRANS

1932　Commerce, trade and monetary units of the Maya. Middle American Research Institute, Publication No. 4 : *531 - 56*. New Orleans: Tulane University.

BLOOM, LANSING B.

1938　Bourke on the Southwest. New Mexico Historical Review 13 : *192 - 238*.

BODE, B. H.

1910　An outline of logic. New York: Henry Holt & Co.

BOLTON, HERBERT E.

1950　Pageant in the wilderness. The story of the Escalante expedition to the interior Basin, 1776, including the diary and itinerary of Father Escalante. Utah Historical Quarterly 18.

BORHEGYI, STEPHAN F. DE

1956　Settlement patterns in the Guatemalan highlands: past and present. *In* Prehistoric settlement patterns in the New World, G. R. Willey (ed.), pp. *101 - 6*. Viking Fund Publications in Anthropology No. 23.

BRAINERD, GEORGE W.

1951　The place of chronological ordering in archaeological analysis. American Antiquity 16 : *301 - 13*.

1956 Changing living patterns of the Yucatan Maya. American
      Antiquity 22 : *162 - 64.*

BULLARD, WILLIAM R., JR.
1960 Maya settlement pattern in northeast Petén, Guatemala. Amer-
      ican Antiquity 25 : *355 - 72.*
1964 Settlement pattern and social structure in the southern Maya
      lowlands during the Classic Period. *In* Actas y Memorias del
      XXXV Congreso Internacional de Americanistas, Mexico,
      1 : *279 - 87.*

BURNES, ALEXANDER
1842 Cabool. London: John Murray.

BUSCHAN, GEORG (ed.)
1926 Illustrierte Völkerkunde. Stuttgart: Stecker und Schröder.

CAREY, BERTRAM S., AND H. N. TUCK
1896 The Chin Hills: a history of the people, our dealings with
      them, their customs and manners, and a gazetteer of their
      country. Rangoon: Superintendent of Government Printing.

Census of India
1931 Vol. II, Burma, Part I, Report. Rangoon: Government Print-
      ing, 1933.

CHAPMAN, ANNE M.
1957 Port of trade enclaves in Aztec and Maya civilizations. *In*
      Trade and market in the early empires, Karl Polanyi, C. M.
      Arensberg and H. W. Pearson (eds.), pp. *114 - 53.* Glencoe:
      Free Press.

CHILDE, V. GORDON
1936 Man makes himself. London: Watts & Co.
1956 Piecing together the past. London: Routledge & Kegan Paul.

COE, WILLIAM R.
1962 A summary of excavation and research at Tikal, Guatemala:
      1956 - 61. American Antiquity 27 : *479 - 507.*

COE, WILLIAM R., AND WILLIAM A. HAVILAND
n.d.   Tikal, Guatemala: physical and social composition. Mesoameri-
       can Cities Project, Educational Services, Inc. MS., 1964.

COHN, B. S., AND McKIM MARRIOTT
1958   Networks and centres in the integration of Indian civilisation.
       Ranchi, Journal of Social Research 1 : *1* - 9.

COMAS, JUAN
1961   "Scientific" racism again? Current Anthropology 2 : *303* -40.

COOK, R. M.
1960   Greek painted pottery. London: Methuen & Co. Ltd.

COWGILL, GEORGE L.
1963   *Review of* A quantitative method for deriving cultural chro-
       nology, James A. Ford. American Anthropologist 65 : *696* - 99.

CURTIS, EDWARD S. (ed.)
1926   The North American Indian, XVI. Norwood, Mass.: Plimpton
       Press.

DANIEL, GLYN E.
1950   A hundred years of archaeology. London: General Duckworth
       & Co., Ltd.

DAVIS, IRVINE
1959   Linguistic clues to northern Rio Grande prehistory. El Palacio
       66 : *73* - *84*.

DEETZ, JAMES
1965   The dynamics of stylistic change in Arikara ceramics. Illinois
       Studies in Anthropology 4. Urbana: University of Illinois
       Press.

DIDEROT, DENIS
1959   A Diderot pictorial encyclopedia of trades and industry, C. C.
       Gillespie (ed.). 2 vols. New York: Dover.

DOBYNS, HENRY F.
1959   Ethnohistory. Unpublished MS.

DOUGLAS, FREDERIC H.

1932 Modern Pueblo Indian villages. Denver Art Museum Leaflets 45 - 46 : *177 - 84.*

DOZIER, EDWARD P.

1958 Ethnological clues for the sources of Rio Grande population. *In* Migrations in New World culture history. University of Arizona, Social Science Bulletin 27 : *21 - 32.*

1961 Rio Grande Pueblos. *In* Perspectives in American Indian culture change, Edward H. Spicer (ed.), pp. 94 - 186. Chicago: University of Chicago Press.

DUMONT, LOUIS AND POCOCK (eds.)

1957 Contributions to Indian sociology, No. 1. Paris-The Hague: Mouton & Co.

1959 Dowry in Hindu marriage as a social scientist sees it. Economy Weekly 11 : *519 - 20.*

DUTTON, BERTHA P.

1963 Sun Father's way, the kiva murals of Kuaua. Albuquerque: University of New Mexico Press.

EDMONSON, MUNRO S.

1961 Neolithic diffusion rates. Current Anthropology 2 : *71 - 102.*

EGGAN, FRED

1950 Social organization of the western Pueblos. Chicago: University of Chicago Press.

EGLAR, ZEKIYE

1960 A Punjabi village in Pakistan. New York: Columbia University Press.

ELLESMERE, EARL OF (ed.)

1848 Guide to northern archaeology by the Royal Society of Northern Antiquaries of Copenhagen. London: James Bain, Haymarket.

ELLIS, FLORENCE HAWLEY

1951a Pueblo social organization and Southwestern archaeology. American Antiquity 17 : *148 - 51.*

1951b   Patterns of aggression and the War Cult in Southwestern
        Pueblos. Southwestern Journal of Anthropology 7 : 177 - 201.
1959   An outline of Laguna Pueblo history and social organization.
        Southwestern Journal of Anthropology 15 : 325 - 47.
1964   A reconstruction of the basic Jemez pattern of social organiza-
        tion, with comparisons to other Tanoan social structures. Uni-
        versity of New Mexico Publications in Anthropology 11.

EPSTEIN, SCARLETT T.
1960   Economic development and peasant marriage in South India.
        Man in India 40 : 192 - 232.
1962   Economic development and social change in South India. Man-
        chester: Manchester University Press.

EVANS, JOHN
1850   On the date of British coins. Numismatic Chronicle and the
        Journal of the Numismatic Society 12 : 127 - 37.

FERDINAND, KLAUS
1959   Preliminary notes on Hazara culture. Historisk-filosofiske
        Meddelelser udgivet af Det Kongelige Danske Videnskabernes
        Selskab 37 : 1 - 51.

FORD, JAMES A.
1962   A quantitative method for deriving cultural chronology. Pan
        American Union, Technical Manual 1.

FOSTER, GEORGE M.
1960   Culture and conquest: America's Spanish heritage. Viking
        Fund Publications in Anthropology No. 27.

FOX, COL. A. LANE
1875   On the principles of classification adopted in the arrange-
        ment of his anthropological collection, now exhibited in the
        Bethnal Green Museum. Journal of the Royal Anthropological
        Institute of Great Britain and Ireland 4 : 293 - 308.

FRANKFORT, HENRI
1961   Ancient Egyptian religion. New York: Harper Torchbooks.

FREMONT, J. C.
1845 Report of the exploring expedition to the Rocky Mountains in the year 1842, and to Oregon and the northern California in the years 1843 - 1844. Washington.

GOGGIN, JOHN M.
1950 Cultural occupation at Goodland Point, Florida. Florida Anthropologist 2 : *65 - 91.*
n.d. Monograph on majolica. Unpublished MS., Department of Anthropology, University of Florida, Gainesville.

GOLDFRANK, ESTHER S.
1927 The social and ceremonial organization of Cochiti. American Anthropological Association Memoir 33.

GOULD, HAROLD A.
1960 The micro-demography of marriages in a North Indian area. Southwestern Journal of Anthropology 16 : *476 - 91.*
1961 A further note on village exogamy in North India. Southwestern Journal of Anthropology 17 : *297 - 300.*

GREBER, JOSEF M.
1956 Die Geschichte des Hobels. Zürich: VSSM-Verlag.

HAFEN, LeROY RUBEN AND ANN W.
1954 Old Spanish Trail: Santa Fe to Los Angeles. Glendale: Arthur H. Clark Co.

HAMMOND, GEORGE P., AND AGAPITO REY
1929 Expedition into New Mexico made by Antonio de Espejo, 1582 - 1583, as revealed in the journal of Diego Pérez de Luxán, a member of the party. Quivéra Society I.

HARRINGTON, JAMES P.
1916 The ethnogeography of the Tewa Indians. Annual Report of the Bureau of American Ethnology 29 : *29 - 636.*

HAWLEY, FLORENCE
1946 The role of Pueblo social organization in the dissemination of Catholicism. American Anthropologist 48 : *407 - 15.*

1950a   Big kivas, little kivas, and moiety houses in historical reconstruction. Southwestern Journal of Anthropology 6 : 286 - 302.
1950b   Keresan patterns of kinship and social organization. American Anthropologist 52 : 499 - 512.

HEGLAR, RODGER
1964   Personal communication.

HEIZER, R. F.
1954   Notes on the Utah Utes by Edward Palmer, 1866 - 1877. University of Utah Anthropological Papers 17.

HEWES, GORDON W.
1955   World distribution of certain postural habits. American Anthropologist 57 : 231 - 44.
1957   The anthropology of posture. Scientific American 196(2) : 122 - 32.

HODGE, FREDERICK W.
1907   Handbook of American Indians north of Mexico. Part I. Bulletin of the Bureau of American Ethnology 30.

HOIJER, HARRY (ed.)
1946   Introduction to "Linguistic structures of native America." Viking Fund Publications in Anthropology 6 : 9 - 29.

HOMMEL, RUDOLF P.
1937   China at work. New York: John Day.

HOWELLS, W. W.
1936   Measurements on two Indian Pueblos. American Journal of Physical Anthropology 21 : 16 - 17.

HRDLICKA, ALES
1908   Physiological and medical observations among the Indians of southwestern United States and northern Mexico. Bulletin of the Bureau of American Ethnology 34.

HUDSON, ALFRED E., AND ELIZABETH BACON
1941   Social control and the individual in eastern Hazara culture. *In* Language, culture and personality, L. Spier (ed.). Menasha.

ILIFF, FLORA GREGG
1954   People of the blue water. New York: Harper & Brothers.

JELINEK, ARTHUR J.
1962   Use of the cumulative graph in temporal ordering. American
       Antiquity 28 : *241 - 42.*

JENNINGS, JESSE D., *et al.*
1956   The American Southwest: a problem in cultural isolation. *In*
       Seminars in archaeology: 1955, Robert Wauchope (ed.).
       Memoirs of the Society for American Archaeology
       11 : *59 - 127.*

JONES, P. D'A., AND E. N. SIMONS
1961   Story of the saw. Manchester: Newman Neame (Northern)
       Ltd.

JOPE, E. M.
1961   Cornish houses, 1400 - 1700. *In* Studies in building history:
       essays in recognition of the work of B. H. St. J. O'Neil, B. H.
       St. J. O'Neil (ed.), pp. *192 - 222.* London: Oldhams Press Ltd.

KANE, PANDRUNG VAMAN
1941   History of Dharmasāstra (ancient and mediaeval religious and
       civil law). Poona: Bhandarkar Oriental Research Institute.

KAPADIA, K. M.
1958   Marriage and family in India. 2nd ed. London: Oxford Uni-
       versity Press.

KARDINER, ABRAM, AND RALPH LINTON
1939   The individual and his society. New York: Columbia Univer-
       sity Press.

KARVE, IRAWATI
1953   Kinship organisation in India. Deccan College Monograph
       Series No. 11.

KELLY, ISABEL T.
1934   Southern Paiute bands. American Anthropologist
       36 : *548 - 60.*

KIDDER, ALFRED VINCENT
1962   An introduction to Southwestern archaeology. Reprinted with
       an introduction by Irving Rouse. New Haven: Yale Univer-
       sity Press.

KLUCKHOHN, CLYDE
1954   Southwestern studies of culture and personality. American
       Anthropologist 56 : 685 - 97.
1962   Culture and behavior: collected essays of Clyde Kluckhohn,
       Richard Kluckhohn (ed.), New York: Free Press of Glencoe.

KRAUS, BERTRAM S.
1954   Comments on Spuhler's "Some problems in the physical an-
       thropology of the American Southwest." American Anthropol-
       ogist 56 : 621 - 23.

KROBER, ALFRED L.
1916   Zuni potsherds. Anthropological Papers of the American
       Museum of Natural History 18 (1).
1925   Handbook of the Indians of California. Bulletin of the Bureau
       of American Ethnology 78.
1936   So-called social science. Journal of Social Philosophy,
       1 : 317 - 40.
1944   Peruvian archaeology in 1942. Viking Fund Publications in
       Anthropology No. 4.
1955   On human nature. Southwestern Journal of Anthropology
       11 : 195 - 204.
1963   The methods of Peruvian archaeology. Ñawpa Pacha
       1 : 61 - 71.

KROEBER, ALFRED L., AND WILLIAM DUNCAN STRONG
1924   The Uhle collections from Chincha. University of California
       Publications in American Archaeology and Ethnology 21 (1).

KURATH, GERTRUDE P.
1957   The origin of the Pueblo Indian matachines. El Palacio
       64 : 259 - 64.

LA FARGE, OLIVER, II, AND DOUGLAS BYERS
1931   The Year Bearer's people. Middle American Research Insti-
       tute, Publication No. 3. New Orleans: Tulane University.

LANGE, CHARLES H.

1952a Problems in acculturation at Cochiti Pueblo, New Mexico. Texas Journal of Science 4 : 477 - 81.

1952b San Juan's Day at Cochiti Pueblo, New Mexico, 1894 and 1947. El Palacio 59 : 175 - 81.

1953a Culture change as revealed in Cochiti Pueblo hunting customs. Texas Journal of Science 5 : 178 - 84.

1953b The role of economics in Cochiti Pueblo culture change. American Anthropologist 55 : 674 - 94.

1954 The analysis and application of cultural dynamics. Texas Journal of Science 6 : 292 - 96.

1955 Significant factors in the comparison of explicitly heterogeneous cultures. Texas Journal of Science 7 : 256 - 74.

1957a Acculturation in the context of selected New and Old World peasant cultures. American Anthropologist 59 : 1067 - 74.

1957b Tablita, or Corn, Dances of the Rio Grande Pueblo Indians. Texas Journal of Science 9 : 59 - 74.

1958a Recent developments in culture change at Cochiti Pueblo, New Mexico. Texas Journal of Science 10 : 399 - 404.

1958b The Keresan component of Southwestern Pueblo culture. Southwestern Journal of Anthropology 14 : 34 - 50.

1959a Education and leadership in Rio Grande Pueblo Indian culture change. American Indian 8 : 27 - 35.

1959b Cochiti: a New Mexico Pueblo, past and present. Austin: University of Texas Press.

1960 Forces of change and tradition at Cochiti Pueblo, New Mexico. Texas Quarterly 8 : 63 - 72.

LATHRAP, DONALD W.

1964 An alternative seriation of the Mabaruma phase, northwestern British Guiana. American Antiquity 29 : 353 - 59.

LEHMAN, F. K.

1963 The structure of Chin society: a tribal people of Burma adapted to a non-western civilization. Illinois Studies in Anthropology 3. Urbana: University of Illinois Press.

LEWIS, OSCAR

1958 Village life in northern India. Urbana: University of Illinois Press.

LINTON, RALPH
1943   Nativistic movements. American Anthropologist 45 : 230 -40.

LONGACRE, WILLIAM A.
n.d.   Archaeology as anthropology, a case study. Unpublished doc-
        toral dissertation, University of Chicago.

LOWIE, ROBERT H.
1924   Notes on Shoshonean ethnography. Anthropological Papers of
        the American Museum of Natural History 20 (3).
1937   The history of ethnological theory. New York: Holt, Rinehart
        & Winston.

LUCE, G. H.
1959   Chin Hills—linguistic tour (Dec. 1954)—university project.
        Journal of the Burma Research Society 42 : 19 - 31.

MCBRYDE, FELIX W.
1947   Cultural and historical geography of southwest Guatemala.
        Institute of Social Anthropology, Publication No. 4. Washing-
        ton: Smithsonian Institution.

MADAN, T. N.
1962   Is the Brahmanic Gotra a grouping of kin? Southwestern
        Journal of Anthropology 18 : 59 - 77.

MAJUMDAR, D. N.
1958   Caste and communication in an Indian Village. Bombay: Asia
        Publishing House.

MANDELBAUM, DAVID G.
1948   The family in India. Southwestern Journal of Anthropology
        4 : 123 - 39.

MARING, JOEL M.
1964   Personal communication.

MARRIOTT, MCKIM
1962   Rejoinder to Métraux. Journal of Asian Studies 21 : 263 - 65.

MAYER, ADRIAN C.
1960   Caste and kinship in central India, a village and its region.
        Berkeley and Los Angeles: University of California Press.

1962 System and network: an approach to the study of political process in Dewas. *In* Indian anthropology, T. N. Madan and G. Sarana, (eds.) Bombay: Asia Publishing House.

MAYER-OAKES, WILLIAM J.
1963 Complex society archaeology. American Antiquity 29 : 57 - 60.

MEAD, MARGARET
1949 Coming of age in Samoa. New York: Mentor Books.

MEIGHAN, CLEMENT W.
1959 A new method for the seriation of archaeological collections. American Antiquity 25 : *203 - 11*.

MERCER, HENRY C.
1960 Ancient carpenters' tools. Doylestown: Bucks County Historical Society.

MERRIAM, EDMUND F.
1900 A history of American Baptist missions. Philadelphia: American Baptist Publication Society.

MILES, S. W.
1957 Maya settlement patterns: a problem for ethnology and archaeology. Southwestern Journal of Anthropology 13 : *239 - 48.*

MILLER, ERIC J.
1954 Caste and territory in Malabar. American Anthropologist 56 : *410 - 20.*

MILLER, WICK R., AND IRVINE DAVIS
1963 Proto-Keresan phonology. International Journal of American Linguistics 29 : *310 - 30.*

MORSE, EDWARD S.
1904 Japanese homes and their surroundings. New York: Harper.
1917 Japan day by day 1877, 1878 - 79, 1882 - 83. 2 vols. Boston: Houghton Mifflin.

MURDOCK, GEORGE PETER
1959   Africa: its peoples and their culture history. New York: McGraw-Hill Book Co., Inc.

MURDOCK, GEORGE PETER, *et al.*
1945   Outline of cultural materials. New Haven: Yale University Press.

NELSON, N. C.
1920   Notes on Pueblo Bonito. *In* Pueblo Bonito by George H. Pepper. Anthropological Papers of the American Museum of Natural History 27 : *381 - 90.*
n.d.   Excavations at Ojito Cañoncito. MS., Laboratory of Anthropology, Museum of New Mexico, Santa Fe.

NEWMAN, STANLEY
1956   Personal correspondence.

PARK, WILLARD Z., *et al.*
1938   Tribal distribution in the Great Basin. American Anthropologist 40 : *622 - 38.*

PARSONS, ELSIE CLEWS
1939   Pueblo Indian religion, 2 vols. Chicago: University of Chicago Press.

PETRIE, W. M. FLINDERS
1899   Sequences in prehistoric remains. Journal of the Royal Anthropological Institute of Great Britain and Ireland 29 : *295 - 301.*
1901   Diospolis Parva: the cemeteries of Abadiyeh and Hu, 1898 - 9. Special Extra Publication of the Egypt Exploration Fund, Memoir XX.
1904   Method and aims of archaeology. London: Macmillan & Co., Ltd.

POWELL, JOHN WESLEY
1891   Indian linguistic families of America north of Mexico. Annual Report of the Bureau of American Ethnology 7 : *1 - 142.*

RADIN, PAUL
1933   Method and theory of ethnology, an essay in criticism. New York: McGraw-Hill.

RANDS, ROBERT L.
1961a   The ceramic history of Palenque, Chiapas, Mexico. Year Book of the American Philosophical Society, 1960, pp. 566 - 68.
1961b   Elaboration and invention in ceramic traditions. American Antiquity 26 : *331 - 40.*

RANDS, ROBERT L. AND BARBARA C.
1957   The ceramic position of Palenque, Chiapas. American Antiquity 23 : *140 - 50.*
1961   Ceramic investigations at Palenque, Mexico. Boletín Bibliográfico de Antropología Americana 21 - 22 (pt. 1) : *218 - 20.*

REED, ERIK K.
1949   Sources of Upper Rio Grande culture and population. El Palacio 56 : *163 - 84.*
1956a   Transition to history in the Pueblo Southwest. American Anthropologist 54 : *592 - 603.*
1956b   Types of village-plan layouts in the Southwest. *In* Prehistoric settlement patterns in the New World, G. R. Willey (ed.), pp. 11 - 17. Viking Fund Publications in Anthropology No. 23.
1963   The beginnings of physical anthropology in the Southwest. Journal of the Arizona Academy of Science 2 : *130 - 32.*

RICHTER, GISELA M. A.
1946   Attic red-figured vases: a survey. New Haven: Yale University Press.

RILEY, CARROLL L.
1955   On the ranking of cultures. Colorado Quarterly 3 : *291 - 303.*

ROBERTS, FRANK H. H., JR.
1939   Archaeological remains in the Whitewater district, eastern Arizona: Part I. House types. Bulletin of the Bureau of American Ethnology 121.

ROBINSON, W. S.
1951   A method for chronologically ordering archaeological deposits.
        American Antiquity 16 : 293 - 301.

ROUSE, IRVING
1939   Prehistory in Haiti, a study in method. Yale University Publi-
        cations in Anthropology 21.
1951   A survey of Indian River archaeology, Florida. Yale University
        Publications in Anthropology 44.
1952   Puerto Rican prehistory. New York Academy of Sciences,
        Scientific Survey of Puerto Rico and the Virgin Islands 18
        (3 - 4) : 307 - 578.
1953   The strategy of culture history. *In* Anthropology today: an
        encyclopedic inventory, A. L. Kroeber (ed.), pp. 57 - 76. Chi-
        cago: University of Chicago Press.
1955   On the correlation of phases of culture. American Anthropolo-
        gist 57 : 713 - 22.
1957   Culture area and co-tradition. Southwestern Journal of An-
        thropology 13 : 123 - 33.
1960   The classification of artifacts in archaeology. American Antiq-
        uity 25 : 313 - 23.
n.d.   Caribbean ceramics: a study in method and in theory. Un-
        published MS., Department of Anthropology, Yale University.

ROUSE, IRVING, AND JOSE M. CRUXENT
1963   Venezuelan archaeology. New Haven: Yale University Press.

ROWE, JOHN HOWLAND
1959   Archaeological dating and cultural process. Southwestern Jour-
        nal of Anthropology 15 : 317 - 24.
1961   Stratigraphy and seriation. American Antiquity 26 : 324 - 30.
1962   Worsaae's law and the use of grave lots for archaeological
        dating. American Antiquity 28 : 129 - 37.

ROWE, WILLIAM L.
1960   The marriage network and structural change in a north Indian
        community. Southwestern Journal of Anthropology
        16 : 299 - 311.

ROYS, RALPH L.
1943   The Indian background of colonial Yucatan. Carnegie Institu-
        tion of Washington, Publication No. 548.

RUZ LHUILLIER, ALBERTO
1959 Exploraciones arqueológicas en Palenque: 1956. Anales del Instituto Nacional de Antropología e Historia 10 : *241 - 99*.

SANDERS, WILLIAM T.
1963 Cultural ecology of the Maya lowlands, part II. Estudios de Cultura Maya 3 : *203 - 41*.

SAPIR, EDWARD
1929 Central and North American languages. Encyclopedia Britannica (14th ed.), 5 : *139 - 41*.

SCHOLES, FRANCE V., AND RALPH ROYS
1948 The Maya Chontal Indians of Acalan-Tixchel: a contribution to the history and ethnography of the Yucatan Peninsula. Carnegie Institution of Washington, Publication No. 560.

SCHROEDER, ALBERT H., AND DAN S. MATSON
1965 A colony on the move: Gaspar Castaño de Sosa's journal, 1590 - 1591. Santa Fe: The School of American Research.

SCOTT, J. GEORGE
1900 Gazetteer of Upper Burma and the Shan states. Rangoon: Superintendent of Government Printing.

SELTZER, CARL C.
1944 Racial prehistory in the Southwest and the Hawikuh Zunis. Papers of the Peabody Museum of American Archaeology and Ethnology 23 (1). Cambridge: Harvard University.

SERVICE, ELMAN R.
1947 Recent observations on Havasupai land tenure. Southwestern Journal of Anthropology 3 : *360 - 66*.

SHEPARD, ANNA O.
1956 Ceramics for the archaeologist. Carnegie Institution of Washington, Publication No. 609.

SHOOK, EDWIN M., AND TATIANA PROSKOURIAKOFF
1956 Settlement patterns in Meso-America and the sequence in the Guatemalan highlands. *In* Prehistoric settlement patterns in

the New World, G. R. Willey (ed.), pp. 93 - 100. Viking Fund Publications in Anthropology No. 23.

SIMPSON, CAPT. J. H.

1876   Report of explorations across the Great Basin of the Territory of Utah for a direct wagon route from Camp Floyd to Genoa, in Carson Valley, in 1859. Washington.

SINGER, CHARLES *et al.* (eds.)

1954 - 58   A history of technology. New York: Oxford.

SMITH, ROBERT E.

1955   Ceramic sequence at Uaxactun, Guatemala, vol. 1. Middle American Research Institute, Publication No. 20. New Orleans: Tulane University.

SMITH, WATSON

1952   Kiva mural decorations at Awatovi and Kawaika-a, with a survey of other wall paintings in the Pueblo Southwest. Papers of the Peabody Museum of American Archaeology and Ethnology 37. Cambridge: Harvard University.

SPAULDING, ALBERT C.

1960   The dimensions of archaeology. *In* Essays in the science of culture in honor of Leslie A. White, Gertrude E. Dole and Robert L. Carneiro (eds.), pp. 437 - 56. New York: Thomas Y. Crowell Co.

SPENCER, ROBERT F.

1940   A preliminary sketch of Keresan grammar. Unpublished M.A. thesis, University of New Mexico.

SPICER, E. H. (ed.)

1961   Perspectives in American Indian culture change. Chicago: University of Chicago Press.

SPIER, LESLIE

1917   An outline for a chronology of Zuni ruins. Anthropological Papers of the American Museum of Natural History 18 (3) : 207 - 331.

1919   Ruins in the White Mountains, Arizona. Anthropological Papers of the American Museum of Natural History 18 : 367 - 87.

1921   The Sun Dance of the Plains Indians: its development and diffusion. Anthropological Papers of the American Museum of Natural History 16 (7).

1922   A suggested origin for gentile organization. American Anthropologist 24 : *487 - 489.*

1927   The Ghost Dance of 1870 among the Klamath of Oregon. University of Washington Publications in Anthropology 2 (2).

1928   Havasupai ethnography Anthropological Papers of the American Museum of Natural History 29.

1929   Problems arising from the cultural position of the Havasupai. American Anthropologist 31 : *213 - 22.*

1931   N. C. Nelson's stratigraphic technique in the reconstruction of prehistoric sequences in Southwestern America. *In* Methods in social science, Stuart A. Rice (ed.), pp. 275 - 83. Chicago: University of Chicago Press.

1933   Yuman tribes of the Gila River. University of Chicago Publications in Anthropology: Ethnological Series.

1935   The Prophet Dance of the Northwest and its derivatives: the source of the Ghost Dance. Menasha, General Series in Anthropology No. 1.

1938   Preface to "The Sinkaietx or Southern Okanagon of Washington" by Walter B. Cline, *et al.* Menasha, General Series in Anthropology No. 6.

1943   Franz Boas and some of his views. Acta Americana 1 : *108 - 127.*

1954   Some aspects of the nature of culture. New Mexico Quarterly 24 : *1 - 21.*

1959   Some central elements in the legacy. *In* The anthropology of Franz Boas, Walter Goldschmidt (ed.). American Anthropological Association Memoir 89.

SPIER, LESLIE, AND EDWARD SAPIR

1930a   Wishram ethnography. University of Washington Publications in Anthropology 3 (3).

1930b   Klamath ethnography. University of California Publications in American Archaeology and Ethnology 30.

SPUHLER, JAMES

1954   Some problems in the physical anthropology of the American Southwest. American Anthropologist 56 : *604 - 19.*

Srinivas, M. N.
1942   Marriage and family in Mysore. Bombay: New Book Co.

Stevenson, H. N. C.
1943   The economics of the Central Chin tribes. Bombay: Times of India Press.
1944   The Hill peoples of Burma. Calcutta: Longmans Green (Burma Pamphlets No. 6).

Steward, Julian H.
1938   Basin-Plateau aboriginal sociopolitical groups. Bulletin of the Bureau of American Ethnology 120.

Stewart, Omer Call
1942   Ute-Southern Paiute. Anthropological Records of the University of California 6 : 231 - 354.

Stubbs, Stanley A.
1950   A bird's-eye view of the Pueblos. Norman: University of Oklahoma Press.

Stubbs, Stanley A., and W. S. Stallings, Jr.
1953   The excavation of Pindi Pueblo, New Mexico. Monograph of the School of American Research and the Laboratory of Anthropology.

Sullivan, Maurice S.
1934   The travels of Jedediah Smith. Santa Ana: Fine Arts Press.

Swadesh, Morris
1954   Prospectives and problems of Amerindian comparative linguistics. Word 10 : 306 - 32.

Tax, Sol
1952   Economy and technology. *In* Heritage of conquest, Sol Tax (ed.), pp. 43 - 75. Glencoe: The Free Press.

Taylor, Walter W.
1948   A study of archeology. American Anthropological Association Memoir 69.
1954   Southwestern archaeology, its history and theory. American Anthropologist 56 : 561 - 70.

THOMPSON, J. ERIC S.
1954 The rise and fall of Maya civilization. Norman: University of Oklahoma Press.
1964 Trade relations between the Maya highlands and lowlands. Estudios de Cultura Maya 4 : *13 - 49.*

THOMPSON, LAURA
1961 Toward a science of mankind. New York: McGraw-Hill.

TILAK, LAKSHMIBAI
1950 I follow after. Madras: Oxford University Press.

TOZZER, ALFRED M.
1941 Landa's relación de las cosas de Yucatan. Papers of the Peabody Museum of American Archaeology and Ethnology 18. Cambridge: Harvard University.

UNDERHILL, RUTH
1954 Intercultural relations in the Greater Southwest. American Anthropologist 56 : *645 - 56.*

WALLACE, ANTHONY F. C.
1956a Mazeway resynthesis: a biocultural theory of religious inspiration. Transactions of the New York Academy of Sciences, Series II, 18 : *626 - 38.*
1956b Revitalization movements. American Anthropologist 58 : *264 - 81.*
1961 Culture and personality. New York: Random House.

WENDORF, FRED
1953 Salvage archaeology in the Chama Valley, New Mexico. Santa Fe: Monographs of the School of American Research.
1954 A reconstruction of northern Rio Grande prehistory. American Anthropologist 56 : *200 - 27.*

WENDORF, FRED, AND ERIK K. REED
1955 An alternative reconstruction of northern Rio Grande prehistory. El Palacio 62 : *131 - 73.*

WHEAT, JOE BEN
1954 Southwestern cultural interrelationships and the question of area co-traditions. American Anthropologist 56 : *576 - 91.*

WHITE, LESLIE A.

1930 A comparative study of Keresan medicine societies. Proceedings of the 23rd International Congress of Americanists, pp. 604 - 19.

1942 The Pueblo of Santa Ana, New Mexico. American Anthropological Association Memior 60.

1943 New material from Acoma. Bulletin of the Bureau of American Ethnology 136 : 305 - 59.

1963 Keresan Pueblo prayer sticks. Papers of the Michigan Academy of Science, Arts, and Letters 48 : 549 - 56.

WHITEHEAD, A. N.

1925 Science and the modern world. New York: Macmillan Co.

WILLEY, GORDON R.

1945 Horizon styles and pottery traditions in Peruvian archaeology. American Antiquity 11 : 49 - 56.

1956a Problems concerning prehistoric settlement patterns in the Maya lowlands. *In* Prehistoric settlement patterns in the New World, G. R. Willey (ed.), pp. 107 - 14. Viking Fund Publications in Anthropology No. 23.

1956b The structure of ancient Maya society: evidence from the southern lowlands. American Anthropologist 58 : 777 - 82.

WILLEY, GORDON R., WILLIAM R. BULLARD, JR., and JOHN B. GLASS

1955 The Maya community of prehistoric times. Archaeology 8 : 18 - 25.

WILLEY, GORDON R., AND PHILIP PHILLIPS

1958 Method and theory in American archaeology. Chicago: University of Chicago Press.

WILLEY, GORDON R., *et al.*

1956 An archaeological classification of culture contact situations. *In* Seminars in archaeology: 1955, Robert Wauchope (ed.). Memoirs of the Society for American Archaeology 11 : 1 - 30.

WINSHIP, GEORGE P.

1896 The Coronado expedition, 1540 - 1542. Annual Report of the Bureau of American Ethnology 14 : 329 - 598.

WISSLER, CLARK

1942   The American Indian and the American Philosophical Society. Proceedings of the American Philosophical Society 86 : 189 - 204.